Hope in the Balance

Hope in the Balance

A Newfoundland Doctor Meets a World in Crisis

ANDREW FUREY

DOUBLEDAY CANADA

Doubleday Canada and colophon are registered trademarks of Penguin Random House Canada Limited

Library and Archives Canada Cataloguing in Publication

Title: Hope in the balance / Andrew Furey.
Names: Furey, Andrew, author.
Identifiers: Canadiana (print) 202002128oX | Canadiana (ebook) 20200212818 | ISBN 9780385692618 (hardcover) | ISBN 9780385692625 (EPUB)
Subjects: LCSH: Furey, Andrew—Travel—Haiti. | LCSH: Team Broken Earth (Organization) | LCSH: Medical assistance—Developing countries. | LCSH: Medical assistance—Haiti. | LCSH: Humanitarian assistance, Canadian—Developing countries. | LCSH: Humanitarian assistance, Canadian—Haiti. | LCSH: Physicians—Travel—Haiti. | LCSH: Physicians—Newfoundland and Labrador—Biography.
Classification: LCC RA390.C3 F87 2020 | DDC 362.10971/091724—dc23

Book design: Leah Springate
Cover design: Matthew Flute
Cover images: arindambanerjee/Getty Images; (sky) Wang Binghua/Unsplash

Printed and bound in Canada

Published in Canada by Doubleday Canada,
a division of Penguin Random House Canada Limited

www.penguinrandomhouse.ca

10 9 8 7 6 5 4 3 2 1

Penguin
Random House
DOUBLEDAY CANADA

For Allison, Maggie, Rachael, and Mark.

For my parents and grandparents.

*For the people of Haiti and other marginalized
people around the world. There is hope.*

Foreword by Alan Doyle ix

Introduction 1

1. I'M HOLDING HOPE IN MY HANDS 5

2. HOW DUST NEVER SETTLES 10

3. WHERE THEY CAME FROM 23

4. SOUNDS LIKE THEY MAY NEED YOUR HELP 43

5. WHERE ONCE THEY STOOD 51

6. LEAP AND THE NET WILL APPEAR 63

7. THE SILENT CHORUS 70

8. THE TWO ISLANDS 82

9. THE LESSON OF BALANCE 92

10. ARM IN ARM THROUGH THE GATE 110

11. TOO MANY TO REMEMBER 127

12. LAND OF A MILLION ORPHANS 153

13. TACTILE NATURE OF CHANGE 171

14. THE STILLNESS OF COMPLETE DESPAIR 185

15. FORCES AT WORK IN THE UNIVERSE 202

16. THE CURRENCY OF HOPE 213

17. ONE POINT TWO MILLION CASES OF COMPLICITY 222

18. EVERY WALL HAS ITS DOOR 230

19. UNDER AFRICAN SKIES 238

20. A LEGACY OF QUESTIONS 249

Epilogue 261

Acknowledgments 269

WHAT DRIVES SOMEONE to do the best of things? What motivates a person to selfless public service? For some, pious notions of religion or spirituality, for others more dubious lusts for notoriety and praise. And hopefully, at least some do it just because it is the right thing to do.

Meet Andrew Furey. Andrew is many things to many people. The son of a senator who rose from the humblest of beginnings and a dad himself to three of the loveliest humans I know. He is a husband to a doctor who is every bit as lovely and remarkable as their children. He is an eternal student whose passion for learning and education has led him from simple undergraduate bachelors programs to the highly touted Diploma in Organisational Leadership at a little post-secondary institution called Oxford University, where in 2015, he was class valedictorian. Not that he'd ever tell you that himself.

He is a humanitarian and has given countless hours to causes at home in Newfoundland and Labrador, and in Canada as co-founder of the Dollar A Day Foundation for mental health and addictions services, and of course internationally with the simply astounding efforts of Team Broken Earth in Haiti and Bangladesh and crisis-struck places around the world. He is a friend, to me and many more, and is always quick to chuck his name in the hat for a fun time, and even quicker to raise his hand to help when times are troubled.

Oh yeah. I forgot to mention that he is an orthopedic surgeon and a man of letters whose full title reads Dr. Andrew Furey, BSc MD MSc FRCSC MSM DipOL. Again, not that he'd ever tell you any of this as he is way more interested in what you are doing and if he can help you do it.

You are about to read a story of a remarkable person who has no idea how remarkable he is. You would be right to wonder how this could be. How could a person so willingly throw himself into a war zone to help the sick, and run to the site of a historically devastating earthquake to actually lift people from the rubble and perform life-saving medical care as the world literally crumbles around him. You would be right to wonder about this because indeed, Andrew is asking himself the same question.

Perhaps this eagerness to help comes from his own family upbringing. Maybe it comes from a personal desire to give back as much as or more than one has been given. It is possible this desire to help and host is actually a part of the Newfoundland spirit and is as much a part of the fabric of the people as songs and smiles. But I will let the readers of these pages decide that for themselves.

Hope in the Balance is a travelogue, really, but not a typical one at all. Among the many travels described here, Andrew journeys back to his parents' young lives, where two of the most unlikely families came together, to the streets of cities not often found on the same itinerary, like St. John's and Port-au-Prince. This is a walk down a very uncommon path to discover why one person becomes who they are. And this person is nothing short of incredible.

At the end of this journey and this book, perhaps we all learn the same wonderful thing. Certainly not always, maybe not even often, and maybe only once in a lifetime, there comes along someone who does the very best of things for exactly the right reasons.

Alan Doyle

MY NAME IS Andrew Furey. I'm an orthopedic surgeon and father of three. I live and work in St. John's, Newfoundland and Labrador, the oldest part of the New World, as I like to call it. I don't consider myself a writer. But I have a story to tell you.

It's a story about coming face to face with the crumbing reality of complete despair. About choosing to put yourself in the middle of a dark chaos and then making a choice: run from it or do something about it. Sounds like an easy choice. A lot of us like to think we'd choose the latter. We make that choice from the comfort of where we are, not knowing that the guts of it, the true messy shredded horror of it, sits in a dark place where few would ever shine a light, let alone step forward.

As the dust still filled the air of Port-au-Prince just days after an earthquake lay waste to the city, killing hundreds of thousands, injuring many more, taking a place from awful to so much worse, I chose to do something about it.

Maybe I was a bit naive at first. In over my head. I had no idea what this would all become. But I remembered something I'd heard once along the lines of "leap and the net will find you."

I have a story to tell you. A story of history, family, balance, and altruism. It's about how one idea changed so many lives, including mine.

The first time I went to Haiti was with a group from the University of Maryland's medical school. Like most, I had seen on the news the devastation of the earthquake. As a doctor, my mind is trained to let the shock settle for only a second before I start determining a response. I knew I had to go there. I had to get up and leave the security of where I live and work, leave the responsibility of my wife and two young kids and seek out the hell that was so easy to just keep at arm's length.

Haiti. One of the poorest countries in the world. The nation shares an island with a hugely popular vacation destination, yet its healthcare is virtually non-existent. Its political legacy is one of corruption. It is steeped in violence and ruled by the streets. These people have nothing, yet in a moment they lost so much more.

Team Broken Earth has its origin in the dust and devastation of Haiti. It was born out of necessity. After my first trip, I knew I needed to go back. *We* needed to go back. Like any medical response, this required a dedicated team.

This is a book about how a small group of medical professionals from Newfoundland and Labrador decided to make a long-term commitment to Haiti. Post-tragedy, the news feeds fill with stories of aid and people pitching in. Sadly, it's usually only a short time before the attention shifts elsewhere. That's not a judgment. That's a reality of the world we live in. When the cameras go, so does the attention. This was Haiti's reality. But when you factor in that this is one of the poorest countries in the world and it's in our own backyard, it's that much harder to turn away from it.

So we didn't.

In Haiti, we had our souls laid bare. We could work 24/7 for the next ten years and still not make a dent in the ocean of need that separates Haiti from the rest of the world. But Team Broken Earth isn't about that.

One thing I realized early on as part of this team was to focus on the treatment if the cure eludes you. And it did in Haiti. Nothing could be taken for granted. Can you imagine a hospital that doesn't have clean water? Infrastructure was only one problem. The first of many.

In this book, I want to show how we came together as a team to bring hope, sustained hope, to those who needed it most. I want to show how the call to service started in Newfoundland and has grown to tap and inspire the desire to serve others in other areas throughout Canada and beyond.

Beyond that, this book is a search to answer the question, why? Why me? Why Newfoundland and Labrador? Why now? Is it more than a personal journey? Is it a genetic and geographic destiny?

I am a very lucky man. I have a family who are supportive and have helped guide me along as I now guide my children too. But like most families, our storied path has not always been smooth. We've had our history, good and bad. It brought me to this point, shaped who I am. But the definition of who I am has now changed because of all this. Leaving one island to help another was not linear. I felt as if the Rock was somehow connected by the thinnest thread imaginable to the Republic of Haiti. A parallel, maybe. People. Place. Conflict. Triumph. Same geographic complications, different outcomes. Or maybe it was just me.

When I was growing up, I never thought about global health. It was not a topic at our dinner table. I always supported those in medical school who went to Africa, but it was not on my chip, not part of my life plan. But neither was a massive earthquake for those living in extreme poverty, a term I didn't appreciate until I was quite literally surrounded by it in Port-au-Prince.

This isn't a triumph story. The battle isn't over. But like the city from the earthquake's ashes, hope gets rebuilt. Hope grows. We grow. Team Broken Earth grew from three people in St. John's to over a thousand from across Canada and it continues to expand to this day. Everyone giving up their vacation time, time with family and friends, to take on something that asks more than they ever thought they could give. But they did. And they still do.

I want people to know they can make a difference. This will sound like a cliché, but there is so much truth in it: one idea can change the world. Or someone's world. That's something we say a lot. It came from one of our original members on one of our earliest missions: *Team Broken Earth is not trying to change the world, just someone's world.*

NOTE: This book has been mostly drawn from my memory as well as conversations with colleagues, family, and friends. If I've missed a detail or recalled an event differently, please forgive me, it was not done on purpose.

1

I'M HOLDING HOPE IN MY HANDS

Port-au-Prince: June 2010

DARKNESS. COMPLETE DARKNESS. My hands hold the bleeding artery of a patient on an operating table and I can't see anything. Beads of sweat roll down my cheek. Each breath a 45-degree reminder that there's no power. There's no air conditioning. There's no light. For a moment, there isn't even any sound.

Then panic sets in. The screaming starts with the nurses, running out of the OR, fearing an aftershock, a collapse, or something worse. But what could be worse? I literally have this man's life in my hands. The anesthesiologist is scrambling to ventilate without electricity. Hardly anyone speaks English. Bursts of Creole are shouted just outside the room.

Then, for a moment, everything goes still again, as if a pause button has been pressed. Frozen. Darkness. Heart beating loudly in my neck. Invisible strangers all around me. A film of dust making everything seem thick. This is goddamn chaos. I've been in many operations, and I've seen some impossible situations. I came here expecting the worst. I was naive. Foolish. And now it may cost so much more than I knew. Every vein in my body tenses as if I'm anticipating a kick in the gut. It's coming. It's coming.

The screaming snaps everything back. A strobe of light returns. On, off. On, off. Tiny beams cut through the plumes of dust. I can feel the scalpel in my hand. I can feel blood softly push its way through the strained artery. Then it hits me. In this moment, on this table, in a dark room somewhere within the cavity of a crushed and broken city—right here: this is hope. I have my hand on the faintest little bit of hope and I can't let it go. The will to live is in there. The body wants to survive this, wants to continue to be part of this, even this hell. Hope is alive. Barely, but alive. My hand is touching it. I won't let it go.

I'm not going to tell you if the patient lived or died. Not yet. Part of me is still in that OR. Still in the dark, waiting, wondering if the situation will change. *Can* change. Are there things that exist beyond saving? You never want to consider that. Doctors are taught to believe otherwise. Or maybe I've seen one too many movies where a hero overcomes the odds, saves everyone, credits roll.

I'd love to tell you that I saved the day. That children smiled again, spared the devastation. That young men waved from wheelchairs. That I signed the cast of a young girl who will live to dance another day. That I made a difference. And when it was said and done, I ran off the plane in my bloodstained scrubs into the arms of my wife.

But that's not the truth. No. I'll tell you the truth. You may not want to hear it. I hardly admit it to myself. Truth is, that first trip to Haiti was a disaster. Chaos applied to chaos. I keep coming back to the guy on the table. How do you stop the bleeding when you can't tell where the bleeding is coming from? You can treat, but your mind is far away from cure. So many elements are needed to stop the bleeding. It's not one person's job. It's that of many.

I'm an orthopedic surgeon. And I teach. Give when I can. I'm a husband and a father to three beautiful kids. They've got dance class and hockey and parties to go to and play dates. I can't put all that on my wife. Allison has her own career. I'm doing enough. Am I?

Who asks that question? The guy on the table does. I feel his artery send a message like Morse code. Or maybe it was written in the twisted rebar in the remnants of some corner shop. Maybe it was in the geography of the countless pieces of rotten tarp strung together by people desperate for any kind of shelter. It could have been in the Creole screams. If only I had listened closer.

Truth is, I couldn't hear anything beyond the voice in my head. And it kept asking: What are we doing to help? The guilt and disgust of my own life came rushing to my thoughts, and all I could think about was how can I turn these feelings into the action of change and hope. This one experience was almost religious, almost political, almost business, almost family. But at its core, at its heart, the experience was simply transforming in all its horrible complications.

Earthquakes occur mainly as a consequence of tectonic plates shifting. As a result, the world shifts and suddenly the earth changes shape. Growing up, I had never thought of doing work in developing countries. I always admired and respected those who did, but I never had a burning desire to get on a plane and travel to Ethiopia, the Sudan, or anywhere else. But when the earth shakes, the world changes shape.

This story is one of experiences. Experiences that started as simple ideas. I would be embarrassed, ashamed, and, frankly, lying to say that this story was mine alone. It's not. Team Broken Earth is a collection of stories and experiences; a collection of people trying to shape more than their own worlds, trying to shape the world itself. Trying to move tectonic plates in their own ways. This is my humble recollection and interpretation of what I have experienced.

Yet this is also more than the story of Team Broken Earth. I think it speaks to the human spirit. We often forget during this fast-paced millennium, where negativity plays more frequently and lastingly than positive stories, that hope and love are what make us collectively who we are.

Simple ideas projected to national and international screens can, and do, have the anticipated consequences. Our story should inspire a state of simplicity when considering larger issues. Issues such as poverty and global socioeconomic divisions are complex, if you let them be, but at the centre of that complexity is a paradoxical, beautiful simplicity. How can nations with so much wealth influence those with less? There's a simple answer: we help them. This is a story of a simple idea with that very premise at its heart, no more, no less.

For me, the simplicity lay in single patients. That is it.

A single life changed is what inspired me. Change can start with helping just one person. Then five. Then thirty. It's a twist on that Lao Tzu quote that the journey of a thousand miles begins with a single step. That first step—that single life changed—is what motivated me and others to start what would become Team Broken Earth. These are some of the stories I recall and some of the ones that deeply affected me. We helped many people in Haiti, and then, as the team expanded its reach, we helped others, in Bangladesh, Nicaragua, and more. There were successes and failures along the way, cases that worked out and others that fell short. But all of it touched and changed me in a profound way.

2

HOW DUST NEVER SETTLES

Port-au-Prince: June 2010

WHEN YOU LIVE in a larger urban area, you can take flying for granted. Not in Newfoundland. Here, it's always a commitment. The first leg of any flight is usually just to get you off the Rock. It can be expensive—more so if you have a family—and it's not something you plan last-minute. I have a career that doesn't involve much travel, so apart from the occasional conference and family trips, I wouldn't say I fly a lot. So it's quite an under-taking to fly to the flattened capital of one of the poorest coun-tries in the world recently devastated by an earthquake.

I find myself paying closer attention to the flight safety demon-stration. I don't know why. No plane ever slipped into the ocean like it was easing itself into a bath. A lap belt can cause massive internal trauma. Sudden depressurization can completely disori-ent you. Would you even have time to put on a mask? The flight attendant in her jump seat stares aimlessly down the aisle. I stare at the cockpit door.

Minutes into the flight I become aware that I've been holding Allison's hand tightly for god knows how long. This isn't something we usually do. Allison being Allison, she sits there calmly, leafing through a magazine she bought before we boarded. Our third team member, Dr. Will Moores, is already asleep. But my mind keeps accelerating as the plane keeps climbing.

I'd requested three spots on the orthopedic team: one for me, one for Allison, and one for a resident. (A resident is a doctor who already has an MD and is training to become a surgeon or other specialist.) In the beginning I wasn't sure about subjecting a student to the unknown, adding another responsibility to the trip. But I knew I couldn't do the surgeries alone and we committed to just going for a week to see how things would go. Orthopedics often requires an assistant. The work can be tough and the lifting can be heavy, literally.

Dr. Will Moores was in his third year residency when I approached him to see if he wanted to join us. Will had graduated from medical school with my sister, Rebecca, and I'd always liked him. He'd initially wanted to do plastic surgery. I always thought he would make a great orthopedic surgeon and when he was in medical school I tried to convince him that it was the career for him. I would pass him in the gym and constantly rib him about why he should choose orthopedic surgery. In the end, he did. Will is from the Big Land (Labrador). The magnitude of the terrain there is dwarfed by the size of Will's heart. As soon as I asked him, without any hesitation he said yes.

But even as the plane reaches cruising altitude, I still wonder if Dad was right. Am I flat-out nuts for doing this? Nuttier still for getting Allison and Will involved too? I thought—hoped— that being on the way would feel different. But there is no excitement. No anticipation of how we are going to help. Just anxiety and a whole lot of doubt. From my bag, I take out a manual about how to react if you are kidnapped. Yeah. That was a mistake. Calm was now a far-off place I was speeding away from.

The final leg from Miami is different. I'm struck by the number of Americans heading to help. The plane is full of people in matching aid agency T-shirts and big smiles. A sense of camaraderie radiates throughout. In stark contrast, it is easy to spot the Haitians. They have that thousand-mile stare, a deep, silent sadness across their expressionless faces. Like us, they have no idea what they are heading into. The difference being, this is their home. My anxiety lessens a little as the motivating feeling returns. I am going to be okay. We are going to be okay. I was, in retrospect, naive.

It's probably a good thing that you don't often get to see a sight like this. Devastation. Ruin. Part dust bowl. Part rubble. This was my introduction to Port-au-Prince as our flight began its descent. Collapsed buildings loosely connected by impassable roads.

The airport was partially collapsed, so we are taken by shuttle bus to an airplane hangar where our bags will be delivered in the middle of a chaotic scene. Bags are sent into this barn along a makeshift conveyor belt. Between the language barrier, the tense emotions, and the routine disorder of an airport scene, everything feels unstable, uncertain. You can't tell the airport employees from the passengers. And it's a mad scramble for baggage, everyone grabbing what you could only assume was theirs.

Then comes the heat. Thick and unrelenting. The barn is not air-conditioned, so you are suddenly aware of your breathing. And the dust. Everything is coated with it and it fills the hot air. You feel it in your nose. You feel it in your lungs with each laboured breath.

We eventually push and prod our way to the conveyor and collect our bags, and then we negotiate our way out the doors of the hangar. As we pass through, the sweat begins to pool and the smells and sounds of Haiti suddenly are very real. The first thing I see is a mass of people behind a chain-link fence. Oddly I first think it's a crowd gathered to welcome aid workers. It's not. They're pleading for money. They're begging for help. I had seen those eyes before. The expression similar to the Haitians on the plane.

We are met by a local driver hired by Catholic Relief Services, an American charity group. His name is Gilbert. He is a tall man who speaks English well and has a wide smile. He is armed. He protects the three of us, conspicuous in our North Face and camping gear, as he leads us through the sea of people. There is no hiding us. We are obviously from somewhere more prosperous. An armed escort leading us to a private vehicle as the locals suffer just feet away: it had a vibe of colonialism about it. The rich, white landlords and their staff. We climb into an armed white truck with the windows rolled up tight and the doors are locked. There is definitely no turning back now.

This first trip through the streets in 2010 is unforgettable, even though since then I've made over twenty-five trips to Haiti. Each time I come I notice how the road from the airport has reclaimed a little bit of its pre-earthquake self. On that first trip, the streets are almost entirely covered with rubble. About one and a half lanes have been cleared from what was a four-lane highway. The amount of rubble on either side of the road is so high, you can't see over its mountainous peak. It's as if a heavy snowstorm had blown through and the plow has made one cut through the drifts. Cars have to stop or pull over to let others pass, and you can't tell what's on the other side of the peak. But you know it isn't something good. The rubble is a fence between us and the true horror of what has happened here.

Seeing the first tent city really jars me. It is not far from the airport. In our briefing we had been told about this. How the tents would be common after such an event. You're never really prepared for it, though. So many together in such a struggle for the most basic of necessities.

It is estimated that over a million people have been left home-less. These are the residents of the tent cities and makeshift shelters, some of which are still being used today, as I write this book. The crowds are so dense, you can only see the first row of shelters, and after that it's anyone's guess how deep or populated they actually are. The shelters are cobbled together from a mix of scrap plastic tarp and twisted sheet metal as well as some tow-els or blankets. Basically anything that can provide even a hint of shade from the relentless heat. There is no clean water. No sewage or electricity. I see a little boy with no shirt or shoes just at the outskirts of this mass of humanity. He is playing in a ditch of stagnant water. Fifteen feet from him, a man stands relieving himself in the same trench.

Almost more striking than the visual of the tent city is the smell. An acrid combination of open sewer, smoke, and rotten fruit. It hits you like a brick wall. It makes everyone leaving the airport gag.

The sun begins to set. Long shadows creep across what's left of the city. I'm not sure what we are on is even a road. We've zigzagged so many times that I've lost any sense of direction as we ascend the hills of Port-au-Prince. There are moments of odd beauty. I can tell there was beauty here. The bones of it still exist and I try to picture it before all this happened.

Between the three of us, barely a word is spoken. Maybe it's a combination of the exhaustion, the heat, and the images, but we travel in silence for what feels like three hours. Around every turn, there is new evidence of catastrophe. Tents, tent cities, the minor commerce of vendors selling everything from batteries to flip-flops, people wending their way through the streets with their children and carrying rations of food and water. I wonder where they're headed. How their day will end.

Turn, turn, and turn again. Pass pockets of people, sometimes thousands of them and varying heights of rubble that reveal no hint of their former selves. As we ascend the hills, the destruction becomes less obvious, the temperature drops, the homes become more established, the streets more manageable, and the volume of people less. These changes, of course, are relative in a worse-is-better-than-worst sort of way. As the sun finally sets, we reach our destination far up in the hills, far away from the airport.

Open fires lighting the side of the road guide us into a commune called Pétionville. (Communes are like townships.) As we navigate the last series of turns, I have a new level of trust in someone I just met. If the doors opened and we were told to get out, I would not even be able to find my way back to the streets, let alone the airport. I keep hearing Dad's words echoing off the rubble back at me.

The truck comes to an abrupt stop and blows the horn in front of a house that is surrounded by a ten-foot wall with barbed wire and broken bottle glass on the top. The gate in the wall is solid metal. As it opens, a flashlight shines out and the silhouette of a large man with a shotgun appears, backlit by the house behind him. It's intimidating. I don't scare easily and maybe I've seen one too many movies, but I can feel the tension in my chest.

We climb out of the vehicle, grab our bags, and head inside the house, passing two guards with large guns at the door.

It is somewhere after 9 p.m. local time. I'm jet-lagged, exhausted, but at the same time wired with tension created by what little I've seen already. Have to dig a little deeper and get a game face on. We quickly meet the team members we'll be working with for the week as well as those leaving from the previous week. Remember that scene in *Band of Brothers* when Easy Company is heading towards Bastogne and they meet the battered soldiers coming back from the front? You could feel the weariness, but everyone still manages a smile and handshake. The team are all extremely nice and energetic, but I'm too tired to remember their names. There's a nurse from Chicago and a surgeon from Maryland. I smile and attempt some small talk.

I have to get some sleep. The security briefing would normally get anyone's adrenaline going, but I'm just too burnt for it to register. Every inch of the house is filled with air mattresses, sleeping bags, and fly nets. The three of us set up our supplies and sleeping bags directly on the floor next to the door. The generator and power are flicking on and off, strobing the light around us. Varied sounds from the street perforate the walls. I ball up a T-shirt as a pillow. Cloaked by a fly net, I lie next to Allison. I feel safe and I close my eyes. I see my daughters and know instantly that this was the right thing to do.

I've always been a solid sleeper but that night I wake several times. It must be some kind of protective instinct to answer my own fears. The hard floor is uncomfortable, or perhaps it is the malaria prophylaxis I took. Regardless, the thin beams of daylight finding their way through the back of the house are a welcome sight.

The things you take for granted in life. Comfortable bed, hot shower. Waking up on a floor in a stuffy room somewhere in Haiti will snap you back to reality pretty quick. The shower is in a bathroom without a light. There is no hot water; the only water is sourced from the roof. Still, the cold water is refreshing. A large cockroach in the corner scurries as I make my way closer. There were strict instructions last night not to open our mouths in the shower and not to brush our teeth using tap water. I won't need reminding.

After I get dressed in scrubs, I take pretty much a second shower in DEET and sunscreen. The DEET is strong enough that it tingles the skin and smears the black ink warnings on the bottle. There are more alcohol wipes and hand sanitizers throughout the house than water bottles.

After a brief breakfast we gear up for the drive to the hospital. I imagine we look like some scout troop, right out of the shop, creases still in our fanny packs. We pass the guards sitting on the steps as we load into the convoy of three white Land Cruisers. Not what I had imagined when I got my acceptance letter to medical school.

As we move through sharp turns back down the same hills of last night, the roads are much busier. The driving is painfully slow. My heart aches for the return of the darkness that hid the destruction. There are more tents than I had thought. As we continue down the hill, I notice there is a valley on the left side. It turns out that the valley is actually a large deposit of homes and other buildings that had slid off the side of the hills they were built into, taking, like dominoes, the houses below until they all collected in the trough. One mass grave.

We drive into a busier part of the city, to a commune called Delmas, a main thoroughfare. The bumper-to-bumper traffic gives us time to digest our surroundings. Beyond the rubble and tents, that same humanity is present. People are trading goods such as clothing and toiletries and food. It looks disorderly but it's an organized disorder. Then there is something incredibly normal: a line of children in clean, ironed, bright white uniforms skipping and playing with books in their hands on their way to school. We pass several of these groups of schoolchildren. They look so out of place. They make me smile. They march as if there is no one watching their playful stride. Their innocence is palpable, their laughter tangible. If they have a concept of the collapse of their city, they do not show it that day. Life goes on.

From the road we can see some of the homes. They are often small, one-room shacks with tent roofs and plywood or scrap metal walls. There appears to be no chance of electricity or water, and I am struggling to see how the floor plan would accommodate a bed. Yet there appears to be room for families to thrive and for hope to be cultivated.

The convoy takes a right turn off the main road. The crowds of people and the masses continue. We stop next to the site of a building that has been absolutely flattened and where Haitian men, in tandem, are carrying away rubble brick by brick. We inch slowly down the side street and then stop, and the driver blows his horn, indicating that we have arrived.

I'm a little confused, as there is no sign of a hospital. There are just two large gates, which are sealed tightly. No evidence of what is beyond the gates other than a hand-painted sign in French suggesting, yes, this is a hospital.

Along this street there are random collapsed buildings among others that have been spared. The convoy is stopped at the gate, blocking traffic. I watch the masses of people pass around us, oblivious to us, just continuing on with their day. Amazing how normal it seems.

Across the street from the hospital gate stands one building that is completely unharmed. The early sun illuminates it. Then I notice the dilapidated hearse outside. It is a funeral home. The irony takes a while to sink in.

Moment drifts into moment. My eyes and thoughts wander. I become aware of the gun sitting near the front seat. My anxiety level increases. Should this really be taking so long? Why the gun? Why a shotgun at that? As if on cue, the gates open to reveal a sunlit courtyard. The engines rev and the vehicles proceed through the gates. The gates close quickly behind us.

First impressions? It is like a hospital without walls. Nurses in white uniforms mill about, and patients and their families are already lined up, waiting to see us. The line seems to be endless. Two large tents, which were obviously meant to be temporary wards, have taken up permanent residence in the courtyard, which also serves as the parking lot.

More than two hundred patients sit under and around a makeshift covering for shade. Attached to this is a triage area built of plywood. It is divided into two major patient areas. This is the emergency room. That feels like it should be a question. The now familiar smell of wet plywood fills the air. This is where Allison will work. Two rooms. My god, it will take forever for her to see all those patients, even two at a time.

It takes me a few minutes to realize that this makeshift hospital sits in the belly of a collapsed hospital. It's a jaw-dropping backdrop. It used to be a four-storey building, with wards for obstetrics, gynecology, pediatrics, and surgery. At the far end of the courtyard I can see a corner of the old roof, draped with downed power lines. Immediately drawn to it because of its gravity, I walk across the courtyard and look around the corner, where the roof is in full view. It's massive. It has collapsed and pancaked the four floors under it and turned to face the courtyard with the top of the roof remaining largely intact. It sits there now like a headstone embedded in the earth.

I try to picture the four floors of the hospital as it was: fully staffed, full of sick patients being cared for, being looked after. Doctors and nurses with families and bills and cars and work duties, caring for these patients, caring with compassion and empathy. Visitors, maintenance staff, and support workers, all of them. And then, in just forty seconds, this place was turned into a massive tomb of crushed concrete walls and twisted rebar. Those who died quickly were the lucky ones.

Around another corner of the roof is a hospital room tilted and twisted on what had been the uppermost floor. The floor is partially collapsed at one end, like a folded piece of paper, but you can see it had been a patient's room. The bed has listed to the side. On top of it is an IV pole with a bag still attached. Its tubing dangles over the edge of the collapsed floor. That tubing had been attached to someone.

Locals said that in the first few days after the earthquake they could still hear screams coming from the hospital. Gradually the screams stopped as the stench of rotting corpses took its place.

You might be asking yourself, Why didn't anyone help them? It's hard to fathom. Having seen the amount of destruction. The body count right in front of you. For the medical staff, these situations boil down to making a decision about who to help first and who is likely to survive. I can't imagine ever having to make that choice, let alone living with it. Triage, especially in a mass casualty situation, becomes a purely logistical exercise. You identify who will die unless they take up too much time and resources, those who will die without reasonable intervention, those who can be saved, and those who can wait. It sounds cold. It is. That's the reality of the situation. Ethics detaches itself from emotion so you can make such decisions.

It is tough to break my gaze from this sight, but we need to do a tour and familiarize ourselves with the patients. We are led down what is basically an outside corridor parallel to the tent wards and shaded by trees. At the end of this natural walkway is a partially collapsed building. To the left of us is just collapsed walls. Past fallen-in door frames, desks, cabinets, and stools are buried under piles of bricks and slabs of concrete. To our right is a two-storey building that seems to have largely survived. It contains what remains of the lab and sterilization unit. There is no power. Peering through the broken windows is like looking into an abandoned warehouse. We step through the door and there are two rooms, a recovery room containing a single stretcher and separated from the main hallway by a bedsheet, and an examination room dimly lit by the flicker of an old X-ray viewing box.

Navigating through this part of the building is easier. It is relatively well preserved. Dirty, but preserved. Also off the main hall is a dirt-floor supply area that houses the donated orthopedic surgery equipment, including plates, screws, scalpels, and saws. It is dark, lit only by small windows. It smells intensely of formaldehyde and it immediately brings back memories of the anatomy lab in med school. I'm not sure if this tour is supposed to make me feel reassured. It does test me.

We pass by the broken autoclave (a machine that sterilizes medical instruments) and reach a room that is partitioned by plastic drapes and a makeshift plastic door. Outside the door we are made to put on plastic booties—an odd twist, given that we are standing on a dirt floor. And they are militant about the booties too. No patients or staff get past the plastic door without them. Later, when we ran out of booties, we made them out of gowns. The plastic door lifts a little in the breeze. I don't know what to expect next. This has been the cinema of the bizarre so far. But passing through that door, I know, is going to be an epic moment. I can feel the tension again. The heat. The dust in my lungs. Sweat trickles down my spine, a tiny reminder tapping me back to the moment. My mind races trying to compartmentalize all of these epic moments into their right places. Someone close by is coughing. The formaldehyde. The plastic door now still. Daring me to make the first move.

3

WHERE THEY CAME FROM

St. John's: 2019

I SPEND A LOT of time in airports waiting for flights. The traffic can be hypnotic. It is on this occasion. Business suits with a charge-forward pace, always on a phone. Teens in pyjama bottoms and hoodies. Part of a youth soccer team congregating around a parent staring at an itinerary, then up at the departures board, then back at the itinerary. One sight makes me smile. Trailing behind their parents single file, two little girls each roll a Dora the Explorer suitcase that I imagine is full of the essentials: Skittles, a favourite pen, a well-worn Harry Potter book, ten different barrettes and a stuffed monkey named Jeans. All these people, and a million stories among them. Where they came from, what they've seen. All these trips being made to or from home.

Home. I go there in my head so often when I'm away. I think my kids are still too young to really understand what I'm doing. Maybe Maggie and Rachael get it, but only because they're a little more used to it. They're twelve and ten, but Mark is just eight. They feel things like absence, and that's hard on us all. I see their faces and can tell you how much of Allison, how much of me, I see in each of them. Like any parent, I always wonder what I'm passing on to them, what lessons they are learning and how those will shape the people they'll become. It worries me. It worries any parent. The one thing you never want to screw up is your kids. You want to prep them for the world as you know it, protect them as best you can, and hope they make the right decisions. You probably never stop being like this.

I scroll through pictures in my memory. Birthdays and Christmases. Family we've made, adopted, lost. There's something of all of this inside us—memories and moments that make up the fabric of who we are. I turn that camera back on myself and try to see what my parents see. It doesn't matter what you've accomplished, how many accolades you've received, deep down you want your parents to see it, *really* see it. To be proud. Maybe then it'll feel real. What they are is what I had hoped I'd become. But have I?

Flight calls echo through the terminal and some people rush by while others calmly look for their gate or a place to grab a snack. One older couple sits nearby, sharing an iPad to Skype with family, making a plan to be picked up. Mom and Dad come to mind again. There's this photograph I've had for years of their wedding day. Just the thought of it makes me grin. The two sides of the family could not look more different. It looks like *That '70s Show* meets *The Crown*.

Mom's side looks so dapper and crisp in their Sunday best. Sharp, fashionable, and somewhat timeless, the way you see photos from the fifties and think it could be last week. Dad's side is in contrast for sure. It's a mix of unbuttoned velvet shirts, odd colours, my aunt Rose in a nun's habit and dark tinted glasses like something out of a movie from 1978. We've had great fun with this photo over the years. It reflects exactly what my family represents: misfits who fit. People with more in common than the picture can ever say. Confident. Sometimes quirky. But together.

Together. I love hearing stories of how couples become couples. The coincidence of it all. Sometimes the fate. Have you ever heard of a meet cute? It's a movie term for the scene when a romantic couple first meet. For my parents, their meet cute came courtesy of happenstance and a lost psychology book at Memorial University of Newfoundland.

Their path starts a little further back. Both Mom and Dad were raised in St. John's. My mother's father, John Bennidict, only ever known as Ted, grew up in the downtown area. He was one of four brothers. His family survived the Depression and lived through Newfoundland losing its independence to Great Britain. They became local merchants. His oldest brother, Joe, started a grocery store downtown, O'Keefe's, eventually turning it into a successful business. This all would mean a segue for Joe into a short career in politics as the member of Parliament for St. John's East and then a career in public service in Ottawa.

At the outbreak of World War II, Ted, who had always wanted to be a pilot but couldn't because he was colour-blind, signed up with the Royal Canadian Air Force and was deployed overseas. Keep in mind this is still pre-Confederation times in Newfoundland, so joining the Canadian military was still like joining a foreign service. I remember as a kid watching those epic movies like *Patton* or *A Bridge Too Far* and being fascinated with the war. I'd pepper my grandfather with questions, imagining him high above the French countryside dogfighting the Luftwaffe as searchlights weaved among the clouds.

My grandfather was a stoic. Always with a cigarette in his favourite chair or on walks through the small town of Holyrood on the Avalon Peninsula. He wouldn't answer my questions. He was never abrupt about it, never mean. He just had this way of gently steering the conversation towards a different topic. I had no idea at my young age of the depth of his silence or the things he had seen. He was not on the front lines but he carried a weight I'm sure only veterans understand.

A grandparents' basement is a treasure trove for any child. In the corner, on a painter's easel, I remember finding an old gas mask and my grandfather's beret. The WWII-era mask with its big bug eyes and a perforated canister for a nose was a terrifying sight for a child. I had to put it on. I needed to work up the courage first, though in my child's innocence I had no appreciation for the horrors that had made the device a necessity. I would also put on his beret (I still have it) and climb into my imagination for the dogfights waiting, trusty gas mask nearby in case things got hairy. Wasn't until years later that I learned that the original gas mask had been invented during World War I by Cluny Macpherson, a Newfoundland doctor.

When my grandfather returned to Newfoundland after the war, he married my grandmother and began working for the local power company. Before going overseas, he had left school and become an office boy for the company, and the job was there when he returned. He then worked his way up to become vice-president and treasurer of what was Newfoundland Light and Power, now Fortis. Today, Fortis is an industry-leading company, generating and distributing electricity in countries all over the world, traded on the New York Stock Exchange and still headquartered in St. John's. My grandfather would have been so proud of that. I always remember driving down Kenmount Road, where their corporate headquarters was at the time, and my parents blowing the car horn and telling us to wave to the building where Poppy worked. I still catch myself to this day thinking of him in there as I routinely drive by. And yes, occasionally I will honk and wave.

Like a lot of Newfoundlanders of that era, Poppy was an incredibly religious and tolerant man. Family was so important to him. He used some of his earnings to pay for his younger brother, Dermot, to attend seminary. In many large Catholic families, it was expected that at least one child would join the church. My great-uncle Father Dermot would eventually reach the rank of monsignor and dedicate his life to the service of the church. A bit of Catholic guilt seeps in here. I often wonder if my departure from a traditional organized religious path would have disappointed them.

My mother was the oldest of four children and by all accounts the princess of the family, and I think there are pictures of her as a debutante. Mom went on to study nursing. It was during a psychology class that my parents' journey together began. A mishandled psychology textbook in the student centre at Memorial University, a chance meeting that led to a date.

After the war, my grandfather had managed to work his way from office boy to the executive level and accumulate a modest wealth. My grandfather had done very well for himself and he made sure his family had a better start than he had. Mom's childhood seemed to be one of moderate privilege. A phone, a car, a summer place, and a trip to London when she was a girl. There were plenty of black-and-white photos of my mother playing the piano with perfect posture and a dress that belonged in *The Sound of Music*. I always imagined life on Elizabeth Avenue, next to a brand-new Churchill Square development, must have been a 1960s middle-class dream, replete with dinner parties, cigarettes, and highballs. I remember as a child being afraid to enter the living or dining room in my grandparents' home. Everything in its place, and no place for children. We were allowed in the living room only at Christmas and in the dining room for excessively formal Sunday family dinners.

My mother graduated with one of the first bachelor of nursing degrees awarded from Memorial University. When we were very young, she was a nurse providing care to some of the smaller communities around the province, like Stephenville Crossing. As our family grew, she checked her career as a full-time nurse to work with the Victorian Order of Nurses for a short while, before deciding to dedicate her life to raising the four of us.

My mother is constant energy, never sitting still, ever. If she is awake, she is moving and trying to accomplish something. On vacations, she is constantly walking, rarely if ever sitting around in the sun somewhere. I guess that's what happens after you raise four children: you get used to the pace and the never-ending list of tasks to complete. When people ask where I get my energy, the answer is clear.

I think of balance when I think of Mom. Dad was always the freer, less risk-averse one; he would often act without thinking things through, resulting, to give one example, in the sudden appearance of a new car that we could not afford. Mom would be left to balance the books and the family as well. Their success in life depends on balance, and Mom sets and maintains the fulcrum to this day.

My father's path started not too far from the lights of old St. John's, in a little part of rural Newfoundland that you've probably never heard of. Avondale is one of a string of communities that cup Conception Bay just a short drive outside the city. These once isolated old fishing towns go back centuries. Eventually they were connected by road, then railway. That was how you got to "town," meaning St. John's. These places are popular subjects for postcards, with their saltbox houses, wharfs, and flakes, all clinging to rocks that sometimes tower above the bay or bow to its powerful will. It's beautiful. It's dangerous. It's complicated.

Like Cleary, like Brown and Walsh, Furey is a proud old Newfoundland name. And the Fureys were certainly well known throughout these communities at the time. Dad's grandmother was an institution. A matriarch. An astute businesswoman, she owned and controlled a hotel, a bus service, a taxi service and, most infamously, a bar called Furey's in Holyrood, then the heart of Conception Bay commerce and activity. She had six children, one of whom was my grandfather.

My grandmother, Nanny Furey, was born a Bruce and came from Harbour Grace, in Conception Bay North. I am not sure of the details of how they met, but they were quickly married and had eight children together, three girls and five boys. Nan was larger than life, always with the broadest smile and a mischievous glint of gossip in her eye. She eventually became the quintessential "townie," combing the obituaries, peeking out her apartment window in Churchill Square in St. John's taking note of which schoolboys were smoking and who was holding hands with whom.

Her family was her greatest passion. You want to see a big smile get even bigger? Put Nan in a room surrounded by her loved ones. The more the merrier. She never wanted any of us to leave. Never liked being alone. I think that's when the ghosts came out. The voices of her past in her ear.

Nan's life in Avondale should've been ideal. She had family support, she was part owner with her husband of some of his family's successful businesses, her children were healthy—all the pieces were in place. Yes, ideal indeed. Of course, as in a lot of these situations, that was the public persona. The private was something else.

My grandfather was an alcoholic. The addiction and the guilt sent him looking for something or someone to blame—a target. My grandfather would come home drunk and take it out on Nan. It wasn't until a few years before she died, after I completed medical school and was asking about her health, that I discovered she was blind in one eye. I later learned it was my grandfather who had been responsible. I never knew. She never once said a bad word about him.

That was the 1950s. And at that time, rural Catholic Newfoundland wives stayed with their husbands no matter what. Divorce or separation were unthinkable. The mention of either could bring on ostracism or a reaction worse than what you were trying to escape. But Nan was different. She had a will that was bigger than the judgment of those around her. It was harder than any hand that touched her. She dug deep and found the courage to get out of the hell she was living in. One fall day, she took her eight children, ranging in age from infancy to teens, and fled into the night.

All she took was what mattered most to her: her children. It speaks to her desperation that she freed her family from a nightmare that would not have had anything resembling a happy ending if they'd stayed. Violence begets violence. Her children would not suffer this fate. No way. And so, without a place to call home, without somewhere for them to sleep, eat, or pray, she departed. With the help of a few relatives and social services, she took the train to St. John's. That's pretty much as far as her plan went.

I had heard variations of this story over the years but never the details. Until I started writing this book, I had never asked

Dad about that day. I knew he had some memories of Avondale. Mostly childhood memories. He was six when they left. That's a couple of years younger than my youngest, Mark. That gives me a painful context for the clash of innocence and reality. How much could he have understood? Being told you're leaving your room, your home, it must have been a combination of confusion, fear, and childlike wonder. Was he afraid? Was he happy?

The church's influence on Newfoundland and Labrador at the time was overarching. St. John's could be a rough place for a single mom. Many doors were closed. Many judgmental looks were shot her way. In my mind I see Nan and her eight kids huddled together like in a scene from a Dickens novel, not knowing what the next minute would bring, what lay around the next corner. For her family to survive, Nan had some unbelievably tough decisions to make. She needed to support herself and her children, but she had few options. She had left Avondale with the kids, what clothes they had gathered and little else. All the businesses and any accounts were in my grandfather's name. They belonged to his family. Women in Newfoundland at that time rarely held titles, deeds or controlled the banking. It was one more obstacle for Nan to face.

At that time there were two Catholic orphanages in St. John's. Belvedere was the one for girls, and it was run by the Sisters of Mercy (known simply as "the nuns"). The orphanage for the boys was Mount Cashel, and it was run by an order called the Christian Brothers.

Well before the Catholic Church was thrown into global turmoil by reports of widespread sexual abuse of children by priests, Mount Cashel shook Newfoundland and gained national and international attention with one of the largest sexual abuse scandals of the 1980s. The shocking details were laid bare in the daily papers and on the nightly news as one of the religious cornerstones of the province was shattered. Mention Mount Cashel to any Newfoundlander or Labradorian today and watch their expression become solemn. The place was a torture chamber for many, where unspeakable acts were carried out by those trusted to look after society's most vulnerable.

When Nan had made her way into St. John's, Mount Cashel was yet to be revealed as the Mount Cashel we know today. It was an institution run by the church and therefore beyond judgment. It was full of boys ranging in age from five to sixteen in varying states of need and neglect. It was understood that this was a place for boys whose parents could not afford to support them. This was the reality for many families. Where else was Nan to turn?

I can't imagine having to make this decision. I look at my own kids now and it's like a knife in my chest to even think it. But Nan had no other choice. The girls, aged five to thirteen, were the first to be sent to Belvedere. Their five brothers, aged two months to seven years, looked on. I can picture them waving. Nan was the only caregiver they'd ever known. She was their mom and now she was relinquishing them to the nuns. My sadness boils to a rage. How horrible must my grandfather have been for this to be an alternative?

Mount Cashel presented another challenge for Nan. They didn't take infants. Ever resourceful, Nan quickly came up with a solution. She negotiated to keep the youngest, Chuck, with her until he was old enough to enter, and in return she would work as a cook for the Brothers' private residence next door. I'm not sure how this deal worked and if it occurred over days, weeks, or months, and what happened at that time. What I do know is that my dad was placed that night in a dormitory room with several dozen boys his age while his two younger brothers were in the younger dormitory and his older brother was in the older one. The dorm was filled with bunk beds. You were told when to brush your teeth. You were told when it was lights-out. Dad, six years old, alone in a bunk bed, surrounded by strangers. Plucked from his home. No sign of his mom to hug and kiss him good-night. No comfort in even knowing that she was just next door.

I try to picture her life then. Her day-to-day thoughts. She was in her early thirties, younger than I am now but wise beyond us all. There she is, raising Chuck as a baby until he could enter the Mount and trying to check in on the boys when she could between meals for the Brothers. Balance that with weekend trips, without a car, to see the girls. Her family was always her life. From every bit of abuse she took, every fist that landed, every adversity she faced, she was there for them. Her family would survive.

The years went on like that for Nan for some time. After the boys grew up and left the Mount, she got a job as a cook in a nursing home. She was a constant fixture in our lives. Every penny she made went into caring for her kids, so she would often live with my aunt on the weekdays and us on the weekends. We loved it when Nan would babysit us. It was just different with her than with any other babysitter. You could tell how much she enjoyed spending time with us, watching TV and playing games, truly cherishing every minute.

Family. For Nan, nothing was more important. She sacrificed everything for her kids. Walked away from everything she knew, from security, but also from a life of abuse, both mental and physical. If it scarred her, you'd never know. She never chose the easy road. She didn't surrender. It just wasn't in her. On her deathbed, with her wedding band still on her finger, moments before she passed, she told Dad, "I'm just not ready to leave you all." She was always wanting to do more for us, right up to her end.

Dad started in Mount Cashel when he was six. The Mount was always part of our family. Even though its name has become synonymous with sexual and physical abuse of children, in a strange way the place saved Dad—saved him from one horror in the shadow of another. I often wonder how the family would've turned out had Nan stayed in Avondale. Would he too have suffered at the hands of my grandfather? Would his potential have been duly recognized and cultivated?

Dad skipped two grades almost immediately and was pushed to be in the same grade as his older brother. I imagine the five Furey boys were a force to be reckoned with within the walls of the orphanage. Children coming from a turbulent background are usually fiercely protective of each other. And I cannot imagine that with Nan close by, anyone—priest or otherwise—would dare touch any member of the family without suffering some retribution from all.

As a boy, well before the institution became synonymous with sexual and physical abuse, I had a romantic idea of the Mount. I never turned away from Dad's history there. Before the Mount's dark history was revealed and the place was closed down, I remember one time being in a bathroom at St. Pius X Junior High School when an older boy came up behind me and said, "Is your dad George Furey from Mount Cashel?" I was terrified. This guy towered above me. I didn't know what to expect other than a blow to the head, a kick to the gut. I was new to the school and had those fears kids have of any place that's new. It took everything in me but I swallowed my fear and said, "Yes, he's my dad." The older boy told me I had nothing to worry about there, that the boys would have my back. By "the boys" he meant the few Mount Cashel boys who were attending the school. I felt a part of something, like wearing an invisible badge. A Furey boy, I imagined, meant you were not to be messed with.

A family history like that often creates more questions than answers. How did he go to bed at night without his mother? How did he reconcile the absence of his father? Did the brothers talk about it amongst themselves? Did they hate the man? Did they know what Nan had gone through? How did they grow as boys into men under the roof of that notorious place? How could he know how to, in turn, be a dad to us, not having had an example to guide him? How does one as a child cope with all of this? Did they rally around each other as they always have?

If it were not for the terrible revelations that ensued, I am sure I would have had some answers to these questions. The day-to-day life of my dad and uncles growing up in that orphanage remains a mystery. I don't know what they saw. What they heard. What they witnessed. I just know they came through it together. The Furey boys. After all, survival stories are about a triumph over adversity, not the adversity itself.

I think about the kind of toughness it must have required to get through those days. Because the truth is, my dad was not tough at all. Dad was a quiet bookworm who lost himself, perhaps as a protective measure, in the vast library at the Mount. He was reading those long, classic novels like *The Count of Monte Cristo* and *Great Expectations* before he was even in Grade 4.

One Christian Brother in particular, Brother Slattery, recognized Dad's capabilities and guided him through his school years. He advanced rapidly. When he was sixteen and ready to leave the Mount and become his own man, Brother Slattery gave my dad the very best advice: before celebrating and going to find your place in the world, go get an education. A real education will open doors you never thought possible.

The normal course of events for boys graduating from the Mount was to be given a hand-me-down suit, a small amount of money, and a pat on the back for good luck. Perhaps it was seeing a diamond in the rough, or perhaps it was Nan's ever-reaching hand, but when it came time for Dad to leave, he was given free room and board in an adjacent building if he promised to start advancing his education at Memorial University.

Memorial is just a five-minute drive from where the Mount once stood. For Dad, I'm sure it felt a world away. While teaching at age nineteen at a school where he was also a janitor, he pursued his bachelor of education. It was during this time that he loaned my mother a textbook on psychology that she somehow lost. It was the perfect excuse for a date. Many good dates followed, leading ultimately to his proposal of marriage.

Back to my parents' wedding photo. Here is where that picture starts to take shape. Two very different families coming together. On one side, a family united by a sense of service and commitment to the family unit, building a place in society and hoping to make a difference. On the other side, a family struggling to stay together, connected by a single mother staying afloat as best she can. Traditional marries untraditional.

It almost sounds like that old Hollywood story: girl meets boy from the wrong part of town, parents disapprove of boy, but he wins them over in the end. My grandmother on Mom's side, Nanny O'Keefe, was less than thrilled at the idea of her first-born dating a boy from the Mount. Was this an act of rebellion? A Jimmy Dean-esque phase? I think she thought it would pass.

I'm not sure what kind of welcome Dad received, but there are rumours my mother's relatives tried to convince my grandfather to put a stop to the relationship. If that's the case, my grandfather would not be swayed. He saw something in Dad. This bookish young man was hardly the rebel/bad influence the family feared. He said Dad was an outstanding young man with a lot to offer, someone who would make a great addition to the family, loving my mother and treating her with respect. I think Dad earned my grandfather's respect with how much he had done with so little to start with. My grandmother would still take some convincing but would eventually come around. My grandfather told the other relatives to mind their own business.

My parents' wedding photo is lopsided: there is a mom and a dad on one side and a single mother on the other. My grandfather is not in the picture. I've looked at this photo many times but I never asked about my other grandfather. I never met the man. In fact, my mother only ever met him one time, by chance, at the hospital. But I guess, subconsciously, he was always there in some manner. I remember getting into a huge fight with Dad once when I was a teen and full of those teenage emotions where it's like you're swinging at anything in front of you. It was Mom who came to me and explained how I should cut Dad some slack, as he was making this up as he went along. Dad's father died of complications of his disease shortly after my sister was born. I think he only saw him one or two times before being called as his next of kin to identify his corpse and make arrangements. Yeah, you could say I cut Dad a lot of slack.

After Dad finished his education degree and Mom finished her nursing degree, the two set out to make a life together and to start a family. Dad went on to finish a masters in education and became a vice-principal in Stephenville and then a principal in Dunville. Dad was a testament to the motto Always Try. He taught band even though he couldn't hold a note. He coached basketball even though he stood just five-six on his tiptoes. To this day, I have patients from both of those communities who tell me what an influence my dad had on them. Some are former teachers, some are former students, but all end the conversation with "What a great guy he was." He still is.

Always looking to take that next step forward, Dad decided he wanted to go to law school. He had saved some money and accumulated a small pension from having started teaching at such a young age. And so, at thirty years old and with two young kids, he packed the family up and headed to Halifax, where he had been accepted at Dalhousie Law School. While there, he added two more kids to the Furey fold.

I can't say I remember all that much of my dad during those years, other than that he always made time for us. I remember coming down the stairs of our duplex at night to see him at the dinner table with stacks of papers studying. I remember him using his university pass on the weekends to take us swimming at the campus pool. And I remember us all travelling in a U-Haul back to Newfoundland after he graduated and after he had given my dog away to a loving family with a "farm."

Returning to Newfoundland as a thirty-three-year-old new lawyer with four kids, two under the age of three, could not have been easy for Dad. But he and Mom made it look easy. Everything felt like a new adventure. A new house, a new yard, summer vacations to Stephenville, crossing the island in the back of a giant green station wagon. Life was ideal in the eyes of an eight-year-old.

Dad's law practice was a traditional small firm. His name was on the door and he had a reputation for giving his clients his full attention. Some of them paid in gifts at Christmas, while others not at all, much to my mother's chagrin. Dad seemed never to be motivated by money. He thrived on new turns in life. To this day he maintains that he is still not sure what he wants to be when he grows up. I've always loved his endless curiosity. Curiosity is better than ambition; it means you want to know more as the basis to be more.

Whether it was through Nan or the Mount, through being a teacher or the law, Dad's life experience taught him a lot about people. He believed that it was through government and good democratic principles that we would advance as a socially just society. He would muse like a Kennedy about the call to public service and how governments could make a difference in the social fabric that is our society. On a drive to Marystown when I was in Grade 5, he explained to me in great detail the idea of government, how it worked and how important it was. He spoke of it almost poetically, and not politically, although he loved that side too.

As in any traditional Newfoundland household, Sunday dinner was like a court in session. Important issues were debated. Sides sometimes drawn. The occasional gravy ladle waved. Our own table conversation would frequently turn to political topics or contentious public policy topics like abortion. Things could get heated and some relatives could get upset, but all viewpoints were listened to equally. I learned a lot there. I learned it was important to be able to listen to other opinions, articulate your own, try to be persuasive and also to know when to quit.

The only thing Dad would not tolerate was a dismissive, negative attitude towards government. He'd vehemently challenge those who would dare suggest that governments are corrupt or self-interested or too big to change. He would not listen to those who would disparage the people who chose to stand up, take account, and offer themselves to be part of the solution in public service. This would, on occasion, be met with intense silence from aunts and uncles, followed by a quick change of topic.

One thing is certain: our Sunday dinner table would always be lively. And at the end of the evening, despite the occasional curse, thrown dinner roll, or raised voice, it was considered a healthy debate and good sport. Some egos may have been bruised, but no feelings were hurt.

Dad was a Liberal and a long-time supporter of Joey Smallwood, the man who brought Newfoundland and Labrador into Confederation in 1949, making Smallwood the last father of Confederation in Canada. Smallwood was the champion of bringing Newfoundland from poverty and despair into the twentieth century. He promised better roads, more schools, and healthcare for all. He is credited with almost singlehandedly convincing the majority of Newfoundlanders, albeit only 51 percent, to relinquish their independent status and join Canada. With a reign of twenty-two years, he remains one of the longest-serving premiers in Canadian history.

As kids, we would attend the former premier's birthdays at his house on Roaches Line, not too far from St. John's. Dad's mission in those days would be to help resurrect the party that was all but dead after Smallwood held on to power with a death grip, leaving it in ruins. Dad successfully chaired several campaigns, both provincially and federally, in the belief that the Liberal Party's ideals could help shape a better province and country for the future. He loved the strategy. He was never one for the limelight and quite relished his role as the man behind the man or woman, the push behind the party.

That all changed in the summer of 1999. I was on vacation when I got a call from Dad. That part of Nan in me says that when they call during late hours or when they know you're away, it can't be good news. But this time it was. In fact, it was the best news. Dad could hardly contain himself. I'd never heard that level of excitement in his voice. He'd just had a call from the prime minister, Jean Chrétien. He was being appointed to the Red Chamber, the Senate of Canada.

We all flew to Ottawa for the swearing-in ceremony, and Nan was just beaming. I'm pretty sure she flew there on that feeling alone. I was old enough to see in her face the reward, the payback she never asked for or expected for the sacrifices she had made. From the Mount to the Senate. Her smile owned Parliament Hill that day.

Dad will always be my hero. And Dad's hero is likely his older sister Rose. Rose was just thirteen when they all left Avondale. She was the oldest of the Furey clan that made the trek in the dark of night to St. John's. She was that second layer of glue that held the family together.

I always had the sense that Rose filled the void of the patriarch and felt the weight of responsibility to help keep the family together. As she graduated from the orphanage, her calling was a spiritual one, and she joined the convent. Rose would say that she answered the call to serve God and the poor.

Rose was not what you would expect a nun to be. I'm certain she caused more than one question among her teachers and mentors. She was by any definition a renegade. Yes, she wore the habit and was immensely spiritual. But beyond the commitment to God, she was devoted to helping the poor and helping young people reach their potential.

Being a Catholic nun in the 1960s through to the '90s could not have been easy, especially for Rose, a trendsetter, an agent of change, and a maverick. She was philosophically and academically a powerhouse way ahead of her time. From driving motorcycles, to setting up an Apple computer lab for a high school in the '80s, she broke the mould. She devoted her life to caring for the poor, travelling to underserviced areas to bring education and spiritual guidance. She was a beacon of change. Don't get me wrong, she was tough too! She was often feared by students, but with a heart bigger than life and an ability to push people to greater heights. When Rose died, in 1996, she was close to completing her PhD in math. I remember being in Grade 4, sitting at the kitchen table while Rose taught me the Pythagorean theorem, not letting me leave until I understood the sum of squares and the purity of math.

She cut her own path in life, often taking us along for the ride to see the first-generation Mac computer, some new camera lens she had found, a new type of garden, or even taking my dirt bike for a long ride. I adored her. I aspired to be like her, and I miss her dearly. She was a woman ahead of her time.

I find myself deconstructing my own DNA in some attempt to understand how I'm the sum of all these parts. My grandmother's tenacity and willingness to always strive for something better for those around her. My father's methodical approach to any problem, his unwavering belief in social justice. My mother's steady hand, poise, and balance. Rose's selflessness when it came to helping those around her, elevating them, inspiring them. All these people are part of my chemistry. Lucky enough to know them, luckier still to learn from them.

4

SOUNDS LIKE THEY MAY NEED YOUR HELP

St. John's: January 2010

HATI? HATIE? HAITY?

I didn't know much about Haiti when I first researched it
online. On the fourth try I got the name right. I knew it was
a Caribbean island. And poor. And there'd been some political
strife over the last few years. But that was about it. Didn't know
anyone who had been there, worked there or was from there. It
was a bit of a mystery to me. It still is.

You'd think locker-room banter before an evening rec game
of hockey with a bunch of guys would be a boozy mix of ver-
bal smacks on the road from insult to injury. There are no com-
pliments among Newfoundlanders. It's not "Hey, you played
a great game!" It's usually "Sure, you were not as bad as you
were last week!" But it's all in good fun. An hour on the ice can
feel like twelve after a day at the hospital. I was half listening to
everyone as I tightened my skates when one guy said there had
been a massive earthquake in Haiti. Thousands dead, he said.
Hundreds of thousands maybe.

Could that count be real? That's a tsunami number. That's a biblical tragedy number. I've spent long hours in many ERs and have witnessed mass trauma events before. But this was an entirely different level. The number of dead, the number of injured. I just couldn't wrap my head around it. It consumed me for the rest of the evening.

On the drive home, something someone said that night kept coming back to me. "Sounds like they may need your help." Help? How the hell could I help in that situation? That's the equivalent of half the population of Newfoundland and Labrador being wiped out. Not to mention the countless injured. How bad could it really be?

As I turned on the TV at home, I have to admit, like watching that second plane hit the second tower, I sat in silence as the footage of the crumbled palace and the debris-filled streets of Port-au-Prince was played and replayed while stats on the death toll and the injured rolled across the ticker.

There I am. Sitting in my big house with a large fireplace keeping me warm and a larger flat-screen TV keeping me company. I'm watching raw, unfiltered images of human suffering on an epic scale. The constant political unrest in Haiti meant that the media were already on the ground. This was being documented in real time. Again, the voice from the locker room. *Sounds like they may need your help.*

Two things struck me. First off—and again I admit I knew next to nothing about Haiti—I was surprised how close it was to Florida. This was happening in our backyard. Second, the people. Beyond the massive destruction, the images of downed power lines and pulverized buildings, it was the people screaming in the streets, the agony on their faces, now live on my television, that stuck with me.

My training usually kicks in to calculate the medical solutions. The victims were going to suffer one of two immediate outcomes. They were going to die of their initial massive trauma—and over 225,000 did die. And the vast number of injured were not going to get the treatment they needed. The impact of this disaster would be felt for generations. See it through a doctor's eyes. If this happened in Canada, with our vast support network, our modern healthcare infrastructure, it would still be bad. From what I could tell, though, Haiti had none of that. This would go from horrible to worse. Sitting here, coffee in hand, I felt like I weighed a thousand pounds. I couldn't move. I couldn't stop watching.

For every person, every mother or child, who died, there were going to be far more who were not going to die of their injuries. Yet they were still going to suffer dreadfully. I've treated children who were writhing in pain with a broken arm, crying their little hearts out. It's a fairly easy fix. I can't imagine the alternative. Left to roam through the rubble with broken bones, looking for help, looking for their family, looking for a place just to lie down and rest. Left to live with the pain.

I lost track of time watching this on TV. Different emotions collided. I could taste acid in the back of my throat. I was angry. I was upset, tearful, and yet driven. I felt strangely guilty for not knowing more about Haiti. More guilty for witnessing this all happen while surrounded by the luxuries Allison and I had worked so hard for. I'm no saint. I could've just changed the channel. Watched *Seinfeld*. Checked in on my two kids sleeping upstairs. Gone to bed. But the weight was still on top of me, keeping me in front of the TV. Keeping my eyes open.

I don't suffer from insomnia. Once my head hits the pillow, I'm out solid. Years of trauma training taught me to do that.

Sleep well, when you can, while you can. But that night, what I'd witnessed on TV kept me up. The taste in my throat did not go away. The question of "Why them?" echoed because there was no answer. When I did close my eyes, I felt a terror of seeing my own kids in the ruins. The weight on top of them. Tiny hands reaching desperately for help. Eyes wide open.

My choice was simple, or so I thought: do something or wait out the news cycle. I had seen natural disasters on the news before, but something about this hit home. Maybe it was the new sense of responsibility I felt with young children of my own. Maybe it was my growing global awareness. Or maybe it was something deeper. Something about knowing what it's like to come from an island with a history of hard times. One underdog to another.

I began looking into it. I had recently graduated from trauma training at R. Adams Cowley Shock Trauma Center in Baltimore, Maryland. I contacted one of my mentors there, Dr. Andy Pollak. He told me the Orthopaedic Trauma Association—the world's leading authority in orthopedic research and education—was organizing to send medical teams to the disaster site. There was an opportunity to be deployed on USNS *Comfort*, an American naval hospital vessel that had been anchored in the harbour of Port-au-Prince.

Any decision on this had to be made with Allison, who knows me better than anyone. She was balancing her support with her hesitation. The support was in knowing how deeply this had touched me. The hesitation was about letting her husband and the father of her two children go into a disaster zone. Maggie was just three, Rachael just a year old. I know deep down she would have let me go if I'd had to push it, irrespective of the workload that would have been placed on her shoulders. That's just the selfless person she is. But I didn't have to push.

Allison never ceases to amaze me. She's not only an accomplished and respected pediatric emergency doctor but she's also the most engaged and caring mother any child could ask to have. Allison is from Portland, Oregon. We met in the first year of medical school in St. John's. How'd that happen? Memorial University was accepting American students for a short time, and by a series of karmic twists this was advertised in Allison's undergraduate college in rural Iowa. She had never heard of Newfoundland and Labrador and was intending to stay only for one semester before returning to study in the States.

Meeting Allison is as vivid today in my memory as it was in 1997. She was calm, cool, and confident, and I just felt drawn to her because of that. She never outwardly stressed about anything. She would just analyze and act. I admired that so much then and still do now. Within a year we moved from being lab partners to dating. My parents were a little surprised that I was dating an American from "Portland, Maine." They both liked Maine. Said it was the Maritimes of the U.S. When I told them it was actually Portland, Oregon, I could see the real reason for their concern. They were worried I would leave Newfoundland.

USNS *Comfort* was the logical, slightly safer choice for going to Haiti for the first time. I quickly contacted the organizing crew. I started looking into getting the shots I needed. I began collecting random medical items and everyday conveniences, not knowing what I may or may not need down there. The prep was under way but I still needed to clear one more checkpoint. I had to sit down with Dad and tell him of my plan. He listened carefully, arms folded, while I told him how this situation had really touched me. He asked one question: was I out of my mind?

My father has been one of my main sounding boards over the years. There is not much that I have done, or not done, without seeking his advice. He thought that the time was not right for this. How could I put myself in harm's way with a young family? I think he even may have used the word *irresponsible*. Dad is a pragmatist. Maybe it's the lawyer in him, or the politician, but his arguments are concise, to the point, and sometimes delivered with blunt-force honesty.

It certainly made me rethink what I'd thought I was sure about. Dad was genuine in his concern. In a decision I do regret, I opted to wait. I wrote an email to the USNS *Comfort* group and turned down the opportunity to go early to the disaster zone. I remember feeling empty as I hit Send.

The weight returned. As did a choking sensation—which I had only previously experienced at the passing of my grandfather—and that acidic taste in my throat. It stayed long after the media cycle was fading back to politics and mundane daily issues.

Still. I knew that I could not ignore it. I couldn't explain it, but I couldn't ignore it. I had to go.

Days at the hospital can be long. There's never downtime in any clinic, especially orthopedics. And there's always a measure of keeping yourself on edge when you're on call. You have to be sharp. You have to be ready. At any moment you could be called into surgery for long hours or make decisions that will affect a patient's life forever.

I had finished a long shift and was headed home in the late afternoon. Pushing through traffic on the parkway, I pulled up alongside a city bus. It was illuminated by a soft blue light that glowed against the dark hours of February. The bus was half filled with university students bundled up for the weather and a senior or two. I thought of my grandmother. I could see her sitting on the train surrounded by her children and heading into the unknown. She'd had no idea what lay ahead. She just knew it was the right thing to do.

I had to go.

I contacted the Orthopaedic Trauma Association. USNS *Comfort* was pulling back, having completed their medical mission. My heart sank as the regret about my original decision grew. But they told me to contact Dr. Pollak again and that the University of Maryland was sending teams to be makeshift surgical units to perform amputations and set broken bones as best they could.

I wanted in. On a cold day in February, without checking with Allison or Dad, I wrote to Dr. Pollak. When a response had not come within 24 hours, I wrote again. There was no way I was missing this.

Finally a response came. They had an opening on what would be the last of twenty-one teams that had been deployed since the earthquake. I said yes immediately.

Was it a hasty decision? Maybe. To be honest, I wasn't sure what I had committed to do. I revisited the idea with Allison, but this time with a twist. She should come too, as an ER doctor. There was a long silence. I can usually read her, but not this time. I thought it would be a big thing, but it wasn't. It was as if we were on the same page without even knowing it. Instead of a hard no, she had questions. What was involved? Where would we work? How would we get there? Where would we sleep? Who'd take the kids to school and their other activities? These were all the responsible questions I should have asked before accepting the offer. But I was no longer going. *We* were going.

A few nights before we departed, I was back on the couch. The news was on and the main story was about the spending for Obamacare. Online, I found a story about how victims of Hurricane Katrina were coordinating relief efforts for the earthquake victims in Haiti. Allison was upstairs with the kids. Everything felt heavy again. I closed my eyes and I was on a train with my grandmother in the middle of the night. Heading into a darker unknown. She smiles at me. I take her hand and smile back.

5

WHERE ONCE THEY STOOD

Port-au-Prince: June 2010

THERE ARE PHASES when time has no edge. Nothing to divide it. Day. Night. Day again. It all blurs to grey and you can't tell how long you've been working because of how hard you've been pushing it. It's been days now since the blackout in the OR in Port-au-Prince. Maybe a week. I don't really know.

I'm standing in the courtyard as sunbeams cut their way through the dust that just doesn't want to settle. There's what's left of a four-storey hospital collapsed to one side of me and the makeshift tents housing patients on the other. I'm holding an X-ray up to the sun. The rays pierce the film to give some hints to the diagnosis. It hurts my eyes, but with sporadic electricity, it's the only way. My mind drifts a little. It wanders out of Port-au-Prince. Out of Haiti. I think of Nan. My daughter's last birthday party. The view out to Bell Island on winter mornings. Then it snaps back. I see the cracks in the X-ray, the multiple fractures, as I think out loud: "How did I get here?"

I didn't know much about this place before I came. Hadn't really given global health a second thought either. I'm not sure how I got here, but here I am. Covered in dust and dried blood in the middle of this devastation. Could I do this? Was I even supposed to be here?

So I go home. Standing there, sweat running down my brow, my mind goes home. I see the cliffs that drop sharply into the ocean outside St. John's. The waves pounding the chain rock and the wind across the dwarfed, twisted spruce trees. The contrast with Haiti could not have been more real. Even in the middle of the relief effort around me, home is an oasis in my heart. Always has been.

Where are you from? "Newfoundland" is instinctually the answer. Don't get me wrong, I'm a proud Canadian. But I was born and raised in St. John's, and when you're from here, it's always a part of your identity, no matter where you go. It's made for some strange looks at customs.

Like any Newfoundlander or Labradorian I wear the badge of origin with pride. The oldest part of the New World. The youngest province in Canada. The oldest overseas British colony. And hands-down the kindest people on the planet. It's sewn into my identity so that I fly it like a flag wherever I go. Like many in my profession, I spent time abroad as part of my education. But even as I finished a year of surgical training in Baltimore, I resisted assimilation to the mainland culture at every turn.

I took pride in teaching my fellow surgeons about my island. The cultural differences and the unique sense of place that is Newfoundland and Labrador. There's an old joke: How do you spot the Newfoundlanders in heaven? They're the ones moaning about how they want to go home.

I just couldn't resist the magnetic draw of this place. It was so strong. I turned down job offers at large academic centres across Canada and the States—the University of Maryland and Johns Hopkins, Emory University and the University of Calgary.

It was surprisingly easy to go home, much to the bewilderment of others. Do you know what you're missing out on? they'd say. Why *there* of all places?

It feels a bit clichéd to say, but if you're not from here, you don't get it. Newfoundland and Labrador is a bit of a mystery that way. The weather is predictably awful. It's a trek to get there from anywhere. It has all the drawbacks that come with remoteness. It's been the butt of more than one joke and fodder for more than one journalist who believes Canada ends at Halifax. It's just easy to dislike. It may be that the province's tourism campaign has perpetuated a myth of this place, but it's grounded in something very true. There's more to Newfoundland and Labrador than just the land that oddly juts out of the ocean as if it was made from leftovers. More than the vast resources she offers to the world. More than the unique culture that goes back centuries, long before Canada, longer than America. Newfoundland and Labrador is its people.

I thought about the people who have inspired me, who have helped shape my path to this ruined hospital. While there were certainly examples of mentors and influencers, there was also an intangible feeling, a feeling of the collective influence of all Newfoundlanders. There is a sense that you are representing everyone, every Newfoundlander, and all of those who stood before you. You feel the collective support that all at home want to see you succeed. Where does that come from? From hundreds of years of only having ourselves to depend on? If there's any benefit to an island's isolation, it is that.

It's just in our DNA. Newfoundland communities always took care of each other, through the famine of long winters, through the brutal elements that claimed many lives, and through economic strife so ingrained we've really known nothing else. Of what separates us, the distinct sense of home and culture, there is the stronger sense of service, not just to each other but to a greater good.

Maybe that's the answer to how I got here. Newfoundland brought me here, put me in a dark OR in the middle of a destroyed city surrounded by the dead and dying. Why? Because it's the right thing to do. More directly, it's what Newfoundlanders do. Out of a combination of necessity and morality, it's the desire to help our neighbours. Families from Britain, Ireland, and France settled Newfoundland over four hundred years ago. They came chasing the rich fish stocks but didn't know the land. They came with no amenities and no idea how to survive the elements. They could only rely on each other. Communities were more than communities. They were families.

The folklore of Newfoundland and Labrador is steeped in this. There's a long history of fishing disasters, large and small. Stories of men leaving in open dories to fish the frigid waters of the North Atlantic, leaving their wives and children early one morning never to return. Communities would rally to care for and protect those grieving. There are folk songs written about it. "Tickle Cove Pond," a song from the nineteenth century, is a beautiful story of a man in late winter taking his chance with a shortcut on ice that is too thin. His horse plunges into the icy water. The neighbours, the Oldfords and the Whites, come to the rescue, risking their lives pulling and hauling through the cold to deliver all to safety.

From Tickle Cove Pond to the heat of Haiti, Newfoundlanders have always answered the call to help. I say "Newfoundlanders" because many don't realize we were not always a part of Canada. Here, we do not forget. We can't forget. Our history reminds us, and we're stronger for it. It inspires a sense of place that motivates us all to contribute, and strive to reach higher than the height of Signal Hill would allow. In Newfoundland, July first has a very different meaning.

In 1914 the population of Newfoundland was only about 250,000, which is roughly the population of the St. John's area today. At the onset of the First World War, Newfoundland, then a British dominion, had to answer the call to arms, and help. They had no equipment or machinery, and so the commitment to Great Britain took the form of manpower. The Royal Newfoundland Regiment had existed before the war, but now its numbers rose quickly, from five hundred to a thousand members. The regiment consisted of young men, often underage, from all over the island. From Joe Batt's Arm and Placentia, from Bonavista to Little Heart's Ease, boys made their way to St. John's by boat, by horse and cart, and by train to enlist. For many it was the first time they had left their homes to travel to the city.

At that time, Newfoundland was a collection of mostly fishing communities linked together by the occasional coastal boat. There were no major highways, just well-worn cow paths and dirt roads. It must have been a shock for some of those boys to travel to St. John's. The population. The commerce. The beehive of activity. And the talk of fighting in places they'd barely heard of with names they could not pronounce. They were not prepared for what came next.

I think about that often when I board a flight to Haiti. What drew them? Was it a sense of adventure? A sense of right versus wrong? Was it a sense of responsibility to contribute and help? Today, the media will give you a pretty good idea of what you're getting into. These boys? They had no idea the nightmare they were headed towards. Yet not even a fear of the unknown could stop them.

The regiment set sail for England. They were referred to as the "blue puttees" because of their lower-leg coverings. These were usually bland colours, but because of shortages at home, blue would have to do. The regiment quickly gained a reputation for its fearlessness in places where there was a lot to fear. In 1915 they saw combat on the Turkish shores, at Gallipoli, where the casualties were heavy, the injuries disturbing, and the likelihood of making it out alive was slim.

Gallipoli was just their first taste of the war. Their truest test, their unavoidable fate, was waiting at the front in France. The Allied forces had been preparing for the Battle of the Somme. The Newfoundland Regiment's objective was to take control of the German trenches near the village of Beaumont-Hamel as part of the third wave of the Allied advance. While awaiting command they dug trenches in the fields and gave them Newfoundland names such as St. John's Road. The regiment occupied the high ground and the Germans were on the other side of the field, a few hundreds of yards away.

On July 1, 1916, the first day of the epic, four-month battle, the regiment was sent over the top. They encountered barbed wire and deep muddied craters. One blackened tree, "the Danger Tree," stood as a marker. Death waited behind it. The Newfoundland Regiment was cut to pieces in the span of twenty minutes. Over seven hundred Newfoundlanders answered the call to duty that day. A mere fraction of these brave souls answered the roll call the next day. Different historical accounts give different numbers. But well over six hundred Newfoundland boys lost their lives in the opening minutes of that battle. A long way from France, a huge hole had been blown through the heart of Newfoundland that would never quite heal.

I know a thing or two about open wounds. About loss and how it changes people. It's a side effect of my day job. But this event, this loss, this was something that was etched into each and every Newfoundlander. It devastated generations. I can imagine how the stories would arrive home slowly, and how the mothers and fathers, at home in isolated communities, received the news of their sons' deaths. Communities were used to loss on the water, but not this kind of loss.

The effect of the war and the loss of a generation of young men reverberated into the economy. With a large war debt and depleted workforce, Newfoundland was forced to surrender its independence. In 1949, the oldest part of the New World became the youngest province in Canada. Today, across the nation, children wear maple leaf stickers on their faces and take their parents' hands and watch the fireworks as they celebrate Confederation on July first. It's different here. It's been a day of mourning since long before we joined Confederation. The day begins with a sunrise ceremony on Signal Hill to remember the loss at Beaumont-Hamel. Don't get me wrong, we're all proud Canadians here too. It's just an unfortunate coincidence that this day brings together these two emotional extremes.

Despite the legend and imagery that has been created around this horrific event, I was not prepared for my visit to Beaumont-Hamel in 2016. There's something haunting about it. After the war, a Newfoundland priest, Father Thomas Nangle, secured the battle site and memorialized it with a bronze sculpture of a Newfoundland caribou standing on a granite cairn. It is a solemn place. Many Newfoundlanders have made the pilgrimage to this hallowed ground. I've always felt drawn to it. Something in me was telling me to go there.

It's strange how some places have this unspoken command for silence. Allison and my three kids and I walked alone through the field, through the trenches, no one saying a word. Somehow my five-year-old son understood the weight of it. There was no temptation to play on the caribou monument, no temptation to roll down the hills into the trenches. It was the most respectful and solemn I have seen my kids. As we approached the Danger Tree, still standing in the middle of the field, my daughter reached for my hand and said, "Dad, that's the Danger Tree. That is where they all died." In the middle of France, a full century later, the impact is still understood and respected.

Here in Haiti just months after the earthquake, surrounded by the rubble, I feel as if I'm in a war zone. There are the collapsed hospital walls, the building itself a mass grave of untold proportions. This event, this tectonic shift, will change the lives of all Haitians. It took just forty seconds to alter the course of history of this island country. Would there one day be a monument remembering the lives lost, the generations altered? If so, I could not see it yet. I could see only the destruction.

Looking closer, I realized that Haiti and Newfoundland have more in common. Both islands were settled by sailors. Both possess the richest of resources and a family-oriented people. Both have been crippled by poverty, though Haiti's is on a scale all its own. Our course has taken us in different directions, and different tragedies have shaped who we are, but I feel there is a deep connection between both islands.

I'm not a sailor, but like all Newfoundlanders and Labradorians I feel an attachment to the ocean. I can't swim in it; it's too cold. I don't often fish in it; I prefer river fishing. I have never worked in the fishery, nor do I travel, as so many do, to the Grand Banks off the coast to work the oil fields. But I feel the sea is still very much a part of my life. There's something calming and settling about it. It's home. It's always there. I catch myself looking for it every time I drive to or from the hospital. It calms me. It scares me. It keeps me company.

Living here means embracing that understanding. The ocean connects us all in some way. Our history is filled with examples of this interrelationship. Whether it's searching for lost fishermen or sealers or a trapped whale, Newfoundlanders and Labradorians can't ignore the service and responsibility that goes hand in hand with living on a rugged coast.

Sri Lanka's independence from the British Empire had for decades been stoking racial tensions. The Tamils and the majority Sinhalese were divided along religious and ethnic lines that culminated in a civil war in 1983. Tens of thousands of Tamils began fleeing the island nation to safe-haven countries. It's amazing to think how, in 1986, 155 Tamil refugees found themselves in a cargo ship half a world away, in the North Atlantic, just off the shores of Newfoundland, where they were put off in an open boat. Three days later, Captain Gus Dalton and his crew spotted the cold, malnourished Tamils in the drizzle and fog. He didn't think twice. He took them aboard. He fed them and clothed them. Answering the call, he saved their lives.

In 1942, the town of St. Lawrence, on the Burin Peninsula, had a population of just over a thousand. Marine traffic in the area had grown to include navy ships passing through on their way to or from the escalating war in Europe. It was on a harsh February day that word spread through the community that an American destroyer, USS *Truxtun*, and her supply ship, USS *Pollux*, had run aground in heavy seas. Both crews were abandoning ship, and men were plunging into the frigid North Atlantic.

Within minutes, the men and women of St. Lawrence and the surrounding communities came to the aid of the seamen, pulling them out of the water and then hosting them in the warmth and safety of their own homes. In total 186 lives were saved.

So here we are. Not on the rocky cliffs of St. Lawrence. Not on the boat of Captain Dalton in St. Mary's Bay. But here in the dusty ruins of Port-au-Prince. My scrubs are filthy. My hands ache. I feel I could sleep for days. The heat is making me sick. But I'm still here. We are still here. On the shoulders of Newfoundlanders and Labradorians before us. I feel one bead of sweat trace down my back. It gives me a chill. I hear a chorus of voices in my head. Voices from the past. I don't compare our efforts to theirs. I hope only to add our voices to theirs.

Self-deprecation is an art form in Newfoundland. Maybe it stems from years of being the butt of many a "Newfie joke" or being the baby province, the latecomer to the Confederation party. Either way, it tends to give us a bit of a complex. Maybe that's why we push harder: we feel we have more to live up to. The bar is set a little higher. When you feel you're being underestimated, you usually double your effort. Yes, Newfoundland has always felt it has something to prove.

I remember that during my first semester at university in Nova Scotia, I would from time to time feel I was being judged. It wasn't paranoia. I worked so hard, probably more so because I was always aware of the misconception of what Newfoundlanders could do. But there was always a little reminder, like when I'd tell someone where I am from and they'd respond with "You don't sound like a Newfie." Or that slight air of condescension in a question like "Is this your first time off the Rock?"

Once, shortly after the Christmas exams, I sat in a corner office overlooking the snow-covered campus waiting for one of the deans of the Math Department. My nerves were a little shook, wondering if I had done something wrong. It felt like being summoned to the principal's office. Then suddenly my math professor, along with one of the deans, approached. They asked if I was really from Newfoundland, because Newfoundlanders do not generally get the highest marks in math. Make no mistake, I didn't take this as a compliment.

So have we proved it? I'm never sure. Never sure if anyone hears anything past the accent. But it's still there, the need to be ahead of the class. A grade above. Standing with the status quo is not good enough to shake the clichés. For me, I use the misconceptions as motivation. I'm not alone in that feeling. Many flights have lifted off from St. John's airport laden with the biggest expectations and the brightest minds.

Those bright minds now help define Canada. For a population of just half a million, we continue to hold some pretty influential and successful positions across the country, in arts and entertainment, in politics, finance, and science. Newfoundland and Labrador is all over the CBC. On *This Hour Has 22 Minutes,* Mark Critch and Cathy Jones have been roasting politicians while turning a satirical eye on current events in Canada for ages. On CBC Radio's *q,* Tom Power has interviewed everyone from Ringo Starr to George Clooney, always signing off with the Newfoundland expression "Later on." And, of course, where would the country be without Bob Cole's hockey play-by-play and Rick Mercer's rants? Not to mention the star power of Allan Hawco and Mark O'Brien, both alumni of *The Republic of Doyle,* now syndicated in over thirty countries around the world?

Beyond the CBC, Canada is shaped by Newfoundlanders and Labradorians. Some promote the culture through entertainment, like Alan Doyle and Bob Hallett. Others quietly strike hard in the corner suites of businesses across the country and the world. People like Brendan Paddick, and companies like Fortis. Chefs like Todd Perrin and Jeremy Charles are the buzz of national culinary circles. There are award-winning authors, poets, critics, and commentators, among them Kathleen Winter and her brother, Michael—who wrote a very good book about the Newfoundland Regiment—Wayne Johnston, Rex Murphy, and Michael Crummey. Olympians such as Team Gushue and the pride of Marystown, Kaetlyn Osmond. Politics in this country has been that much more lively thanks to the sharp wit of people like John Crosbie and the never-back-down attitude of Danny Williams.

All these people share that common drive, deliberate or not, that redefines the expectation of what it means to be from here. Believe me, we all sing the Canadian anthem loudly with pride, but we all stand a little straighter, and sing a little louder, when the "Ode to Newfoundland" begins.

God, I'm homesick now. Would give anything to be taking the kids to the rink or heading down to Mallard Cottage with Allison for a feed of cod cheeks. (That's right, cod cheeks. Don't knock it till you try it!) But being here, amid the rubble, the pain? This is my call right now. I know in my heart it is. My hands speak of Newfoundland with every incision made, every bone set.

Through the X-ray, I wish I could see beyond the fracture and into the future. To trace a finger along a map that takes you from a field in the north of France to the craggy coast off St. Lawrence to a makeshift hospital in the middle of Port-au-Prince. There are ghosts. Pointing a finger. Nodding a direction to take. I lower the X-ray and the sun fills my face. I step towards the hospital and the chaos waiting.

6

LEAP AND THE NET WILL APPEAR

St. John's: August 2010

IN THE BELLY of the hospital in St. John's, there are few windows. St. Clare's Mercy Hospital was opened in 1922 by the
Sisters of Mercy (the same order my aunt Rose belonged to).
Some sections are so old you can't see it raining. But oddly you
can hear it. Or maybe that's some echo in my head. Here, the
white noise also varies depending on where you find yourself.
Not quite raucous, not quite quiet—something that ranges in
between. Being paged breaks my train of thought. Muscle memory takes over. Immediately the routines line up. I head to the
OR and begin to scrub. Put on my mask, pinch my nose to position it, and open the door.

Over thirteen years I've walked through these doors a million plus times now. There are few surprises. It's a fairly stan-
dard operating room. Full of light and the distinct smells and
sounds of any operating room anywhere. Everyone imagines
the TV version. But there's no darkness with a single light cen-
tred on the middle of the table. There are no big huddles over a
patient or nurses falling over the surgeons. In fact, the doors are

transformative in many ways. Egos, attitude, beefs, gripes, and grudges all stay outside. This is a well-oiled machine. It's a thing of beauty when it works well.

I'm still in awe of it. I sometimes pause at the scrub sink and ask medical students and residents, Can you believe we are about to do this? A nervous medical student will usually become a little pale or blush, wondering if this is a trick question. But what I mean is, this is a concert of efforts, like air traffic control or the production of a play. It always amazes me that it works. So many moving parts. So many steps need to happen in order to make one operation work.

I look at it with new eyes lately. Haiti had resparked all those things I professionally, even personally, sometimes take for granted. Everything's a comparison. It's a dialogue usually had in my head. No one needs to be constantly reminded how good we have it. But in the OR on this occasion, while repairing a hip fracture, Dr. Will Moores and I were reminiscing about how different the backdrop of Haiti had been and yet the diagnoses and treatments were often the same. Dr. Jeremy Pridham, the anesthesiologist, was nearby quietly listening to this back-and-forth. "When are you guys planning on going again?" he asked while looking at the ventilator. Will and I just stared at each other for a moment. The question had not really come up yet. We knew we would at some point, but it wasn't till someone else suggested it that it suddenly became real. Jeremy said, "I'd go, if you're looking to put a team together." He couldn't see the smile under my mask.

I've known Jeremy for a while now. He's in his fifties but wears it like he's thirty. Confident but not cocky. Smooth and incredibly sensitive to his surroundings, including the people around him. He has possibly the highest emotional intelligence of anyone I know. Despite being a come from away, he fits in. He's one of us. Talking to him, you'd swear he was born and raised in Newfoundland. From endless empathy to always being calm yet compassionate, he has these exceptional qualities that you often cannot describe but that you want to see in your children.

I say that I've known him for a while, but it was more professionally than anything else. We hit it off right from the start. Friends in context at this point. One of my only previous experiences with him was when Nan had her knee replaced. Jeremy was the anesthesiologist and I was happy he was the one looking after her. Seniors can have an adverse reaction to anesthetics. There was a complication, in fact, but the way Jeremy handled it, and my family, led me to admire him even more. His empathy. His calm nature.

As the case was finishing, Will was closing the incision, so I went to the OR lounge to sit down with a coffee and chart the procedure. Jeremy came in as well and really began asking questions about Haiti, what was it like, why did I do it, was Allison okay with it, and so on. He was serious. This was not a fleeting interest at all. Again he told me that if I ever went back, to keep him in mind.

Go back? It hadn't seriously crossed my mind. We'd said it when we left, but it was in that "see you soon" kind of way. Being there was one of the hardest things I've ever done. And it took a lot out of Allison and me to do it. The old fears crept in. My father's voice too.

Another page echoed through the halls, and again I snapped back into work mode.

———

Haiti didn't come up again until a few months later. I was stopped in the hospital hallway by Dr. Arthur Rideout, a plastic surgeon and one of my former teachers. We discussed the topic of relief work. Art had volunteered on numerous missions over the past ten years, in places like India and Honduras with organizations such as Operation Smile, which specializes in fixing cleft palates in underprivileged children. Art had heard about our original trip. He had never been to Haiti. We talked about the earthquake and the overwhelming need it had created. Art is one of the most laid-back people I know. And in his characteristic casual tone, he mused about maybe going to Haiti with some people from Newfoundland and Labrador.

There's something you need to know about Art Rideout. He's quite the prankster. Many of us have fallen victim to him. He will frequently page people to wrong numbers, sew arms of lab coats together, and take advantage of any emails left open on any computers in the OR lounge. Art's sense of humour makes people want to be around him and laugh with him. That humour is matched only by his huge heart and his technical skill in the OR. Art is from New Brunswick. His father was an anesthesiologist and his mother was from the Philippines. He moved to Newfoundland and Labrador for medical school and never left. He was also once my boss and someone I always wanted to be like. His commitment to his patients while maintaining a sense of family, and his great sense of humour—this guy gets the balance right. Everyone felt it. He was our Hawkeye (if you remember $M^*A^*S^*H$) and we all tried our best to be like him, or at least be in his company.

Go again? To Haiti? The thought kept gestating in my mind. The healthcare system there was left in tatters after the earthquake. It was dismal to begin with. The attention the devastation had brought was now waning, and I knew the need would still be there.

I immediately remembered Jeremy. I wasn't sure if Art was serious or not, as we often joked, but what he said resonated. It got my mind racing again. A team, I thought. A *team* could do this. A team *should* do this. We could build a model, a team model, bringing many specialists and surgeons from home. That was the light-bulb moment. The moment in the church in *The Blues Brothers*. The band? The band! A team of us could support each other. This would be a Band of Newfoundlanders, and that got my blood flowing.

Art had mentioned that Dr. Catherine Seviour, an ER doctor, had been to Haiti after the earthquake and maybe she would return as well. I did not think much of it at the time, until I was suddenly standing next to her at a Great Big Sea concert. The band was playing their annual Great Big Christmas Show in St. John's and, as we say here, it was a time! Catherine and I were making our way to the bar when I asked her about her time in Haiti and if she would ever consider returning with an all-Newfoundland-and-Labrador team. It took a split second for her to think about it and reply. She was in.

This was quickly becoming Ocean's Eleven. Are you in or are you out? So far, everyone was in. One big difference: I had no plan. No strategy or vision. And I was now actively recruiting people for a trip? Whoops. I distinctly remember standing in the audience as Alan Doyle hit the chorus on "Ordinary Day" and everyone was jumping. No ordinary day, you got that right!

Inviting Catherine was the first step in making it real. More than an idea, more than an OR lounge discussion, it was becoming real. I felt a knot in my stomach, but not the same as before. I was a little giddy. Maybe a little buzzed. A million images raced

by. My patients. My family. Allison, who was four months pregnant at the time. My father's voice. That collapsed hospital in
Haiti. The heat. The dust. The need.

By January, the concept had momentum. It seemed like a
simple enough idea: ask people we work with on a daily basis
to travel with us to Port-au-Prince. Surprisingly, and inspira-
tionally, filling the roster with members was nowhere near as
difficult as I had expected. A few phone calls and we had our
team of doctors. Emergency room doctors, surgeons, anesthesiologists, pediatricians, and plastic surgeons. There even began
to develop a wait list of people interested in going.

But this team of high-powered individuals was for all intents
and purposes useless. We needed nurses. Nurses do a lot of work
without doctors, but truth be told, we cannot do very much without them. This effort would be no different. And when asked,
the nurses answered. Skilled, experienced nurses like Jackie
Connolly. She's an excellent nurse who worked with Allison at
the Janeway Children's Health and Rehabilitation Centre.

One day Jackie had an appointment to bring her dad to see me
about his knee. A sweet man from Petty Harbour–Maddox Cove,
he was the quintessential seventy-year-old Newfoundlander. I
proceed to take a history and examine his knee. Then skipper
said, "B'y, I don't really know why I'm here, I barely finds my
knee," as he stood and swung his knee back and forth. At which
point Jackie said, "Yes, Dad. Now Andrew, I hear you're doing
this thing in Haiti. I want in and I am not taking no or Dad from
this office until you say yes." How could anyone say no to that? I
knew then that Jackie would be the heartbeat of this team.

I will forever be surprised at how quickly the team came
together. I had doctors and surgeons crossing a variety of special-
ties. I had experienced nurses ready to take on a new challenge.

People jumping with me. Jumping and not knowing if there was a net to catch them. Almost all had never done work like this before. Some had never been outside of Canada. But in the end, they were following me, or Art or Jeremy. They were heeding that Newfoundland and Labrador instinct to help. It's just in their DNA. They were not jumping off anything. They were simply opening a new door.

Not so much time had passed, but already so much had changed in Haiti. The hospital we had operated at previously had been condemned. We could not go there. So I had a team ready but no place to go.

Finding a location proved to be a bit of a challenge. Some hospitals only did obstetrics. Some didn't have X-ray capabilities, which orthopedic specialists like me needed. Some locations didn't have an autoclave, which meant we wouldn't be able to sterilize operating instruments. Through calls to organizations such as Project Medishare and Doctors Without Borders, I managed to locate a trauma hospital in Port-au-Prince that could use our help. All I needed now was to book the plane tickets, make sure everyone had the right vaccines, buy fly nets, get insurance, organize surgical supplies, arrange money, find places to stay, and a million plus one other details now lost in the moment. Nothing to it. And through it all, this ragtag team was all in, all the time.

What a one-eighty from that first trip! I was still nervous, but it was a different kind of nervous. Like rollercoaster nervous. And just like that, we were on our way.

7

THE SILENT CHORUS

Port-au-Prince: June 2010

THE PLASTIC DOOR creaks on hinges rigged with paper and tape. Inside, the floor is plastic, with three sweaty concrete-block walls. There are two operating tables and one anesthesia machine. Two procedures could be done simultaneously, one with a ventilator and one with spinal anesthesia. There are two oxygen saturation monitors and multiple large cylinders of oxygen. The surgical beds are old and feel cold. As I am thinking that the room is well lit, the lights flicker and dim.

An overworked air conditioner (which rarely worked) hums somewhere. An anesthesia machine beeps. Two Haitian nurses stand by in silence. All I can see is their eyes. Quiet eyes. Thousand-mile-stare eyes.

The anesthesiologist on our team mulls over the machine, the general surgeon examines the trays, and our nurses look around the room. Dr. Will Moores and I begin poking around what would be our side of the room, looking for things that we might need in the next few days.

We leave the OR and pass through a corridor and into what used to be a birthing suite. It feels like a prison cell: four concrete walls, a small window, and a small door. There is no air conditioner, and it's dark. There's enough room for a single bed, and little more. We could use this, but only for minor procedures. I leave the building, my nose stinging from the formaldehyde.

The sun is cutting through the treetop canopy that covers the waiting area outside the operating room building. It's around ten in the morning and it's getting hotter by the second. We proceed to tour the rest of the facilities.

We pass quickly through the tent wards, listening like interns. Will frantically takes notes. This has suddenly moved from a tour to work. The tent wards have flaps for walls. The patients roll the flaps up or down depending on heat and rain. The electrical hook-ups are all makeshift, and the lighting consists of bare light bulbs, swinging like pendulums in the breeze.

With the flaps up, we catch flashes of the flowering plants and trees that fill the parking lot. There are strong aromas swirling under the tent—combinations of sweat, urine, and the distinctive scent of wounds—that become quickly tolerable. It's amazing the things you can grow accustomed to in life. The tents are jam-packed with people. Beds line one or both walls, leaving narrow corridors for nurses, doctors, and families to pass along.

By a desk at one end of the second tent sits a single woman who appears cachectic—a word we use for emaciated—fatigued and quiet. From afar she looks to be in her late fifties, but as we get closer, I see she can be no older than twenty-five. She sits in a chair by a bed with no sheets on it, the green plastic mattress fully exposed. She leans against the bed, and her white night-gown is falling off her skeleton, which is all that is left of her physically. Her eyes are far different than the large silent eyes I have seen in others. They are sunken and yellowed. She looks so alone. The bustle of the other tent is eerily absent.

Later on, after we see the other patients in the front of the tent, we step outside, and the local medical staff tell us that the lone girl has AIDS and likely TB. I have limited experience with the end stages of HIV. I know what happens but have never experienced it first-hand. And in this situation? It's horrifying to think of this poor girl's fate. The disease, the accompanying soli-tude. Where is her hope? Her sunken eyes are ingrained in my mind forever.

Inside the next makeshift building is the pediatric ward, where children and babies alike are being tended to by families and nurses. Allison smiles at the sight of a crib, and seeing her smile eases the sight of the girl from the last tent.

As soon as rounds are over the team disperses and the sur-gical team retreats to the formaldehyde-laden corridors of the operating room building. The team is nervous; you can sense the tension. We had only just met the local crew and I can barely remember the names of the nurse and the anesthesia provider. Yet here we are. Will and I sit, my legs bouncing rapidly up and down, as the next patient gets ready in the pre-op assessment area. We review the X-rays of the fractured hip and take pictures with the camera to document the case.

Everyone's a bit anxious as we wait for the beginning of the series of steps and prep that routinely lead to an operation. Allison is introduced to her translator for the week. Wicharly Charles is a young man of short, slim stature. He has a big smile and a bouncing energy that seems to lift everyone around him. Over the week, Allison and Wicharly become great friends, exchanging stories of family members and daily routines. Worrying about your kids feels universal in these moments.

Wicharly and the other translators, along with Gilbert the driver, eat with us every night as we regroup. They're a critical part of the team. Wicharly eventually tells us that he is a painter, and at the end of the week he gives Allison one of his paintings. It still hangs in our kitchen in Newfoundland.

The blue booties are on, a gown is on, the patient is placed on an ancient gurney, and we roll into the OR through the plastic door. The air conditioner is not fully working, but it is cooler here than in the other rooms. There is a procedure already under way, with the general surgeon repairing a trapped hernia on the table with the anesthesia machine. The hip will be done on the other OR table under spinal anesthesia. This will be a first for me. It's like a scene out of *M*A*S*H*, where the surgeon at one table can talk to another across the way, nurses circulating to help both patients.

The gurney wheels screech to a halt and the patient is transferred onto the cold OR table and placed on his side. He winces with the move but is otherwise stoic. The anesthesiologist places an IV in his arm and then a needle in his back. We firmly attach the patient to the table so he can't move or fall, and the nurses do the prep. Will and I leave the OR to get ready. The masks go up, eye protection goes on, and as we stand in silence and scrub methodically, all the potential things that can go wrong rush through my head. Is the X-ray accurate or did we miss some detail? Are the levels correct for sedation? It's a feeling I have not felt since being handed the knife as a junior resident. Big breath, hands up and dripping, we head through the plastic door back first. We are quickly gowned and gloved. The patient is draped. There is a calm and all doubt leaves. One benefit of surgical experience is that, as gut-turned stressed as I am, my hands are steady. The knife confidently and firmly goes through the skin.

The case is over, and thankfully it was not a particularly tough one. But I still have this lingering excitement, as if it is the first time I have ever walked into an operating room. I am at home. Surgery knows no boundaries of geography or language, and surgery is pure medicine. We replaced a patient's hip in conditions I would never have dreamed possible. I take a moment as I am leaving the OR to let this sink in. Hoping we changed a life. I cannot describe the feeling; it is one I am sure not many experience. A fisherman returning from a good day, a farmer after a bountiful harvest? I don't know. I give myself this moment. This little oasis of self-satisfaction. I keep repeating in my head: I can do this, I can do this. The heat reminds me of where I am and there is no escaping the sweat. My scrubs are drenched, and it looks like I just showered in them. I have never been this hot or this energized.

The euphoria of the good start lasts all of a second until the reality snaps me back to where I am and what lies ahead. Outside the OR, the lineup of patients stretches out of the courtyard. Allison and the rest of the team are working feverishly to push through as many patients as possible, and there's a subset of patients with broken bones for us to triage.

We go through the cases and try to prioritize them as best we can. There's no light box, so we hold X-rays up to the bright sun to illuminate their findings. Will and I know we have our work cut out for us with each broken, cracked, or shattered bone we see. It's a serious mess, and these people have been in real pain for a long time with not so much as an Aspirin. We organize the list with the nurses and settle an order for the cases this week.

The next case is a man whose leg was broken in the earthquake. For five months he has been struggling to walk, and we think we can help him. Still on a high after our previous case, we discuss the surgery with him and get ready to take him to the operating room.

Just as the tourniquet goes on, all hell breaks loose. We lose power. The local nurses dash out of the operating room, knocking things over in the dark, their screams filling the room and the hall. It gets worse. There's a bleeding artery. We have no control, no light, no help. The room feels ten times hotter. Panic. Blood moving in the dark. Focus returns before the lights. Muscle memory kicks in again. Deep breath. Keep it together till the case is over.

"Surgery in an oven" crosses my mind. My focus is redirected as the team leader tells us we need to plan to leave the site in ten minutes. There is an urgency, as we are all aware of the setting sun and what safety concerns come with darkness.

We wend our way through the streets of Port-au-Prince, slowly tracing our way back up the hill to the safe house, our home for the week. Somehow, within twenty-four hours, what started as a foreign place with armed guards and barbed wire, broken glass sitting on top of a one-foot-thick wall, became home. I looked forward to navigating the jumble of backpacks, fly dope, and scrubs and finding my place on the floor to sleep.

My head is still spinning, and I'm not sure if I'm seeing things through the same lens as I did this morning, which feels like a lifetime ago. The evening traffic seems deflated, less energized. There are no children in bright school uniforms, only what seem to be abandoned people surrounded by ruin.

In my head, I'm still in the OR. It's a surgeon's worst nightmare. The paralysis of uncertainty. Did I do any good today? How can I go back in there? There's no cheering section, no reassuring voices. You fixate on your last mistake. In fact all you see is a flood of all your mistakes. I'm conscious not to let this inner turmoil make its way out. I know we're not supposed to bottle things up, but in this instance, in this place, it's important to keep calm for the team. My self-pity expedition is exhausting, and despite the chaos that surrounds me, and the uncertain security, I fall asleep as we traverse the mountain roads.

I stir awake when the convoy pulls to a stop, and we proceed, with our armed escort, back into the heavily guarded house that feels more like a compound. We all sit exhausted. I am still trying to remember everyone's name. Tonight we will sleep on a bed under the hum of a generator and the scent of the mosquito net. I lather up in fly repellent, grab a slice of pizza and a cold beer, and within minutes I am nodding off again. The lights still on, everyone else awake.

As I drift off, I'm revisited by some faces from the day. The despondent girl with AIDS in particular. I wonder where she is tonight. What was her life like before all this? Where, if anywhere, does she find joy? Those eyes, though. They said, Don't bother, hope left here long ago. The thought stings. I stare at the wall ahead, the collage of faces projected onto it like a home movie.

This place is beautiful—the political history less so, but the people, the scenery are truly beautiful. Even the smells are strangely perfect. I think about some of the faces in the lineup outside the OR. The pain they are in but the smiles they somehow manage to find. I have never witnessed hope in the eyes of patients like I have in Haiti. There's the unwavering family commitment to each other, their undying pride for the people they are and the land they love. That's so hard to explain to anyone who hasn't experienced it. I see the woman with AIDS again. Smile. Please smile. Give me something that looks like a hint of hope.

The next day starts on a positive note. It feels like some order is making its way into the disorder. We wake, shower, and descend towards the hospital. It takes about forty-five minutes in the endless traffic, and we decide to set out earlier tomorrow to avoid the craziness. As we pull through the hospital gates, the funeral home is present in the background. We spend less time getting ready today and jump in right away as the team scurries to their duties.

Will and I begin rounds, checking on patients we operated on the day before. The tents feel hotter and seem fuller than the day before. I'm sure the patients don't know what to make of us. Are we saints? Demons? Just outsiders? Some composite of all three, maybe. The degree of trust they placed in our hands without being able to speak the same language. Is it trust or just a lack of options? The sweat is beginning to pool on my back and neck. We still have not mastered expediently getting through patient rounds in tents; more time with patients means it takes far longer than we would like. It is now almost eleven and we have not operated yet.

The first surgery case is another hip replacement. The patient, we are told, has had a broken hip since the time of the earthquake and has been in a tent hospital since. He is lying there with a pin in his shin attached to a well-worn rope that hangs off the end of the bed with a bucket containing rocks at its end.

It's primitive traction. It catches me off guard and I find myself staring at it as if it's a display in a medical museum. Traction is a form of treatment used years ago to prevent broken bones from moving so they would heal. It is usually rigged with a series of pulleys and is not meant to be used for long. But this man had been lying flat on his back with the bucket pulling on him for months. If left much longer, it will pull him to his death.

The realness comes back when I notice his bedside companion must be his granddaughter. She can't be any more than eleven, in a dirty dress, pigtails, and the serious face of someone far older. She did not leave her grandfather's side the entire time. Most kids her age would be riding their bikes and going to school, just being kids, not providing this kind of care to their grandparent in such a grave situation.

Will begins explaining the surgery to the patient and the girl through an interpreter. The girl stands still, focusing on the risks and benefits that are being mentioned. She's intense, and it gives a different vibe to what would be a normal hospital procedure back home. Once we are finished the explanation, she nods her head, there is a conversation in Creole, and they agree to go ahead. She walks alongside her grandfather being carried on the stretcher to the operating room and waits outside with the bucket in the tree-shaded courtyard.

Things go smoothly. The procedure is routine and I'm confident in the outcome. But the whole time I am aware of the young girl's presence, as if she's right on my elbow as I work, close, the way kids stand when they want to see what you're doing. The procedure goes well, with no complications. Will and I walk with the patient to the makeshift recovery room. We will wait until he is stabilized before making the journey through the collapsed portion of the hospital to get his postoperative X-ray done.

The surgery has taken a few hours, but as I walk out of the building, the young girl is still sitting there. There is no translator near. When she sees me, she leaps to her feet. I slow my pace and smile. Her previously serious face returns the smile. For the first time she looks her age. I give her the thumbs-up, and she sits back down with the smile still on her face.

All I can see is my own daughters sitting there, waiting for news from a surgeon. I get fidgety and I'm suddenly uncomfortable with my emotions, so I turn away and wait for Will.

We take the patient on an unruly stretcher across the uneven pavement of the courtyard. On our way, we are stopped by other team members to look at X-rays and hear of patients to be seen. We balance the stretcher carefully as we pass through a makeshift gateway that leads into one of the most damaged areas of the hospital, through a room where a large chunk of rubble has collapsed directly onto a hospital bed, the green walls still bright.

On the other side of the room lies another outside courtyard. Standing among garbage and rubble is one building that looks relatively well preserved. It is the X-ray suite. Outside the doors, in the direct sun, hang X-ray films drying in the Caribbean heat. It is a far cry from even the old developing labs that used to exist in our hospitals. They are pinned up with clothespins, the Kodak agents dripping onto the ground beneath, creating the distinct scent of a dark room.

There is a delay in the doors opening, as the X-ray personnel are busy listening to a soccer match on the radio. Life goes on. Eventually our patient is taken in and the doors close. Will and I are left to pass the time near the ruins. Around the corner, there's a large room that is collapsed except for one intact wall with windows. Peering through a broken window, I see it is—or was—a cafeteria. It looks like any cafeteria: there are trays scattered about, seats, and the metal tubing in a line to push your tray along. The rest of the room is masses of rubble and darkness. Peering in gives me a childhood feeling, one of misadventures in a basement or graveyard. I get goosebumps and quickly turn away.

Luckily the patient is ready for transport back through disaster's maze. The X-rays will take time to dry and we will need to come back. The disturbing image of life at the time of a disaster is replaced by the smile of the young girl as we come to her grandfather's bedside in the tent. The smile, the hope in her eyes, the commitment to her grandfather, the universality of family. She smiles in spite of her surroundings. She smiles to see the familiar face of a loved one. It is contagious. Person by person around her, we all light up.

I am buoyed by this case and it sustains me for the remainder of the days of that first week-long trip. The faces become an amalgam. The young woman with AIDS. The granddaughter. Every nurse, patient, orderly, everyone waiting in line for treatment, the drivers, the guards, all of them. They become a silent choir in my head. The long stares are their song. Part melancholy, part "Ode to Joy," part funeral procession. It is the answer I don't say when asked what I'm thinking. It accompanies me through the rest of the week and only builds in its quiet numbers. They want me to speak. To say something. They don't want my pity. Nor tears. Nor anger. They watch my hands set bones. Fix things. But the stares never change.

The long ride back to the airport is a mix of relief and that energy you sometimes find in complete exhaustion. Allison wonders aloud about our kids. Will checks his phone. I watch the landscape pass and think about the flight descending towards St. John's, its clustered lights like some forgotten colony hidden among the stones that tower out of the ocean. My silent chorus finally speaks. "What will you do?" they ask. "What are you going to do?" I close my eyes tightly, trying to remember the sound of my grandmother's voice.

8

THE TWO ISLANDS

Cap-Haïtien: October 2014

THE ORIGINAL TEAM and the expanded teams have been back to Haiti many times now. With each trip I notice the subtle differences. Another road cleared of rubble. Construction scaffolding. Progress. The scope of our missions had been progressing as well. So much so that we decided to expand our reach to areas of Haiti beyond the capital region.

During one of these trips, Dr. Art Rideout and I found ourselves in Cap-Haïtien. We decided to walk to the Citadelle, a large seventeenth-century fortress and UNESCO World Heritage Site. I've been to sites like this before. Tourist traps, with rows and rows of souvenir kiosks selling odd knick-knacks to flocks of people. But this was different. It was an hour-long hike to just reach the base of the old fortress. When we arrived, there wasn't a soul in sight. No one. No selfie sticks. No shops. Nothing.

We started the walk up a series of switchbacks. Along the beginning of the trail, in the cover of forest, there were suddenly lots of children and goats. Under the tree canopy and mounting heat, we noticed there were huts on each side of the trail, with pale-eyed merchants peddling small hand-crafted wooden souvenirs. Closer still, it became obvious that these huts were not local stores. They were homes, with dirt floors, roofs of scrap wood and leaves thatched together. Tiny, rustic huts with no dividers and no bathrooms or kitchens. It was a reminder that, UNESCO or not, in Haiti you are always this close to poverty.

I still expected to see tourists, but there were none. Art and I had the entire Citadelle to ourselves. This gigantic fortress has a nose the shape of the bow of a boat. My vision blurred a little from a combination of sweat and sunscreen in my eyes. Suddenly we could see the ocean and could not help but wonder how this place was built. I mean, it was a good ten-hour walk from the ocean, which is where the cannons, cannonballs, and other supplies would have landed. Art and I were soaked in sweat, and all we were carrying was our phones. But someone made the trek here. Someone carried those loads in this heat, swarmed by mosquitoes.

Until this point I had only considered the recent history of Haiti, the coups, the occupations, the reigns of terror of some leaders. I had not given much thought to the history of this country we were trying to help. Our presence here had been an immediate reaction to a current crisis. I've been back many times since the earthquake. The trips are always jam-packed with work. But these moments, like standing here near the dark stones of this old fortress, make me more curious about pre-earthquake Haiti. I have come from one island to this island. Both have had centuries of experience with colonialism, but their paths went in radically different directions.

Being an islander is its own special thing. And only islanders truly understand it. Something about the sense of isolation manifests itself in how we treat each other. How the world treats us. I think that's part of the reason why Haiti resonates with me. The historical paths could not be more different. The plight of the population in both places could not be more different. But there are similarities in how our long, complicated, often truculent histories have shaped who we are into the identity of where we are from.

Haiti was discovered by Columbus during his epic voyage of 1492. John Cabot is said to have made landfall in Newfoundland five years later. Haiti was claimed by the Spanish and called Hispaniola. Like Newfoundland, she had vast resources, not from the sea but of the land: sugar, tobacco, and coffee. In the 1600s the French established colonies around the world. When the French began to settle in Hispaniola, Champlain was exploring Canada and the French claimed ownership of Newfoundland and Labrador.

In 1697 the island of Hispaniola was divided between the French and the Spanish. The French claimed the mountainous west side while the Spanish maintained the more hospitable eastern foothills, now the Dominican Republic. As in North America, these lands were already inhabited by natives, and, in an all too familiar story, they were wiped out by violence and disease.

The French part of the island, known as Saint-Domingue, became one of the most profitable of the French colonies. Throughout the 1700s almost eight hundred thousand African slaves were brought to the colony to work on the plantations. That is estimated to be about twice the number brought to North America during the same period. *Twice*. That stat gives me chills.

Around the same time, settlers from Europe began pouring into North America. While plantations ruled the south, the north was ruled by trapping, logging, and fishing. In Newfoundland in 1610, British settlers established one of the first permanent overseas settlements, in Cupids, followed by settlements throughout the seventeenth and eighteenth centuries in Carbonear, St. John's, Twillingate, and others. The early settlers were often servants or "planters" or common fishermen who had completed a period of servitude to merchants or the Crown. Newly independent, they either married locally or brought their wives and families from Europe.

While the new inhabitants of Newfoundland were battling the elements, and those in the upper colonies were battling for territory and protecting their own land from Americans, Haiti had a much different problem: zombies. You read that correctly. Working and living conditions for the slaves were so bad that they literally worked until they died; the mortality rate has been estimated at 50 per cent. When one slave died, a new one was imported. The cruelty and the endless work caused some to take their own lives. The Creole and voodoo folklore of the time maintained that slaves who died would be returned to their homes in Africa, whereas those who took their own lives would be destined to wander Haiti as a soulless body, undead, a slave to the island forever. These zombies can be summoned today by voodoo priests to roam the streets and follow their commands. A far cry from what we see in zombie movies today, but the sad origin is part of Haiti's dark history.

Repression can only end in one of two extremes: annihilation or revolution. So whether it was the gruelling heat, the punishing work, the threat of death by crucifixion or drowning, or worse still, becoming an eternal slave and zombie, things began to boil over. News of the French Revolution had made its way to the island. Unrest grew, and in 1791 the slaves mounted their own revolution, against not just their owners but a formidable suppressive leader, Napoleon.

Much of the revolution was fought on the northern parts of the colony, in places like Cap-Haïtien. The French and their allies grossly underestimated the tenacity and intelligence of the slaves and were outmatched in the jungle. Touring the battle sites today, it's hard to imagine the French landing on the beaches straight from Paris, wearing their traditional heavy sailor attire in the blazing heat, only to fall victim to the same violence, disease, and malnutrition they had inflicted upon the slave population.

Uprisings are the stuff of legends, from Moses to Spartacus to William Wallace. Henri Christophe was one of the heroes of the Haitian revolution, and there are many monuments to him today in Cap-Haïtien. He led the slaves in the north, and when the French demanded the return of the city, Christophe took control of a fortress and threatened to burn the place to the ground. Some of the Haitian rebels surrendered to the French, believing their promise of the end of slavery and a guarantee that the former slaves could join the French army. This was a lie and eventually led to heightened guerrilla warfare.

The French forces, led by Napoleon's brother-in-law, eventually lost thirty-two thousand troops to the effects of yellow fever, with twenty-four thousand dying from the disease. In 1803, after twelve years of conflict, Napoleon ceded Saint-Domingue and French territory in North America. Haiti declared its sovereignty in 1804, becoming the first black independent nation in the world. It was renamed after the indigenous word for a mountainous land, Haiti.

At the same time, Newfoundland itself was in conflict, with the French, British, and Spanish all claiming ownership over some of the richest fishing grounds in the world. In 1762, the French landed in St. John's, only to be defeated by British forces. The French—and French fishermen—were eventually granted access to and ownership of the islands off the coast of Newfoundland, Saint-Pierre and Miquelon. They still belong to France today, and even though you can almost see them from the shores of Marystown, you need your passport to land there.

In 1867 Canada became a nation with the support of Britain and with the diplomatic and peaceful agreement of Upper and Lower Canada. Newfoundland rejected union with Canada in an election in 1869 and was destined to become her own dominion in a peaceful, organized fashion.

Whereas the wheels of diplomacy and negotiation calmly turned in Newfoundland, Haiti had no such luck. Napoleon refused to recognize the country as independent. Other countries, fearing their own slave-led revolutions, joined in supporting France's position. The persecution, torture, and killing of the five thousand remaining white inhabitants of Haiti resulted in crippling trade embargoes and threw the new country into political, financial, and social disarray. France and the international community refused to recognize the Republic of Haiti unless financial compensation was made to the tune of 150 million gold francs for lost property and slaves. Haiti was faced with a decision: to continue to suffer under the intense embargo or settle the debt. Haiti took out high-interest loans to pay France and the embargo was lifted. The loans would not be repaid until 1947. The revolution had been meant to lift Haiti from poverty, but instead it set the course for the country to become one of the poorest in the world.

Haiti struggled to recover from the sanctions. A series of failed governments and growing German influence in the country were cause for concern. As the country fell into further turmoil, the United States worried that Haiti would default on its loans, and so it occupied the country from 1915 until 1934. The U.S. Marines were the main occupying force, and they built roads and other infrastructure, drawing a debt of manual labour from those who could not afford to pay tax.

Fresh off the first successful transatlantic radio message from St. John's, Newfoundland became independent when Britain granted it dominion status in 1907. Despite the non-revolutionary path to independence, Newfoundland would suffer a heavy burden early on. The Great War drew on Newfoundland's men, money, and resources. With crushing losses in Beaumont-Hamel and a crushing war debt, the new dominion could no longer meet its payroll. Bankrupt, it surrendered independence back to Britain. A commission of government was established with a surrogate decision maker for the newly defunct nation. Though not occupied by foreign soldiers, Newfoundland was crippled with debt, and many who lived in the small communities and fishing towns of the Rock struggled to survive.

In the 1940s two paths were forged for both island nations. In Newfoundland, there was great debate about what path was best to take for the future of the place. Should we remain independent, join the United States, or remain attached to the Commonwealth? All options were on the table, and a great deal of political manoeuvring and posturing culminated in a referendum in 1948 that, with the narrowest of margins, created a new Father of Confederation in Joseph Smallwood. The result of the referendum divided the population for years. There are those who felt the 51/49 per cent outcome was rigged and to this day still prefer the flag of the old republic.

In Haiti, the situation was less amicable and much less fortunate. The Americans pulled out, leaving a void in authority that led to a compounding and escalating concentration of power. The only form of government that tends to benefit and flourish in those conditions is a dictatorship. Attempts at more quasi-democratic control consistently failed.

The juntas took control and attempted to re-establish governance. That too failed, and what followed was a period of quick turnovers of multiple presidents. In 1957 "Papa Doc" François Duvalier, one of the world's most notorious criminals who also, unfortunately, happened to be a doctor and former minister of health, was elected president. He ruled by concentrating power and using a paramilitary force that would eventually threaten, rape, or kill over thirty thousand Haitians. One of the most corrupt, torturous, and deadliest rulers of the Western Hemisphere came to the attention of the Kennedy administration, which stopped aid to the troubled country.

By comparison, Canada's newest province continued unprecedented development. Cities, roads, hospitals, bridges, medicines, vaccines, and safety regulations became more modern as Newfoundland industrialized. Yes, there were pitfalls and some legendary bad deals, but I don't think anyone could logically dispute that we were better off as part of Canada.

At this time the population of Haiti was approximately four million, and you could have fit the country of Haiti fourteen times neatly inside the boundaries of Newfoundland and Labrador.

In Haiti, things always seem to go from bad to worse. You'd think when a gruesome murderer dies, things would get better.

But on Papa Doc's death in 1971, he passed the murderous knife to his nineteen-year-old son, the infamous "Baby Doc." Baby Doc shared his father's flair for repression. Although the killings may have been lower in number, the financial abuse of the people was worse, as Baby Doc allegedly pocketed millions that had been meant for aid. After Pope John Paul II called out the dictator in the early 1980s, the U.S. demanded that Baby Doc resign. He was exiled to France in 1986, only returning to Haiti in 2011 and dying there in 2014.

I saw him once in my travels. We were at a restaurant in Port-au-Prince with a Haitian friend who calmly said the man a few tables over was Baby Doc. I wasn't sure what I expected to see, perhaps a large military figure, an imposing force. Instead, sitting at the table was a shell of a man, a wilted frame, his face thin, shoulders narrow. A man whose cruelty to the Haitian people is unfathomable was sitting there being served a cup of coffee. I couldn't believe that it was Baby Doc until we went outside and saw the guard and the kind of vehicle reserved for government officials.

I tend to see things through a medical filter. I can't help it. I've thought a lot about these parallel journeys of two island nations. In some respects, it's a lot like a child. How it turns out is very much a result of how it is treated in its infancy. Is it nurtured and cared for well? Is it fed properly and given the medical necessities? The thing with the birth of a baby is that once we get through it and come out the other side, the hope is that we can raise a child to become better than his or her parents. We all are a product of our history. We stand on the shoulders of all of those who have gone before us. It takes a village to raise a child.

For these two island nations, the paths could not have been more different.

My hand touches the weathered stones of the old fortress. It stands there in silent witness, built by slaves and having known only decline, repression, and violence ever since. I think about Signal Hill in St. John's and going there on a school trip years and years ago. The tiny stone Cabot Tower where the first transatlantic wireless message was sent and received. A positive herald for the future. Progress is coming. Hope's coming with it. But here, on this island, there is only the sound of the surf in the distance, a few vendors chanting their offerings as the heat continues its relentless assault.

9

THE LESSON OF BALANCE

St. John's: Summer 2010–Summer 2011

WHEN YOU HAVE kids, they're always somewhere in your mind. No matter what you are doing or where you might be, inevitably your thoughts will turn to them. What are they doing? Are they happy? Are they safe? Those thoughts were amplified during my first week in Haiti.

I don't wear my heart on my sleeve. As a doctor, you honestly can't. But at the mention, the mere thought, of my kids, I'm holding back tears. I know Allison is feeling the same thing. We don't talk about it. Feels like a mutual-assured-destruction situation if we bring it up. We're exhausted. We both stare at the seatbacks in front of us. That first hug will be like badly needed medicine. Those little faces looking up at us. Innocent. Full of joy. They have no idea where we've been, no comprehension of the hard things we've seen.

Of the feelings I carry, guilt is always one. Even though this was by all accounts a successful mission, I feel these odd pangs of guilt. Guilt for leaving when there's so much more that needs to be done. Guilt for the life I'm returning to from the abject poverty I merely visited. I keep thinking of that little girl waiting for her grandfather outside the surgery. Her eyes so full of hope. There was an irresistible comparison to my own children's eyes.

How easy it is to fall back into routines again. Kids' homework, an upcoming recital, the drive to work, the cafeteria coffee. The long faces of those shuffling in and out of the hospital. The blank stares of those waiting at the clinics. I'll be sitting in my office, reading a file, readying to see the next patient, but my thoughts are still in that dark operating room. It hits me that I have changed. I'm noticing things that I did not before. There is a new clarity. I have a new appreciation for the law and order of simple things: the simplicity of traffic, people moving in an orderly fashion, being able to brush my teeth with tap water. The lingering organic smell of the ocean. How our community functions like a hive. I feel the extent of my naivety. The weight of guilt.

I keep reliving moments of the previous weeks in high-definition flashbacks. The contrast is blinding. I live in a big, comfortable house. I drive a nice car. I don't fear violence beyond the walls around me. I eat when I'm hungry, or even when I'm not. I take long showers. I eat fresh oysters with friends before heading to a show. What the hell is this? Was this the point of that first trip to Haiti? To make me feel awful about what I've accomplished, what life has brought me? Nothing was ever handed to me. I've worked so hard for everything I have.

Yet the guilt exists.

It exists because I've seen behind the curtain. I've been beyond the wall. There's a whole world suffering that no one is talking about beyond Band-Aid solutions and nightly news reports just after the weather. It feels like no one realizes the suffering that is happening.

———

Back home in St. John's in the summer of 2010, I saw my first patient, a middle-aged man. He was slightly overweight and admitted that he had not maintained any real level of fitness. He was complaining of back pain. Lower back pain is such a common complaint that it is almost considered to be normal, so much so that is it is abnormal to go through life and not experience it.

The patient said it hurt to stand at work and that this was probably being caused by his job. His self-diagnosis aside, I have to admit that I wasn't feeling very empathetic at the time. It wasn't about him, it was about me. I've got a pretty good poker face so I listened but part of me wanted to tell him flatly that he didn't have a real problem and he shouldn't be here. Looking back, I know that would've been me projecting feelings I had about the situation in Haiti upon someone who knows nothing about it. I wanted to take out on him the poverty, the lack of healthcare, the uncertainty.

Here he was, complaining of lower back pain and asking if he should take time off work to recover. I was silent for a long time. Then I told him he would be fine and could go back to work.

It wasn't his fault. This situation became the lightning rod for the tension that had been building inside me. God, I felt bad for even thinking this way. He was just looking for a little help. And I would like to say that this was the only such episode during those first couple of weeks after I got back, but I can't.

What the hell is this feeling? This guilt? What purpose does it serve anyone?

I didn't choose the circumstances into which I was born, and the opportunities they provided me is not something I chose. I shouldn't feel guilty about it. I won't. What I will do is flip the feeling. Everything that's gone into making me who I am must now drive what I will do. What I can do. My grandmother didn't spend a minute that I know of feeling sorry for herself. She willed change to happen. Her inner strength—which I pray I have even a fraction of—fuelled her resolve. And the patient with back pain? To him, his back pain was as important as the broken bones were to the patients in Haiti. Lesson learned. I could be angry, depressed, and deflated. Or I could do something about it.

Scariest question: Where to start?

When I was putting together a team for our second visit to Haiti, the first problem was that we had nowhere to work out of. The hospital where we had been based on the first trip, St. François de Sales, in Port-au-Prince, had been condemned. So I started researching the various medical agencies at work on the ground in Haiti. There were quite a few, but I was looking for a group with a long-term commitment and vision. They had to be the right fit. I was going all-in on this, so I wanted to make sure I made the right choice.

That's when I remembered hearing about a neurosurgeon who had started a project in Haiti years before the earthquake. After the earthquake he quickly changed his focus to trauma. Dr. Barth Green was from Miami and his project was called Medishare. I contacted the team to see if we could partner with them, or at least at the beginning try a trip to their hospital. They were incredibly enthusiastic about the idea.

By that time, Medishare had moved from operating in tents to working out of a hospital in downtown Port-au-Prince, Bernard Mevs. The hospital is named after a famous Haitian physician from one of the most influential families in the country. It started as a home but had grown into a 30- to 40-bed hospital and out-patient clinic. After the earthquake, it was one of the only places in the country providing trauma and critical care. It was a perfect fit. After the first trip I have come to know Dr. Green very well. He's a kind, charismatic, industrious visionary who has his heart and mind set in the right direction. It seems every move he makes is with empathy and compassion for his patients and the people of Haiti. Our partnership with Project Medishare is a perfect symbiotic fit.

I will always marvel at how the first team came together in 2011. We didn't really ask many to be involved, yet suddenly we had a team of over twenty-five. There had been a buzz at the hospital about our original mission. And then that very Newfoundland thing happened: everyone wanted to help. We now had a combination of highly skilled nurses, doctors, and physiotherapists, all ready to help a country they had never been to and knew little about. Each knowing they were giving up their vacation time to step into the unknown. It was overwhelming.

You won't see this on any tourism commercial, but the wind in Newfoundland is a beast. In winter it just cuts right through you. It was one of those nights. Dark and just howling outside. Snow whipping and shaking the house like it was going to take flight. I was going through notes and countless to-do lists in my head. I was also kicking around a name for our team. Did we need one? Giving the team a name would make it feel more real. And by "more real" I mean sustainable. Not just once. Not an event. An entity. A team. Teams have a name.

One of our team members was married to a woman who had visited Haiti before the earthquake and knew some Creole. I asked her if she had any ideas about a name, preferably one without *Haiti* in it in case we wanted to replicate the initiative elsewhere. Within hours she came back with *"raze tè,"* which means "broken earth." It was a reference to the earthquake but spoke to the heart of what we wanted to do. To help. To heal what's broken. To bring hope. This was it. Broken earth. Team Broken Earth.

So here we are again.

This time feels a little easier. Hearts are not as heavy because family and friends know why this trip is so necessary. The big difference this time is the number of people we have with us. Twenty-seven. This brought a new sense of responsibility I do not know if I'm prepared to handle, like organizing a big wedding or some complicated school trip. This was a leap of faith. People trusted me, trusted my guidance. Truth is, I felt like I was making this up on the fly.

Had I overpromised, oversold? Would everyone be safe? How high were their expectations, and could they even be reached? But the wheels were in motion. And when these things move, they move as fast as Newfoundland wind. The effort to organize this group was gigantic, yet it was so rewarding that it felt effortless. After a few pre-departure meetings, we were off.

In the summer of 2011, more than a year since the earthquake, the airport in Port-au-Prince is the same as we left it. The disorder has not dissipated at all. We all slather ourselves with hand sanitizer and fly repellent. We are hurried through customs and wait for our bags to be thrown into the barn-like hangar. In the stifling heat, our Team Broken Earth T-shirts quickly become like wet towels. Pushing through the crowd of passengers, we manage to collect our bags and proceed outside into the blazing summer Caribbean sun to wait for our companion.

Soon enough we are packed into cube vans in a ritual that will become common. Our bags are thrown in after us. We move slowly through the sweltering heat and chaos of the streets of Port-au-Prince. There have been some recognizable changes, but the place is still very familiar. We wind through a round-about and pass a massive tent city adjacent to the airport. There seems to be far less debris, and traffic now travels in two directions, a small win. I am acutely aware of everyone's impressions and reactions to their surroundings. Oddly too, I'm also compulsively counting heads.

We pass brightly covered tap-taps (local cabs) and some motorcycles with three people on them. The UN presence is ubiquitous now, blue helmets and armoured vehicles throughout the streets. Surprisingly the UN presence makes me more nervous, not less. Something about the cold and unfamiliar feeling of armed men in armed vehicles is so foreign, it makes me uneasy.

The pungent smell and taste of the air near the tent city is unchanged and equally rich. I notice some of the team members gag. Others try to conceal their shock. Rubble is still piled high along the roadsides.

I have the long drive from my first trip in my head, and I'm prepared for it this time. But the drive to this new hospital surprises me. After only a few minutes, we take a turn onto an unpaved road, past an enormous steaming mound of refuse. On this street people are selling and trading clothing and food. Normal life on the streets of Port-au-Prince.

We are on the outer perimeter of Cité Soleil, an incredibly poor and densely populated area in downtown Port-au-Prince. It is a confusing mixture of homes and street vendors that started as a makeshift shantytown and has grown to have over three hundred thousand people living in it—the poorest of the poor in Port-au-Prince. (I later learned this was in the red zone of the city, one of the most dangerous areas in the world. Visitors, even UN staff, are advised not to go there under any circumstances. What an opportune place for doubt to creep back in.)

The gates of the hospital are closed. They are massive green metal gates with arching tops that have a curiously inviting feeling to them. The horn blows, and two heavily armed men open the gates to reveal our new home for the week. It doesn't look like a hospital. It has a vast courtyard, with multiple stand-alone buildings, all connected by an overriding decorative arch that has defied the forces of the earthquake and remains standing. I take that as a good omen.

We are hurried into a room for an operational briefing where we discuss security and the plan for the week before a tour of the hospital. There's little time to digest our surroundings. A bunch of Newfoundlanders and Labradorians sit in a hot room talking about the week ahead. The gravity of it is intensely real.

The briefing is cut short. There is a trauma in the OR. The hospital has a small staff of general surgeons but they need an orthopedic for a broken femur that has torn through the skin. I hurry to find the patient and quickly change into my scrubs. Before I have any time to figure out where I am in the compound, I am scrubbing my hands. Welcome back, I think. The familiarity of the ritual is actually calming. There are Haitian nurses, and anesthesia has already been started. It all goes like clockwork. I'm drenched in sweat but relieved that the first case is soon over. This baptism by fire surprises the rest of the crew. I pull off my mask and manage a smile.

The team is still doing the tour of the facilities when a few of us stop to help a very sick man who has pretty much stumbled into the courtyard. He is pale and frail. At the request of the local doctors, our team inserts the breathing tube. Opinions are discussed. Someone realizes the man has cholera. The hospital is not a cholera centre, and those patients are ordinarily directed to specific cholera centres. There is panic as the patient is whisked away. They are stripped out of their clothing and hosed down with diluted bleach. The patient later dies from dehydration.

Baptism by fire? No. This is baptism by flamethrower. And we haven't even unpacked our bags yet.

No one expected four-star accommodations, but twelve of us are jammed into a room where bunk beds take up every square inch. Only two people can stand at once. The floor is dirt and uneven. A single light bulb hangs down, teasing that it may provide some light. There is no bathroom, and we are left to try to find these facilities throughout the rest of the compound when needed. It is a good time to remind everyone not to drink the water, open their mouths in the shower, or brush their teeth with the tap water. Oh, and to not flush paper of any sort down the toilets.

We are finally given a real tour of the operating rooms. It's all much better than I was expecting. There are two rooms, with an operating table and anesthesia machine in each. Both sets of equipment are battered, tape holding them together, but functioning. I know this because the anesthesia machine is making that familiar sound they do when they are plugged in but idle. Bop-beep-boop-boop, over and over until the machine is turned off or put into action. When you sit in an empty operating room, it is often the only thing you can hear. It's comforting, a tiny comfort of familiarity.

There is no autoclave. Instead, in a corner next to the recovery room, there is a desk-top sterilizer, usually used in dentist's offices or small outpatient surgical centres. It's not much larger than a microwave oven. On the ground next to it is a gigantic pile of used surgical tools and equipment. This will be a project for the week. I see the operating room nurses' shoulders slouch with the weight of the task.

The rest of the tour takes us to pediatrics, a long room full of children in different stages of illness. Their cage-like cribs are crowded together. On the wall is a painted picture of a Sesame Street character. At the end of the ward is a separate room used for neonatal resuscitation or recovery of hydrocephalus patients. It's a simple square room, and the patients in their cribs appear to be breaths away from death. It is one of the loneliest rooms I have ever been in. Their moms hold bedside vigils.

From there we tour the medical surgical wards, consisting of two small rooms. The wards are completely full, poorly lit, and each has an industrial-sized fan in the middle, pointed at the ceiling, and spewing recycled hot stale air. The beds are in varying states of disrepair; some are propped up on books to level them, and some don't even have sheets. Some of the patients have blood-soaked bandages and casts, and their families hover around their beds. It looks like a scene from a horror movie. There is not enough room to turn around, so we observe from the door. The smell is tough to take.

Attached to one of the medical surgical wards is the emergency room. It's not so much a room as it is a two-bed space that is separated from the ward by a half wall that doubles as a workstation. It contains two gurneys. Both are occupied by patients being treated by local doctors and nurses. They glance up and wave at us.

It will be in these tight quarters that the team makes some of our closest relationships over the years, working shoulder to shoulder, elbow to elbow, in the foxhole of that cramped ER.

Here I will meet one of the kindest, most gentle and efficient doctors I have ever worked with. Rivette Louis Juste is a young Haitian doctor who has tight curly hair and carries a balance of maturity and motherhood that only comes with experience. I am constantly reminded of Allison whenever I see her.

Dr. Rivette is one of many Haitians who will become an integral part of the team over the years. She's a hands-on, dedicated doctor in the ER. Methodical. Calm. Never panics. Always steady. Not only will she work side by side with the team, but she will help us organize and teach our trauma course in Port-au-Prince. She will bring balance to an otherwise shaky place.

Once we are settled, the team's nurses get down to organizing the OR, the anesthesia team checks out the machines and drugs, and the ER doctors and remaining nurses go to work in triage at the makeshift workstation. The week starts with a bang and keeps going heavily throughout the days and nights. I like watching the team gel. It's pure medicine. Many moving parts working as one. More than a team, really. A family.

About halfway through the week, I am sitting in a darkened room, head light on as I rummage through my backpack. We are all feeling pretty good by this point. We feel that we're making a difference, even if it's only in a small way. Most of the team is off-site, at the UN compound for dinner. Downtime is important. It gives people a chance to leave the compound, stretch their legs and their minds, reset their compass before coming back to hard work and long hours. We had decided early on to make sure there was always a smaller team of essential people left on-site should an emergency arise. This has proved to be a good idea.

I am interrupted by a Haitian nurse, asking me to come to the ER. An eighteen-year-old girl who had been shot in the abdomen is becoming unstable.

I hurry into the sweltering ER room. This girl, I think, is too young to be lying here. She is getting worse. Her blood pressure has dropped and her heart rate is rapidly increasing.

I examine her and find a small hole in the right upper side of her abdomen, a little below her liver. She is breathing more rapidly now despite the oxygen we are giving her. She does not speak English. She does not need to; her eyes speak volumes. She is panicked and afraid. She needs to be taken urgently to the operating room. Her abdomen is filling with blood and causing her blood pressure to drop. She will need surgery to stop the bleeding.

Back home in Canada, this patient would have a blood transfusion of as much as needed to help her through the surgery and recovery. Here, no such luxury exists. There are no blood products, only saline to help maintain her blood volume as blood spills into her abdomen.

Another problem: the general surgeon and one of our anesthesiologists are away at dinner. We quickly call them and arrange for a driver to bring them back. This will take time. The patient is dying in front of our eyes.

We decide not to wait. We start the procedure. This case will push my surgical skills beyond my capabilities until the cavalry arrives. I estimate that by the time I have the abdomen prepped, the surgeon will be here. The patient does not have time or blood to spare.

We move as one. It is an impressive feat when a medical and trauma team mobilize. Life-and-death decisions are made in seconds, portions of seconds, and like a military unit, the execution is rapid and precise. I remember during my fellowship, being in the trauma bay and just watching, standing back and watching the method, the chemistry. If each and every decision was allowed to hang, a systemic paralysis would set in. But a team moves flawlessly, supporting each other, following decisions at the speed of light. An orchestra at work. It's magic. It's the reason I became a surgeon.

No time for masks as we rush the girl to the small operating room. The doors of the OR fly open as we push the patient through like in a TV drama. They crash loudly against the walls on each side. Papers fly off a desk as we strike it with the gurney. The anesthesia resident, with another anesthesiologist, is waiting with a kit of drugs ready to deliver. We don't even stop to log in the patient. The light is dim and the anesthesia machine makes its presence known with a beep. The air-conditioned room is a welcome relief to me but must seem so foreign to the patient.

The patient's breathing is now more shallow and rapid. She looks directly into my eyes. She is terrified. She is alone, looking into the face of a white surgeon with a maple leaf scrub hat. She is grimacing in pain, and her eyes are fixed on mine, locked in a stare. She is searching for either comfort or reassurance. I'm not sure what she wants but she is searching for some response from me. The reassurance I am trained to provide, that I should be providing, eludes me. She instead is seeing my despair and fright. I can't shake the look on her face. Those eyes locked on me. I feel as if I am failing her.

Eighteen years old. What were her dreams? Where's her family? What path brought her here? I don't even know her name. But here she is in the cold operating room. A team prepares for sterile technique while the anesthesia team prepares to put the patient to sleep. Drugs flow through the plastic tubing and she takes a last breath on her own. From now on that will be controlled by our doctors and the technology of a breathing tube and the anesthesia machine. Now it is over to the surgical team.

Her abdomen is prepped and draped as I scrub my hands with two assistants. We are informed that the general surgeon is on his way. I'm nervous but there is not much choice. We push through the OR door, hands raised, masks on, gowns on, a time-honoured ritual. Nurses are ready, anesthesia is ready, I'm ready.

Dave Pace, the general surgeon, has arrived. Scalpel firmly in hand, I push into the girl's skin, making an incision for opening her abdomen. Her heart rate is rapid, and the beeping of the machine is equally paced. Jeremy Pridham has both hands wrapped around a bag of fluids, pushing it through the IV tubing as fast as his muscles will allow. Dave Pace joins the surgical field as we open the girl's abdomen. Several litres of blood gush out onto the table. Through the sea of red we find the source. She has been shot in a critical artery under her liver, as well as other areas. Dave instructs me to clamp the artery between my fingers. The bleeding stops. This is a complicated repair, and she has lost a lot of blood. If you completely ligate, or tie off, the artery, she will die. If you do not repair it, she will die. But to repair it, she will need blood.

When I take my fingers off the artery, it is still pumping, but now it is pumping clear fluids. The same fluids that our team are giving her through her IV are now being squirted into her abdomen. She has no red blood left. It is obvious her young heart has outlasted and outperformed. It doesn't know the game is over. Eventually these fluids stop squirting. There is a gentle beat of her heart on the machines, but it too is fading. Then silence.

Heads down, hearts heavy, we know we have done everything we could have, but it doesn't lessen the blow.

Eighteen, I keep thinking, just eighteen.

We proceed to suture her wounds. Everything now feels cold and strange. Nurses help clean up, the surgical drapes are removed with dignity, tubes and lines are removed. The team is defeated, and we leave the girl motionless on the table.

I return to the OR and sit down, head down in my hands. The lack of movement is eerie, and in the background the anesthesia machine does its bop-beep-boop-boop. I leave with Dave and try to find the girl's family and an interpreter.

Delivering bad news comes with the job. Medical school even preps you for it. But this is different. Haiti has a way of doing that, of turning what you think you know upside down, inside out. I have grown accustomed to the responses. But in Haiti the screams seem louder. The pain that much deeper. It's as if it originates from the cellular human level. It is followed by the thrashing and collapsing of arms, falling to the ground, and hard, loud crying. Family gathers. Some join in the grieving and some offer comfort.

Defeated, angry, and sad, I go to the cafeteria for a drink and then head to bed. The lump in my throat remains. I look at the pattern of the blood on my scrubs. It looks like a map of Bell Island. Or maybe I'm just thinking of home. Bedtime cannot come quickly enough, even if it means being crammed into a small room with eleven other people.

"You okay, my boss?" I lift my head to see Phillip, one of the cleaners at the hospital. He's a familiar face and a friend to the entire team. *"Oui, mon chef,"* I reply as he raises his hand for a high-five. This is our routine. Phillip's work ethic is admirable. He never stops. Always cleaning yet never complaining. In between shifts at the hospital, he sells knick-knacks near the entrance. Seeing him always lifts me. Good timing.

———

The sun breaks over the arches of the hospital. Another day. There is a young man in the ICU who has been getting rapidly weaker and now struggles to breathe. Jeremy Pridham and Jane Seviour put their heads together and suggest the diagnosis could be myasthenia gravis, a rare autoimmune neuromuscular disease that can be treated with a common anesthesia drug.

The patient's breathing has been heavy and laboured. He is becoming fatigued and is on the verge of needing a breathing tube when they decide to give him a test dose of the drug. People huddle around the head of his bed. The ICU is a twenty-by-ten-foot room with four patient beds crowded in. There are three nurses. Aged monitors hang from the wall, and there are supplies in the corner. The small air conditioner works intermittently.

Jeremy gives the dose of the medication as the crowd watches with hope and anticipation. The drug flows through the syringe into the clear IV tubing and into the patient's veins. Within minutes the patient is sitting up in bed under his own power. The next day, he walks out of the ICU.

Selfishly, I needed this. I needed a reminder about the balance at work in the universe. How we influence it but don't control it. How it reveals itself sometimes when we need it most. And this kid? This kid was the answer. His name was Dimy, but we read it wrong on the patient record. We called him Jimmy and it stuck. When Jimmy sat up, he smiled. And when an interpreter helped explain the diagnosis to him, his smile grew. However, it is a disease that requires regular medication, and that costs money, of which Jimmy had none. Jeremy and nurse Jackie Connolly arranged for the life-saving drugs to be paid for and donated to Jimmy.

Fast-forward to 2014, and there was a proud moment for Jimmy and us as we watched him graduate from school, a feat that would not have been possible without our team's help. I know he's just one person, but these small victories add up. If anything, they are the ultimate morale builder. We still look for the next Jimmy in the faces that come and go from the hospital.

For me, the lesson has a personal side as well. Balance. Balance governs everything we do, whether we realize it or not. We cannot afford to be overwhelmed or sunk by the defeats; we need to be buoyed by the small wins. We are not going to change the world by going to Haiti for a week, but we can change *someone's* world, and that alone can make all the difference.

The week comes to an end sooner than I thought possible. In true Newfoundland and Labrador style, in just one week in Haiti, team members have developed friendships with local staff. Beyond simply knowing names, our team has come to know hospital staff's family stories and developed meaningful relationships. We all say our goodbyes, and I hear people promising we will be back. We will be back? Was that a part of the plan? Balance, Andrew, balance.

We pile into the vans, dirty, sweaty, tired, and punch-drunk as we head to the airport. As we sit and wait for the flight to board, I'm overcome with a sense of pride and relief that we accomplished something special and did it safely. Everyone was getting back on the plane in one piece.

After midnight, we land at the airport in St. John's aching for our own beds. As we file off the plane, we're greeted by families

and friends with signs and hugs like a championship team returning with a trophy.

We are all feeling it—that crazy energy you get after a long
jog. That excited feeling to keep going. The city is asleep as we
all head our separate ways. There is a sense in me again that this
can be more than just one trip. Maybe we could capitalize on
this small win and do more, much more.

It is a fleeting thought until I arrive home and check my text
messages. It is the middle of the night and my team members
are not even in their own beds yet after the crazy week we just
put in. And yet they are messaging me about doing more. About
returning to Haiti as soon as possible. At first, I think it is just
one enthusiastic member. Within minutes, there are texts from
many doctors and nurses.

Something had happened there. We all got a taste of the
change we could be, the difference we could make. The phone
gives the only light in the room. I swear I can hear bop-beep-
boop-boop. I smile at the thought. Welcome back.

10

ARM IN ARM THROUGH THE GATE

Port-au-Prince: January 2013

THE TEAM IS getting into a rhythm on these trips. And I have tried really hard to ensure they understand what to expect before heading to Haiti. We have developed a bit of a protocol around it, making sure the teams hear the information three times and ensuring that we are always available for any questions. What should I pack to wear? Should I bring my own food? What shots should I get? Are there any medications I can bring to help out at the hospital? What range of patients is to be expected? I feel like a veteran of the experience already when issuing my usual warnings about the heat and the constant reminder not to swallow any of the water that comes from the tap, even when brushing your teeth.

The one hard truth about these trips is this: they will break you. You can be the toughest, hardest, most seen-it-all surgeon there is and Haiti will still find a way to break your heart. That's not a scary statement. That's a reality check as to where you are going and what you will see. It's why we put a lot of thought, time, and effort into selecting who goes.

I want to let you in on a little secret: medicine can be full of egos. No different than any other profession. But one misplaced ego on a trip like this could set the whole thing in the wrong direction. It is important that everyone gel with the team. For the team to thrive, it must function as a unit, not a dictatorship. That's not for everyone.

At the end of any pre-departure meeting, I tell everyone that if we get there and it turns out the experience is not for them, if it is not what we described, or they simply need to get out, then we will arrange to get them home, no questions asked, no judgment or guilt. I would rather have a functioning team with fewer parts than a full team that cannot function because of one part.

Sometimes I forget that this is a new experience for people. Often this is their first true exposure to a poor country. Many have been to the popular Caribbean destinations—Jamaica, Cuba, the Dominican Republic—and have seen what they think are the real streets as they are taken by bus to their all-inclusive resorts. But very few have been to a truly poor place or seen the truly poor side of wherever they vacation. I have to remind myself that this is all new to them: the first drive from the airport past open sewer pits, the first time seeing a tent city, or the remnants of buildings, the makeshift homes of sheet metal, or the masses of people on the streets not knowing there is another world beyond Port-au-Prince. I go back to my first long, terrifying ride here. Yet despite all the discussions and warnings, I never know how the individual or the collective group is going to respond until we hit the ground.

Incidents happen. We've had several episodes where a doctor or nurse got overwhelmed, whether by the heat, the poverty, or the overall environment. The hard part is that you can't really leave it behind. At home, family can offer some comfort when there's a trying work condition or a sad case at the hospital. Maybe you head out for some comfort food or to a friend's place for the healing power of a few laughs. In Haiti, though, you live at the hospital, which is an armed compound in one of the poorest parts of the city. The farthest away you can get is to go on the roof. Grab a Coke and some air. Then, back to the grind ten minutes later. It just surrounds you.

On one of the earlier missions, an ER doctor had approached me early on the second day and said that she was having a problem adjusting to Haiti and needed to go home. We had barely settled in the compound and our bags were not even completely unpacked. That will be fine, I said. But I asked that we go to the roof first to chat about what was on her mind.

Travel to Haiti can be draining in itself. We had left St. John's at six in the morning, meaning everyone had to meet at the airport at three. So she had been up since at least two the night before. She had not slept on the plane and had started working a shift in the ER basically as soon as we landed. She was clearly sleep deprived, and as a result her emotions were running high. As part of your medical training, you learn to be as sharp on the twenty-fifth hour as you were on the first. The variable here is the place.

She said it was not the work or the people; she was just so overcome by the poverty, by seeing people in the streets with nothing, no home, no clean water. And then there was the raw sewage and the stench on the way from the airport. Most of us think we know what poverty is, mostly from UNICEF commercials or maybe a panhandler outside our favourite coffee shop. But coming face to face with the poverty of places like Haiti? That can hit you harder than you think. I remembered that the first drive from the airport, the one I had done so many times now, could be overwhelming. But those sights, sounds, and smells were now so familiar to me. I had forgotten my own gut-turning first experience.

I tried to reassure this doctor that she just needed some sleep and asked her not to make a decision without some solid rest. I encouraged her to make a call home to her partner and then to lie down for a bit. I also reassured her that, afterwards, if she still wanted to go home, we would arrange for her to be on the first available flight. I could see some of the weight lift. The perspective from the hospital roof can do that. It's become a bit of an oasis for us.

After a few hours' rest, she came to find me. She felt better, she said, but was still not sure if this was for her. I wasn't convinced she had rested enough to clearly make this call. In my heart, I felt she would have a profoundly meaningful week if she stayed. But no problem, I told her. We would get her a plane ticket. But first, I had to go pick up pizza for the team. I suggested she come along. Sometimes the compound insulates you too much from the world around you. It can be claustrophobic. It can also leave you thinking the worst of what lies beyond its walls.

As we drove through the busy streets, we talked about the job, the future, what we wanted. When we got to the pizza restaurant we had to wait for a bit, so we had a beer and chatted more about life, Haiti, and whatever was happening with different people we knew. She looked more relaxed and had a smile on her face. She was going to be just fine, I thought. She took a sip of her beer and stared at the label for a long time before she said that she was probably just overtired and overcome. She told me she'd try to stick it out for the rest of the week. Not only did she stay, but she became an incredibly important and valued member of the team. At the end of the week, she gave me a smile and quietly thanked me for the beer.

One of my heroes in this adventure has been an ER doctor I know whose incredible family had adopted a boy from Haiti a few years before the earthquake. The boy is loved and cherished and completely integrated into the schools and communities where we both live. I think of that kid every time I drive through the streets of Port-au-Prince. I have this notion that one of these adopted kids is going to return to this country and make a profound change. That sounds like a movie plot, but it gives me hope.

I've worked with this doctor, and we know each other's families the way dads at barbecues do, so I wasn't surprised that he approached me about going on a mission with us. A steady buzz was growing in medical circles about what Team Broken Earth was doing. He had never been to Haiti, and his wife hadn't been back since they'd adopted their son. He wanted to give something back.

I thought this was a home run. This was what it was all about. A panoramic give—how powerful. That idea and his profile would bring even more attention to and support for what we were doing. It also distracted me from asking the questions I usually ask: Is this person the right fit? Should this person go? I had been organizing these trips for two years now, and in this case, I dropped my guard.

Once again, we had all arrived a little sleep deprived and anxious and this doctor went on shift right away. It was busy. Haiti busy. Meaning too many patients, not enough staff. The ER was full of pediatric patients. There was one little boy who had fallen from a tree and had a significant brain injury. He was about the same age as the doctor's adopted son.

It struck a deep chord with him. I checked in on the operation and watched as he cared for the little boy with incredible poise and professional expertise. This work was as if he was a seasoned pediatrician, his hands steady though his heart was breaking.

A few hours later I was walking through the courtyard in the blistering heat when our plastic surgeon, Art Rideout, stopped me. He said we had an issue with the ER doctor, who was pretty shaken up about the pediatric patient. I went to find him and we had a long talk at his bunk. He was composed and seemed cool and collected, but was fixated on the thought that this physically and emotionally draining relief work was probably not for him.

He told me about the time years ago when his wife went to pick up their adopted child from an orphanage. Knowing what they rescued him from, the drive from the airport alone had brought so many hard emotions to the surface. On top of that, he'd had to treat a boy the same age. That boy might not survive. He could have easily been their new son.

There were no tears, only fleeting moments where he seemed anxious and uncertain. He has a doctor's temperament, but it wasn't hard to see he was experiencing something profound. He said he was overwhelmed and did not think he could be a productive member of the team for the rest of the week. It made sense to me. I wondered if, in the same situation, I would have had such composure and insight. I doubted it very much.

We made sure he spoke with his loved ones at home and got some rest. But he could not shake the visual of his own son at home. No one could blame him. We booked him a ticket home. As he was leaving, he told me he was concerned that he had let the team down, let Haiti down. I tried to reassure him nothing was further from the truth. He had done something truly special for Haiti. He had given a child, an orphan, the gift of a loving family.

That gift is one that I certainly cannot recreate with a scalpel. But change is a chameleon. It comes in many beautiful forms.

Since that mission, we have remained friends and colleagues. He maintains that it was not our fault that he had to leave— although I think I could have done a better job of vetting him— and he believes in the team and what we are trying to accomplish. But on that day, in those conditions, it just cut a little too close for him. Fair enough. Lesson learned.

So the selection process changed. But even then we sometimes take a gamble on some team members. One such member was Dr. Jim Rourke, the dean of the Faculty of Medicine at Memorial University. He has always been incredibly supportive of our work. I had to make a point of ensuring he knew exactly how difficult the situation was in Haiti. But I also wanted him to see how, in meetings and emails, we were championing the residents and the medical school and making education a pillar of our model. He was always an encouraging voice.

Jim is a medium-height, balding sixty-year-old family doctor from Ontario. Not what you would describe as an imposing figure, but looks can be deceptive. He came to the university in St. John's and within months had everyone shouting his praises. He has the rare family-practice quality of being able to listen and direct conversations and agendas while avoiding confrontation. So when he approached me about coming to Haiti, I admit I was both worried and a little suspicious. Was there a hidden agenda here? I wasn't a hundred per cent sure how everyone in our local medical community was feeling about, or even truly understood, what we were trying to accomplish with Team Broken Earth. And I was not sure I could even explain it fully at that point beyond saying, "When you go, you'll know."

But this was the dean of medicine. I was sure of one thing: if there were any problems, he'd no doubt see them. He'd also see our overall vision and our pragmatic approach to providing care. I was worried he would have an academic approach, asking for five-step plans. I could picture working groups on safety concerns, reams of academic papers about either the return on investment of such a project or the ethics of providing care in a developing country. I had nightmares of drowning in bureaucracy. Our model simply did not work that way.

We decided he should come on a trip. In retrospect, I am not sure we had much of a choice. Your boss asks if he can help, what are you supposed to do? Had we said no, he was fully capable of shutting down the university's involvement. At least with a yes we had a chance to show him what we were doing, what could be done, what we could all accomplish together.

As I've come to know, the dean is a humble man. He attended all the pre-departure meetings with the entire team. I remember at the first meeting he sat at the back of the room and introduced himself to everyone as Jim—not the dean. This is going to work, I thought.

I did have a lingering concern. In administration and academia, clinical experience often fades. You trade your front-line clinical skills for organizational ones, become really good at directing at the expense of doing. We were very much into doing. Jim had been in administration for a while. Although he prided himself on his rural medical experience and working without support, that was all a good twenty years past. The intensity of these Haiti missions can be a shock to the system.

Upon landing in Haiti in January 2013, we made the now routine journey to Bernard Mevs Hospital. Jim looked unfazed. The rest of the team had been to the hospital before, and we were all used to the cramped living conditions. Doctors are notorious for their poker faces, and I was certain that the sight of twelve bunk beds in that tiny room would test that. No reaction at all. Then, as if we'd planned it to test Jim's mettle, we got a call: a patient was ready to deliver.

The hospital is not set up for obstetrics and gynecology. We barely have the equipment to do what we are trying to do, let alone expand services. But on this night, the closest hospital for this woman in labour was ours. She arrived in a panic in the back of a pickup. An urgent call went out to all team members asking for someone who could deliver a baby. Most of us had done this in medical school, but that had been a long time ago, and for most it was a distant memory. None of us practised obstetrics. None except for the dean. Jim had routinely delivered babies in his rural practice before he entered administration. When the call came, without hesitation and while most of us were nervously looking at our shoes, Jim stood up and said, "I can do that."

In a dimly lit room at the end of the corridor near where we all slept, Jim and a Haitian nurse sat with the patient and coached her through the labour. We all knew the situation was difficult. There was no plan B if there were any complications. This situation would make any seasoned surgeon nervous. We all waited for what felt like forever. But within an hour, Jim stood there, sweat rolling off his head, holding a brand-new baby. Jim's smile said it all. He looked like a combo of a first-year medical student doing this for the first time and a retired athlete proving beyond a shadow of a doubt that he still had it.

It was something I have seen before in Haiti. Pure medicine. The reason most of us went into this profession was this exact experience. Raw, the way it is supposed to be practised. No bureaucracy or hair-pulling policies. A medical problem, then a solution and execution. It has been an addictive feeling for many of our team members along the way. In addition, we get to do things outside our day-to-day routine. In an environment like this, we get to use all our skills. It reinvigorates the passion and enthusiasm that are sometimes dampened by the routine at home.

Any concern about Jim evaporated in that moment.

On that trip, Jim and I became good friends. He has been a sound, experienced voice and has joined our board and provided direction and advice. I frequently approach him for counsel, sometimes on matters not related to Broken Earth. He has become a champion for us, publishing articles and recognizing the needs of the environment, and most recently securing the contract for a medical records system for our patients.

As much as you plan, as much as you think you know how people will behave and personalities will interact, you just cannot know how an individual is going to react to being in a place like Haiti. Especially, as in those early days, coming from the somewhat isolated comfort of Newfoundland and Labrador. You can't predict the workload. The spectrum of cases you'll see. How the team will perform or who will step up.

One thing is certain, though, and that is the positive effect the teams have at home. It is something we didn't think about at first. It's a serendipitous side effect of what we have started. And the shared experience goes beyond individual acts of heroism.

We take highly skilled and trained individuals, used to handling the highest-quality tools and living in the best country in the world. Then we drop them in the middle of one of the poorest countries in the world, expect them to live in cramped quarters without running water to drink or reliable showers, point out the lack of reliable equipment, and ask them to deal with the same life-threatening conditions that they do in their fully equipped modern hospitals at home. Add forty-degree heat. This kind of stress can break you. Personally. Professionally.

But here's the power of a team. Everyone is protected by the collective effort. I've seen stoic surgeons used to dealing with life and death at home go silent and have to take a knee. I've witnessed nurses pull away by themselves for a bit and shed a tear. I've shed my share of tears throughout. But what prevents us all from collapsing and crawling into a deep, dark hole is the team. The nurse who pulls away is quickly comforted by his or her peers. The surgeon is quickly helped back up by the anesthesiologist. I've seen it happen time and time again.

I remember one afternoon, there was a sudden commotion outside the hospital gates. A car had lost control and struck several people. The team assembled on the roof to assess what was happening. A crowd was gathering, screaming for help.

It's okay, I thought. It's happened literally adjacent to the hospital, and we should be able to help this person. We quickly assembled a team. Several men lifted the patient through the gates and lowered her onto the ground in the courtyard. She looked to be around twenty years old. But something was not right. There were flies everywhere, more than normal, circling the young woman's head, and very little blood. She was dead.

I took her feet while others helped with her head and body. Trying to give her some dignity, we placed her on a stretcher and took her to the morgue, a dark concrete area at the end of the courtyard. We looked through her personal belongings, to identify her. As one of us was holding her cell phone, someone began texting her. Watching the text come in punched me in the gut.

Someone on the other end, a loved one, a friend, was texting, not expecting that they would never hear her voice again.

One of the team said, "She is somebody's somebody."

Staring at her phone, I had to wipe a tear. Twenty years old. Outside the hospital, walking somewhere, living life. I'm sure this same situation plays out all the time all over the world in some form or another. But here, in this bunker in this hospital compound, the tragedy felt bigger. More real. I don't know why.

I say it all the time in my line of work: in trauma, your life changes in milliseconds. There is no time for second chances, no time to reconsider, no time to say "whoops." How different this young woman's life would have been if she had taken a different turn, stopped for a Coke, even taken two steps to the left a moment before. The randomness was strikingly unfair. *Somebody's somebody.* Those words hang there, suspended in everyone.

One event like that can paralyze a team. We gathered for supper, everyone seeming a little less bright, a little slower, our eyes focused down. The mood was more subdued than I had seen in a while, even though we see life and death all the time. Doctors sat quietly; nurses looked into space; no one wanted to look at their phones. Then something happened. People gently started talking about the experience. Others, deflecting a little, broke into discussions about the NHL or kids' activities at home. There it was happening right in front of me. The strength of a team. Healing itself. Lifting when all you feel is the fall.

I think if we had to do a textbook formal debrief on that patient and dissect feelings and thoughts, it just would not have worked. The team protects the individual, and we all grow stronger for it.

We try our best to keep to our best practices from home. We make sure to have quasi-formal debriefs, where the group gathers to share experiences, talk about what we could have done better and lessons learned. A sort of post-mortem.

There was one particularly tough day when we lost three children. None of us had much experience with the death of a child, let alone three in one day. The pediatric team was devastated. Loss is tough. Young loss is worse. Multiplying that, in the space of one day, is the hardest punch to take.

One of the pediatric team leads decided to do a formal debrief. It was a good idea, given the emotions involved and the level of despair on the team's faces. I stood back and watched as they gathered. You could see the humanity being spread without words. Literal and figurative shoulders being offered. But for me it was less about the procedure and structure—not to dismiss the importance of either—and more about the essence of the team. It made me think of home.

I remembered attending a wake once that felt more like a celebration and a buffet. So many dishes and desserts. Stories being told, and that dance of laughter and tears that those who mourn understand. I'm sure this isn't just a Newfoundland thing. But here in Haiti, the team gathers the way families would. You feel that things will be okay.

I have been asked how this affects us at home. I think these shared experiences, good and bad, and the power of the team make us better doctors and nurses. If nothing else they supercharge an already high-powered team of medical professionals at home. When you find yourself working with someone you worked with in Haiti, you have an automatic bond. An understanding. A trust. You know things will be more efficient, more effective. And ultimately, the patient reaps the benefits.

You also bring home the difficult memories of certain patients you worked with, the situations you faced, and the stress that can cause. It's something I do not admit often. As stoic as I would like to think I can be, as calculating and decisive as I pride myself on being in the operating room, occasionally the memories get the better of me. It happens at the most random of times. Self-doubt takes over and a screen goes up. On it flashes faces, moments, scenes of trauma or the haunting quiet of loss. I see my grandmother surrounded by her children and grandchildren. Smiles. Warmth. Did we do enough? Did I? Could we have done more?

I'm not going to call this PTSD. I have too much respect for what our veterans and first responders have been through to do that. But there's something in me, a tension I've been carrying since that first trip to Haiti after the quake. I remember once being back in St. John's and receiving an email from a team member complaining about what I considered a minor issue. I decided to go for a run before replying, clear my head and resist the temptation to fire off a curt reply. I am not an expert runner, an amateur jogger at best, but I like to run to clear my head.

St. John's is beautiful in the fall. The trees are changing colour and the temperature drops to single digits. Not too cold or too warm, perfect running weather. The east end of St. John's has a series of ponds with manicured running trails. This is where I grew up. As a boy, I spent countless hours around those ponds, skimming rocks at waterside, riding bikes on the trails. This is the ideal place to help me hit reset. It was a little wet and grey that day but there was no one else on the trail and I felt like I was alone on the planet. I was suddenly confronted by a memory of a boy we saw in Haiti. Not sure why it sprang into my consciousness, but there he was, as vivid as the day I saw him. My pace and heart rate accelerated.

He was around sixteen. He had a bone tumour in his leg, the same kind Terry Fox had. We could save this boy. We could simply cut the tumour away, perform an amputation, and he would go on to live a long life. A twenty-minute procedure that would allow him to survive, have children of his own someday. Without it, he faced certain death within years.

My colleague, Dr. Frank Noftall, and I explained to the boy's father that this was a life-saving operation and that, although an amputation was not ideal, it was certainly better than the alternative. In my memory, we are standing in the heat of the courtyard. The boy, his father, an interpreter, Frank, and myself. The father stands next to his son, who is seated in a makeshift wheelchair, as his leg is too sore to stand on. You can see their expressions change as the interpreter translates and tries to convey the gravity of the situation. You can see the panic grow in the boy's face. Perhaps we should not have included him in the conversation. Was he too young to hear this? No. He was sixteen and he deserved to know that we were going to save his life with a twenty-minute procedure. There would be a happy ending.

I was losing sight of the running trail and all I could think of was this young boy's face. His face as his father becomes impassive and folds his arms and refuses the surgery. He does not believe us. I can't tell if I am sweating from the heat or the pressure of the situation. I walk the father through the situation very slowly and carefully, assuring him of my training and skills. I even have a prosthetic technician come and show them how the boy can be fitted for a prosthesis.

There is some deep objection to this procedure. The harder I try to convince the father, the more he seems to believe that it is not the right course of action.

I beg the hospital administrators to help and they try, but to no avail. It's futile. Frustrated and almost fist-clenched angry, I walk away. I head up to the sanctuary of the hospital roof to calm down. I'm standing up there looking down into the courtyard at the several local staff trying to persuade the father. He motions for his son and they leave. They go out through the gates before I am able to scramble down to stop them. If I even could.

From twenty feet above I watch them leave, father and son, arm in arm, through the gates. Everything drains out of me. Things will get worse for this boy. More suffering. A certain death. And for what? Why? Why didn't the father believe me?

I tripped and fell on the wet root of a tree, hitting the ground hard. Stunned for a moment, I rolled over and looked at my legs. Wiping the dirt from my jacket and hands, I sat frozen for minutes on end, not in shock from the fall but absorbed in the memory of the father and son walking arm in arm through the hospital gates so far from here. Was the father living with the guilt and regret of his decision? What became of the boy?

My breath was heavy. Adrenaline had kicked in. My heart pounded against my collarbone. I saw the young girl in the yellow dress, the one who sat vigil for her grandfather as we operated. I saw the hope in her eyes. I closed my eyes and nodded a thank-you. Dusted off a little more and started running again.

I have had other episodes like this and have been pulled to my feet by the team at home. Just being with Allison and the kids. A conversation with Art or Jeremy, Frank or Michelle, Dick or Jim. They all seem to come at the right time. They've all been there. I hope I am able to do that too. To be that shoulder, that pick-me-up to others along the way. Because even though some will walk out of the gates, you have to be there for the ones who stay.

I start running back in the direction of the hospital. The leaves add a dampness to the air. Someone is burning wood nearby. I think again about that email from the team member and the work that has to be done. I keep running.

11

TOO MANY TO REMEMBER

St. John's: March 2012

I'M LACING UP my skates. The dressing room has the smell all sports dressing rooms have, some combination of deodorant and stale beer. Around me are lawyers, doctors, actors, musicians, people from all walks of life. I feel most at home in these moments. There's no hierarchy, just the game. I've often wondered how many big decisions have been made in such places and what can be more Canadian than that.

Paul Duffy and I trained together in orthopedics at Memorial University. He was my chief resident, and after residency we continued to be great friends. We've frequently hit the ice together and have played in tournaments throughout Newfoundland and even in Las Vegas. We remain tight even though he now practises surgery at the University of Calgary.

Paul was back in town, so naturally we found time and reason to head to the rink. We were sitting in the dressing room of Prince of Wales Arena in the midtown of St. John's. Paul had been invited to speak at the Newfoundland and Labrador Surgical Society meeting. I like to think the real reason he was there was to play in the annual hockey tournament. Yes, it's the infamous Maroun Cup, a grudge match for bragging rights between orthopedics and general surgery. The game is named after an eighty-four-year-old neurosurgeon, Falah Maroun, who came to Newfoundland for a short visit in the 1960s and has been here ever since.

We were sitting in the dressing room relishing orthopedics' win when Paul noticed the Team Broken Earth baggage tag on my hockey bag. He asked what it was all about, and in that sweaty beer-filled dressing room we had a conversation that would change the lives of so many. Paul knew that I had been to Haiti several times now but had no idea how much our commitment had grown.

I talked about the idea of the team, about Haiti and the hospital that we adopted, and about the variety of patients we had treated. I told him about the poverty we witnessed there but also the humanity and those tiny flashes of hope. Paul was still staring at the baggage tag when he said that this was something Calgary could do too. I always knew we'd add teams but always thought it would be other teams from Newfoundland. But why not Calgary? I assumed he would ask me or someone else from the Newfoundland team to join him. But before I had the chance to offer, he said this could be Team Broken Earth Calgary.

It felt like a logical fit. I know Paul. I trust him. Despite the distance now, he is one of my best friends. And they could use the team name, our travel arrangements, our tax-receipting, and our relationships at the hospital in Haiti. We would make it as easy as possible for them. Tell them what to pack, what supplies to take, what team composition to aim for. Everything we've learned. We could eliminate as many hurdles as possible for them.

Looking back on it, we were creating a template for how to proceed. We would make it possible for any new team to link into what we had created as seamlessly as possible. Whatever potential problems they could come up with, we more than likely had already solved.

I was still running on the adrenaline from the game. And as I sat there with my skates still on, drinking beer from Dr. Maroun's Cup, it hit me that this could be something so much bigger. The Newfoundland and Labrador team had created something that could so easily be replicated. I started a roll call of names in my head, doctors and nurses I've worked over the years in different parts of the country and around the world. I was getting ahead of myself, but we could do this. Grow this. It fit with that one truth I knew from my time in Haiti: that what they really needed was a sustained medical effort. Not one-offs, but commitment. A broader idea of Team Broken Earth could provide that.

Paul and I decided that it was a good idea for me to go to Calgary and give grand rounds to the surgical department at the Foothills Medical Centre. Grand rounds is a gathering of all specialists at a hospital during which someone will often present recent work or interesting cases. Frequently there will be a visiting professor or specialist who will come to discuss research or a new technique. It is a staple of academic medicine. The larger the hospital or university, the grander the rounds. It is usually pleasant, and people exchange ideas and provide constructive feedback about the topic being discussed. Occasionally things can get heated when ideas are challenged.

I had given grand rounds on our experiences in Haiti before. It was light in the beginning, but then people began challenging the effectiveness of Team Broken Earth, the sustainability of it and the real benefit to the Haitian people. Were we not medical tourists, cowboys making ourselves feel better as we rode into town to save the day? Wouldn't the cost of the trips and the talent involved have a better return on investment elsewhere?

I had thought about these questions myself, and I thought I had answers, but I had not been fully prepared to deal with how personally attached to the project I had become. I always maintained a professional demeanour, being able to separate my emotions from the work at hand. But these challenges? This I took personally. I felt like people were questioning my personal character and integrity. I would find my heart rate going up faster than my back, and I am sure I did not hide my agitation well. But although irritating and more than a little humbling, it was a gigantic life lesson. If I was going to be in this environment, I clearly needed thicker skin. I had to be able to take the comments for what they were. Some good, some not. Some had valuable lessons hidden in them.

My trip to Calgary was my first time taking the idea and the pitch outside the province. I did not know if it would work. Admittedly, there was a bit of that Atlantic Canadian inferiority complex weighing in there, the feeling that what we do is somehow not worthy of attention. But I put that aside and set out to make a compelling pitch to the University of Calgary while telling the Broken Earth story.

Travelling from Paul's house is like moving through the most beautiful painting. The snow-capped Rockies form a magnificent backdrop. But I hardly noticed. I was getting nervous and nauseated. Suddenly, there I was with a suit, a PowerPoint, and using words like *pitch*. I am a surgeon, I kept telling myself, what did I know about this stuff?

When I was younger, I suffered a bit from stage fright. I would start to talk and my eyes would start to shake so that the room was bouncing up and down to the point where I felt like my head must have been bouncing too. Or that everyone could see my eyes moving up and down like on a marionette. That anxiety came back to me in Calgary. I was sure the audience was going to be full of people with more experience than me. That they would look down at an idea from Newfoundland and Labrador. My anxiety was the loudest voice in the room.

Halfway through my presentation, which was webcast to other hospitals in the Calgary area, the eye-bobbing stopped and I could see people were interested in our story. During the Q&A afterwards, a myriad of hands shot up. There were the expected few about sustainability and were we actually making a difference, but more about how people could get involved. There was genuine interest in signing up. I could have recruited dozens on the spot.

Within minutes, Paul had secured enough interest for a Calgary team to go to Haiti as part of Team Broken Earth. For me, that was a seedling pushing through the crust of the earth. The moment of growth. This can be bigger, I realized. *Will* be bigger. It brought a smile to my face.

Paul Duffy has always been an incredible leader. As a New-foundlander, I would like to think this comes from his Torbay roots, although I suspect there is more to it than that. He has an innate ability to draw people to him, a magnetic kindness that is certainly in the DNA of those from the Rock. He immediately had a team of emergency doctors, nurses, surgeons, and physiotherapists. In what was remarkably similar to our experience, and has become a theme, there was no advertising and no marketing, but as soon as word of a team going to Haiti moved through the halls of Foothills Medical Centre, he had a team together with minimal effort.

Over the summer of 2013, we helped Paul and his team put the pieces in place to make their mission a success. I remember running a conference call from a grassy pitch while watching my oldest in Timbits soccer. I was answering questions, planning a budget, and making travel arrangements. We landed on a date that would follow a team from Newfoundland, and Art Rideout and I would stay an extra few days to help them through any growing pains. Any work the team did not finish we could leave for the team from Calgary. A seamless hand-off. We would also coordinate teaching so that local doctors and students could build on the lectures of the first week.

I now began to think seriously about the sustainability of Broken Earth. We could create a medical relay, a continuous train of hand-offs. Hand-offs of patients and education. All the while coordinating with local surgeons and staff and making sure they were fully involved. We could create a model of continuous care just by asking every medical school in Canada to take one week. One week a month and we would have continuity, sustainability, and hope.

This model could work. *Would* work. It would mean a strong, integrated partnership with our Haitian colleagues and friends. We'd need to work in concert. Sometimes this would mean direct hand-to-hand training. Other times it might mean answering an email at a dinner party on a Friday night from a Haitian surgeon asking for an opinion on an X-ray. We could do this.

Newfoundland and Labrador were on the ground working hard. We had secured and installed a new autoclave, this one as big as a fridge. Through everything from pub nights and bake sales to a gala concert with Great Big Sea, we had raised funds for this in St. John's and now it was plugged in and working in Port-au-Prince.

Before this, we'd sterilized the surgical instruments with a fluid called Cidex or in the old microwave-sized sterilizer. Although it seemed like a small addition to the hospital, it was a monumental change. It meant not just that more cases could be handled, but more cases with guaranteed sterility.

There was a large caseload that week. There was an unusual level of trauma and really sick people. During a lull in the action, the surgical team, who had not been off the compound in a few days, decided we would take a much-needed reprieve and go with the rest of the group to the UN compound for dinner. We left behind a small team, including Jeremy Pridham and an ER doctor and nurse, to cover the ER and hospital. We piled into the back of a few Toyota Land Cruisers, the vehicle of choice for the streets of Port-au-Prince, and headed through the winding streets.

Once we arrived at the UN everyone felt normal again. Our team were in shorts and T-shirts, flip-flops, and hats that weren't scrubs. But most important, we were outside the walls of the gun-guarded compound. They serve great cheeseburgers and pub food at the UN compound. Everyone was just relaxing, hovering around a TV watching NFL football while waiting for our food, when a call came in. It was Jeremy. A bus carrying American tourists and some locals had rolled over and multiple casualties needed to be assessed. We all had to go back.

I could smell my cheeseburger. I really thought it was a cruel joke, but it was obvious in Jeremy's tone that there was no joking here. I thought I was going to be attacked delivering the news to the team. But as the words were coming out of my mouth, everyone's demeanour changed: the fun faces were off and the professional ones back on. All hands on deck, not a single complaint. Everyone piled back into the Land Cruiser. Cheeseburgers could wait.

As we drove through the gates we could see the relief in the faces of our waiting team members. Straight to work. We immediately proceeded to triage all the patients from the bus accident. Some needed only minor wound care, and others would need surgery that could wait until they returned to the States. Others needed immediate surgery. One Haitian in particular, a dual citizen who lived in the States, required immediate surgery for an unstable pelvic fracture, a life-threatening injury. Some patients were medevaced out to the U.S., while others were sent by commercial airline back home.

The Haitian with the pelvic fracture needed immediate temporary surgery but would require advanced surgery in the States. Paul and his Calgary team would be arriving in a few hours, and I thought they could maybe help and avoid the costly transfer (which happened anyways). I emailed Paul with the X-rays and asked his opinion.

Paul and his team arrived in the early evening. Art and I had just earlier that day said goodbye to our own team from Newfoundland. All were wearing Team Broken Earth T-shirts, all were experiencing Haiti for the first time, and all were ready to dig in and make a difference. All the preparation, all of the conference calls, all the emails—none of it fully prepares you for that first walk through the gates of the hospital. Had we done a reasonable job prepping them? Would they fall in love with the work, with the place, with the people the same way I had? I held my breath.

Much like our own first trip, they were immediately thrown into action, their orientation tour cut short by a trauma in the ER and an emergency plastic surgery case in the OR. It was an interesting experiment to watch, to see Paul experiencing the same issues that I had as a team lead in dealing with the personalities, the professional differences, and the stress of working in these conditions.

We spent a few days with Paul and his team. They worked hard and pulled together. It was obvious to us that this model of one-week multidisciplinary teams handing off to each other was workable. The new team gelled, leaned on each other for guidance and emotional support. It was brilliant to watch.

Paul and his crew made a huge difference, and I couldn't wait to hear their feedback when they returned home. I felt fully exposed. If they did not think our model was viable, it would reflect directly on me. As it turned out, they thought it was a huge success. After he got home, Paul received the same feedback that I had after my first team trip. All members wanted to return, with new ideas, new members, and the desire to make an even stronger Team Broken Earth Calgary. Within weeks three more teams were built and ready to go later that year. Each team would consist of between fifteen and thirty people, ranging in skills from emergency medicine and critical care to plastic surgery and physiotherapy to nursing and anesthesia.

One of those wanting to return was Spencer McLean, a young final-year orthopedic resident. He fell in love with Haiti immediately. He was passionate, was empathetic, and he defined team play. I was fortunate to meet Spencer before this trip and got to know him a little better in those few overlap days. His personality was contagious. The *Globe and Mail* published his article about the trip.

Then something unthinkable happened. A few weeks after the team got home, Paul called me to ask what our tuberculosis protocol was. Spencer was not feeling well, and preliminary tests had revealed some swelling in his abdomen. One possible diagnosis was TB. My heart sank. We always knew there were risks, and

TB was one of them. This was terrible for Spencer—terrible for all of us.

I quickly called my friend Natalie Bridger. Nat specializes in infectious diseases and thought it was incredibly unlikely that Spencer had TB. My relief lasted only a millisecond, because if it was not TB, it had to be something else.

Over the next few days, tests revealed that Spencer had incurable end-stage renal cancer. Months before he finished his residency, weeks before he was ready to start the rest of his life, he was given a terminal diagnosis. It was unfathomable. Unfair. My heart sank lower than I thought possible.

Spencer died on June 24, 2013, just days before he would have finished his residency. He left a void in many lives. One of his final requests was that any donations in his memory be made to Team Broken Earth. It was a humbling example of his empathy for those in need.

The Dr. Spencer McLean Fellowship was set up to bring Haitian orthopedic surgical residents to Canada to work alongside Canadian residents and learn the skills needed to improve the quality of orthopedic surgical care in Haiti. Spencer's spirit is alive and well in the lives we change in Haiti.

Since that first Calgary trip, there have been many more missions. Believe it or not, each time we returned from a trip, we faced criticism. Sometimes it came from people in the medical community, sometimes from academics. It tended to focus on the short length of our trips. What difference could we actually make in one week? Wouldn't the money be better invested elsewhere? I have acted on some of the criticism we received, but I never understood this line of thinking. For me, medicine is about individual patients, their lives, and the impact on their families and in turn their communities. Helping one patient never had a sticker price. Should it? Perhaps because I'm Canadian or because my specialty deals with one patient at a time, my lens is fixed on the individual. And from one individual, great things can happen.

I started answering these questions pre-emptively in presentations to schools and universities. I would use one of Art's cleft lip patients as an example. I'd show a picture of them before the operation and ask what issues the patient could have. They would struggle to eat and talk and would be bullied if they survived. The next slide would be a picture of the same child after the operation. You could barely see the scar from surgery. When critics asked what we can accomplish in a week, I figured this picture would answer them.

I always loved Jeremy Pridham's response to this criticism: "We are not trying to change the world, just someone's world." That sums it up better than I could ever articulate. Yet I still fixated on this criticism. One trip, it hit home why.

We were at the end of a mission when someone came in with a fractured femur. That's the thigh bone, the largest bone in the body. We had the ability and tools to fix it, but we were scheduled to get on a plane in a few hours. In Canada this kind of fracture would be fixed within twenty-four hours. The patient would be up and walking with physiotherapy the next day, discharged and home within seventy-two hours, back working and playing sports within six months. But in a developing country like Haiti, this injury typically means six months in bed in traction, assuming the patient even survived. Even then, the fracture may not heal, or may heal incorrectly, and the patient is often left with a disability and unemployed.

Here was a case that we had the skills, equipment, and desire to fix, but no time.

No time. How could I create *more time*, and finally silence the critics with their "What can you do in just one week?"

It was on that plane home I decided that expansion was the only way to create really effective time in Haiti. Sustainability. We could build on the hand-off model. It could be more than just periodic visits by Calgary and St. John's. What about if every province in Canada had a team? I could see how that would build and the weeks would blend, one team handing off to another in an uninterrupted rotation: that's true sustainability.

From there things began to grow organically. We were not yet soliciting any teams or asking for new members. Yet we were seeing natural growth across the country. Just as this idea was floating in my head, and the success of the Calgary trip was still percolating, I got an email from Chad Coles, an orthopedic surgeon and a professor at Dalhousie University in Halifax. He was wondering if I would come and give orthopedic rounds at their hospital about what Broken Earth was doing in Haiti.

I've known Chad awhile now. He had a reputation throughout Atlantic Canada for being smart, intense, and excellent at his job. He had never been involved in work abroad. I had been intimidated by Chad in the past. We had both completed prestigious surgical fellowships in trauma; he had gone to Seattle and I went to Baltimore. I remember calling him for advice on the fellowships when I was a resident. I was nervous calling him. There was no small talk; it was all business. He provided succinct, accurate advice on how to apply for training in the U.S. and what to expect. It was all very by-the-book and brief. Helpful? Very. Social? Not really.

After that encounter I got to know Chad a little more as we taught courses together across Canada. He is an amazing teacher and now a good friend, but always struck me as being very serious and methodical—great traits in a surgeon! I wish I had more of those traits myself—and I wondered what he would think of my talk. Would he think the work we were doing was subpar? Would he criticize how we were doing surgery or the results we were getting? I was unsure, but determined to see if we could get another province to buy into what we were trying to achieve.

Halifax is a beautiful city, especially in the fall. My father went to law school at Dalhousie and I started elementary school in Dartmouth, so I have always had an affinity for the place. Growing up in St. John's, Halifax was the big city, and Dalhousie might as well have been Harvard in my mind, the way my father spoke of the place. My aunt and uncle still live there and the connection I feel has lasted.

I took some comfort in that feeling of familiarity as we were crossing the Macdonald Bridge that connects the Dartmouth side to Halifax. It was a grey, drizzly autumn day that reminded me of home. That eased my tension. The city rises on your left side and always looks inviting in that come-in-the-kitchen-for-a-drink Maritime way. The waterfront was lined with schooners and naval vessels, giving it an old New England vibe.

I met Chad in the lobby of the hospital. He is a tall, sturdy man, and incredibly cordial, and he greeted me with a smile and warm welcome. There were thirty to forty people waiting in the rounds room. I stumbled around in front of them all. Me in a suit, which I rarely wear—and it was the only one I own—trying to hook up the computer. This was the first time I'd presented this talk since Calgary.

I was introduced by the chief of the orthopedic surgery department, Dr. David Amirault, a sixty-year-old balding man who leans forward when he talks to you, listens intently when you answer his questions, and seems from across the room to have the largest of hearts. He put me at ease immediately, and off I went. Let's see if they think this idea has merit. At the end of my presentation I threw this challenge to them: if Newfoundland and Labrador could do this, certainly Nova Scotia could as well? Then I opened it up to questions. Chad was one of the first to raise a hand. His question was not about the specifics of fracture care in Haiti but about how his hospital could get involved. A sigh of relief.

Not long after my presentation, Chad had assembled a team. In the fall of 2013, Team Calgary did a hand-off of patients and teaching materials to Team St. John's, who a week later handed off to Team Halifax. Who could argue with what you could accomplish in three weeks?

Since then Chad and Dr. Amirault have led several trips to Haiti, and Chad has also been on all four of our orthopedic trauma teaching courses. He and his wife, Jodi, an OR nurse, have taken leadership of Team Broken Earth in Halifax and have successfully completed several fundraisers, including their annual Lobster Boil.

Jodi is one of the nicest people I have ever met. Originally from the west coast of Newfoundland, she settled in Halifax but always retained her Newfoundlandness—the magnetic personality and the talkative, empathetic, compassionate traits that Newfoundlanders on the mainland usually not only retain but nurture. She continues to work as a brilliant part-time nurse while running a household and helping organize the Team Broken Earth missions for Dalhousie.

I attended their first Lobster Boil for Haiti, in June 2015, and sat with Chad and Jodi. The room was filled with kind, generous, and supportive people. No one knew who I was, nor did they care. This was *their* Team Broken Earth. They had made it their own. And that was exactly how it should work. It was an aha moment for me. Each team needs to feel that the team is their own. They are not just channelling our identity, like a franchise—they need to make it their own.

I thought that would be the end. Halifax was close to St. John's, and we had lots of common connections in the medical community. Calgary had the personal connection and a large pool of people to draw from. I thought even if the whole thing collapsed now, we had done some great things in contributing to aid and assistance in the aftermath of the earthquake.

Not long after, while I was vacationing in Oregon with Allison's family and trying to figure out how to find a contractor for a new building in Haiti, I received an email from a nurse in Vancouver asking for more information about Team Broken Earth. I had never met Kristi Lange, and I didn't know how she'd heard of us, but I immediately gave her my cell number. Turns out she was in Oregon as well, on a mountain bike trip. What are the odds?

Central Oregon in the summer is absolutely amazing. The sun splits through the fifty-foot pine trees and the ground is covered with pine cones and needles, often hiding any hint of grass. I was walking among those towering trees with Mark, still in a diaper, holding my hand when Kristi phoned.

She was so full of energy, an OR nurse with a can-do attitude. She wanted to know more about the teams, the hospital, and the kind of care we were providing. I think initially she phoned to see if she could be part of a team. I said I thought she should lead a team herself. There could be a Team Broken Earth Vancouver, and, as we had done with the Halifax and Calgary teams, we could help her with the logistics, the flights, what equipment to bring, relationships on the ground in Haiti, and so on.

Kristi was hesitant at first, but within weeks she was committed to delivering a team. By our next conversation, she had sourced people at her hospital, where the response had been similar to the one I'd seen initially: an overwhelming desire to help.

I did not meet Kristi in person, and I never went to Vancouver to give a talk to their group. That was a first, and I nervously wondered how it would go. I'd been so hands-on for so long that having this all move beyond me was both liberating and scary all at once. But their trip was a resounding success.

One of the doctor leads, Jim Kim, was in St. John's shortly after the team, returned, and we met up at Jeremy's house. He was full of enthusiasm and had all kinds of great new ideas for the hospital and the team. Team Broken Earth was continuing to grow.

One of the exceptional memories for me was learning, after the fact, that one of the Vancouver teams had organized an anesthesia critical care conference that, over two days, taught fifty anesthesia residents and staff from across Haiti how to perform intubations and anesthetics. This was a team taking the initiative to build on something we are all passionate about: education. It was another indication that we were onto something universal and special.

Darryl Young, an orthopedic surgeon in Ottawa and another expat Newfoundlander, heard about what we were doing and asked me if his hospital could send a team as well. A pediatrician at the hospital was married to a Haitian and wanted to know if they could join the effort. This was the momentum early on. It caught me a little off guard. Darryl led the first Ottawa team, and it was again a success. As quickly as they were home, they wanted to book a second team, this time set for just a few months later, in January.

From the start, security has always been something we take very seriously. As much as we feel we are making progress at the hospital, we have to keep in mind how volatile the situation can be just outside the walls. If there was ever any question of safety or any threat of instability, we maintained that we would not allow a team to proceed, regardless of the cost implications. Always safety first.

We have several sources we rely on for checking the safety situation in Port-au-Prince, from the Canadian and U.S. embassies to local security firms and local sources at the hospital. Some are very conservative in their assessment, while others are more cavalier. Experience has taught us that a balance of all provides the most reasonable assessment.

The Haitian presidential election had been scheduled for the fall of 2015 and should have been long since over by the time the Ottawa team hit the ground. In Haiti, voting for the president is a complicated business. It starts with a large number of candidates and a haphazard vote, after which certain candidates fall off and those in the lead stay on. Voting is repeated until one candidate breaks a threshold and is declared president. After each runoff vote, there are inevitably protests. It's a mixed group composed of angry losing candidates claiming fraud and corruption as well as front-runners jockeying for future positions. The protests fill the streets and often become violent.

This election was delayed and was now scheduled for the day that the Ottawa team would be arriving. After several checks, all sources said, without hesitation, do not come. This was the first time I had heard a unanimous recommendation. Without a doubt it was the right thing to do, but I was concerned how the Ottawa team would react. Fifteen people had taken time off work and altered their schedules to volunteer. This would not be easy for them, as they had already been rescheduled once before. But it was the right thing to do.

We picked another date. Tickets were rebooked, although because we were rescheduling and not cancelling, the cost was not too bad. Of all the hiccups we'd experienced so far, this felt relatively minor. Onward, I thought, this will work out.

The election results ended up being voided and the whole process had to start again. The Ottawa team would have to be bumped yet again. But we had exhausted our time frame to reschedule flights and might have to absorb the whole cost of the trip. Approximately $50,000 spent without as much as a suture to show for it.

I could not let that pass without an effort. I spoke with the brass at Air Canada, who were very sympathetic, but because the last leg of the trip was on American Airlines, there was nothing they could do. American Airlines is a huge company. I was sure they couldn't care less about our Haiti tickets. I was losing hope.

In a Hail Mary attempt, our travel agent, the brilliant Barbie Hutton, sent an email to American Airlines describing our organization and where we were from and what the situation was. Turns out one of the women who received the email had a friend from Newfoundland and was happy to extend our rescheduling time frame. It's a running joke in Newfoundland and Labrador that everyone outside the province thinks we all know each other. In this case, the two degrees of separation saved the day.

Now that we had softened the financial hit, we needed to make sure the team was still engaged. I was headed to Ottawa to visit family and asked if members of the Ottawa team could meet. I was worried I'd have to address complaints about the loss of money or the waste of time off or questions about how to improve our system.

Darryl picked me up early in the morning. I was suffering from the flu, but as I got into his SUV, the runny nose stopped and an adrenaline rush kicked in. I'm not a fan of confrontations. Who is? But I was bracing for what was to come.

I could not have been more wrong. Darryl was completely understanding, and as we drove through the beautiful mist-covered Ottawa Valley, it was clear that, if anything, he'd been worried that *I* would be upset.

We arrived at the house of one of the team's ER doctors, Tonja Stothart. Tonja is a kind and caring physician, and an incredible mother of two young kids. I was effusive in my apologies, but the five team members who had gathered at six in the morning were more than happy to brush that off and start planning the next trip. It was a gigantic relief and a much-needed boost. We left with a plan.

Team Ottawa returned to Haiti in the winter of 2017 for a successful second mission, with other missions planned after that. Tonja and I have also travelled as a part of a Canadian team to Nicaragua, and she continues to be an active member, as do Darryl and the entire Ottawa crew.

In an event that was all too familiar by then, I received an email from a surgeon in Saskatoon, Huw Rees, who wanted to chat about how they could join the effort. Sometimes you just connect with people right away. I had never met Huw, but in our first phone call it was as if we were long-lost friends. There was something very familiar and comforting about his approach. He had a balance of empathy and pragmatism, the perfect combination for a team lead.

Before I knew it, I was arriving in Saskatoon to give rounds to their surgical and anesthesia department at the Royal University Hospital. Henni, a pathologist and Huw's wife, insisted on picking me up at the airport. Her energy and kindness were equalled only by Huw's.

I had been to Saskatoon only once before, for eighteen hours in the dead of winter when I was interviewing for a residency position there. I am not even sure if the sun had been out that day. As Henni was driving to the hotel, I was dumbfounded by the beauty of the place. The sun was bright, and the city gently appeared from the plains of the prairies. It was as if the Tragically Hip's "Wheat Kings" had been cued in my head and was providing the score for this trip.

Rounds next day was a success. People were interested and engaged. After my presentation, I was invited to a team gathering at a member's house. I thought it would be a good chance for people to ask questions about what to expect, how to plan, what to take, and other logistical issues. It was almost poetic as we drove across the plains, past farms, and down a winding road to a farmhouse that could have been straight out of a movie. Inside, all the team members were gathered for a potluck. It felt like a Newfoundland kitchen party. For hours I sat and answered questions. I barely had time to take a bite of food.

This team was already well organized, and I left Saskatoon with little fear that not only would they be a welcome addition to the Team Broken Earth family but they would be champions of the cause. And Team Saskatoon did not disappoint. They provided amazing clinical care during their first week, they helped organize the mass of equipment we had been accumulating over the years, and they provided solid feedback on how to improve the overall process of how the teams work in Haiti. They also ended up with a significant surplus from their fundraising, which allowed us to fund a Project Stitch for one year. This was a special project created for paraplegics, who are often marginalized in places like Haiti. The program teaches them how to use sewing machines and make garments to sell, allowing them to provide for their own families.

Project Stitch was the vision of the chief medical officer of Bernard Mevs Hospital and a close friend of mine, Joanna Cherry. She recognized that the burden of spinal cord injuries in Haiti was massive. In Canada, paraplegics often struggle with adjusting to life, finding employment, and managing family life, as well as daily needs and sense of self-worth. In Haiti, the struggle is amplified that much more. There's little in the way of meaningful work for those who use wheelchairs, so they can't provide for themselves, let alone their families. There are few paved roads and no sidewalks, making it difficult for them to get around, and at home there is often a dirt floor with cardboard as a bed. They have medical complications, such as pressure sores, that often confine them to hospital beds, but their loss of sense of purpose is often profound. For those in wheelchairs, Project Stitch picks them up in an accessible van and takes them to work. You can see the newfound sense of purpose on their faces. Their ability to contribute was just as important to their healing as any surgery or medicine.

In June 2016, I was the keynote speaker at the Bethune Round Table, an international forum for global surgery that convened that year in Halifax. After I finished my talk, a gentleman approached me in the lecture theatre. His name was Dimitri Litwin and he was originally from Saskatoon but was now chief of surgery at the University of Massachusetts. He was very complimentary and wondered if I would be interested in sharing the Broken Earth story with the UMass medical school.

Surely, I thought, this offer was just vacuous flattery. A university of their calibre should be teaching *us*. Within hours, however, while on the plane home, I received an email from Dimitri asking me what date would work best.

Just like that, I found myself standing at the lectern at that revered university and delivering our idea to surgeons in the audience and throughout the state on a live feed. The story was easy for me to tell by now. It had more chapters, more successes. But there are no hard numbers, really. The metrics and science are often missing, and with an audience like this, I was worried they would be demanding the statistics.

But after my talk, instead of questions, the conversation turned to my experience with the hurdles of the project and how the audience could get involved. A university of this size, with its esteemed reputation—I have to admit I was a bit star-struck. Yet I still had this nagging feeling that I was being patronized, that this wasn't for real. This was world-stage recognition, and I didn't know how to process it.

By the time I returned home, emails and conference calls were already in full swing with the details about booking in a mission for UMass. We would need to obtain U.S. charitable status. It was getting real. Real real.

It was decided that their team would send five or six representatives on a reconnaissance trip when Team St. John's was in Haiti to see first-hand how we functioned and what they could expect. After we deplaned and cleared customs, thirty-four of us joined up with the UMass group, and we all drove to the hospital. I gave them a tour of the hospital and the volunteer quarters and showed them the equipment we had. We talked for a while about future plans and different expectations. They were incredible people, kind and gentle but at the same time goal-directed, determined to make this trip a success and grateful to have the support of Team Broken Earth.

Since then, Broken Earth has expanded more than I ever expected. From Barrie to Montreal to Corner Brook, more teams have been joining up and heading off to make a difference in Haiti. As our coverage and numbers grow, I still feel that, at its core, those early values are still well intact. So many people have stepped up and helped us push this forward. Today we have over fifty-five teams and approximately twelve hundred volunteers in developing countries.

The generosity of so many helps to restore my faith in the world. Not that it was ever really shook. There's a Newfoundland truth in there. We always hope for the best. No matter what's thrown at us, what obstacles we may see in front of us, we always believe that the best is just ahead. I used to take pride in knowing the names of every team member who volunteered. Oddly, I am even more proud that there are now too many to remember.

Reflecting now on Team Broken Earth's rapid growth, from three people out of Newfoundland and Labrador to well over a thousand from across the continent, I'm still at a little bit of a loss to explain it. There are other organizations like ours—Doctors Without Borders, Project Medishare. They're doing amazing work around the world. Some of our team members have participated. But what makes Team Broken Earth different?

It was something local. Something people felt they could own, embrace, be a part of. More than aspirational, it was tangible. These were our hands touching these lives. It is something that just caught fire and spread.

I was once trying to distill the secret of the success of Team Broken Earth to a friend. I talked about the timeline and the growth in both the number of volunteers and the places we now went beyond Haiti. I said that we initially didn't set out to create this. We didn't set out to compete with other organizations in the not-for-profit sector. To be honest, beyond Doctors Without Borders and Medishare, in the beginning I didn't even know what else was out there. It felt like we stumbled into a niche. *How* did it happen? It just happened.

I talked, too, about the commitment possibly being the differentiator. That, unlike some other organizations, we were only asking people to give up a week to ten days and to work with colleagues, friends, or simply just people from the same place. The collective force of many people doing this would unlock the power of scale.

I remember after my residency contacting some of the well-known medical volunteer missions, and they needed a six-month or a year's commitment. Don't get me wrong, I admire and respect anyone who's able to do that. It is an amazing sacrifice. But not everyone who wants to do work like this can commit that amount of time. For me, as a newly minted surgeon, full of doubt and debt, with a new mouth to feed, it was simply not an option. I had to get established in my profession. And I can only imagine Allison's reaction if, as we were discussing buying a house in Newfoundland, I added, "Oh by the way, I'm leaving for Africa for a year." On those first trips to Haiti, we all used our vacation time. That made sense. That's a reasonable amount of time to ask nurses, doctors, and other health professionals to dedicate their talent.

Having each team come from the same geographic area really worked, as team members knew most of the people they were going with. There's safety and efficiency in that. Some of the other organizations out there, even those offering short-term opportunities, want you to work with teams of people from all over the country or around the world. People you don't know and, more importantly, may not trust. For trust is a critical part of any successful medical team. Many hands work in sync towards one goal. If you don't trust the anesthesiologist to regulate the patient or the nurse to anticipate each move, things fall apart quickly. Art Rideout and I witnessed some dysfunctional if well-intentioned teams early on before Team Broken Earth, and we committed to making sure that this would not be part of what we were developing. We would rather have no team than a team that didn't work. So, having the familiarity of travelling with and working beside people you knew was comforting in a tense foreign place. The support of a "home team" was inspiring. The ability to lean on each other when things got tough on the ground proved to be beneficial. Not a lot of non-profits can claim that.

One other unintended consequence of our team model was that the communities each team came from rallied behind their team for fundraising. It was a point of pride, really, Halifax or Calgary or Brantford supporting their local doctors and nurses as they volunteered their time and talent to some of the poorest countries in the world. It became our fundraising model. There are corporate donations to Team Broken Earth overall, but each team also looks to their own communities to help the cause.

Team Broken Earth also developed a brand and relationships that people in Haiti trusted. As I have said many times to new teams, believe it or not it's easy to find people to do this, to find donors and equipment, but the biggest barrier, the highest hurdle to jump, is building relationships on the ground. That is what makes it easier for Broken Earth. It is impossible to build and maintain trust and a relationship in a week, but scale the weeks through Team Broken Earth and it becomes a reality.

The combination of being dynamic, smaller, and nimble has also meant Team Broken Earth can roll with the punches a bit more, experiment and adapt. I'm surprised when we find, not infrequently, organizations that can't do this.

Finally, and one of the toughest life lessons for me, in the not-for-profit environment there are less than altruistic motives. Competition for space, for recognition, and ultimately for funds is fierce. We never wanted to be like that. We all strongly believe that organizations trying to accomplish the same goals are stronger together. Synergies need to be nurtured, not stifled through competition. No matter where we go, it is about partnership. Not competition, but collaboration.

My friend, whom I was trying to explain all this to, took a long sip of his coffee. And then he said, "So, you didn't really have a plan for all this." It all evolved, I thought. Trial and error. Learn as we go. I smiled back at him and replied: "Leap and the net will appear."

12

LAND OF A MILLION ORPHANS

Holyrood: August 2016

NEWFOUNDLAND AND LABRADOR can be a place full of the most bizarre and magical coincidences. Connections that run generations are suddenly rediscovered over a cup of coffee or a pint. Many conversations here begin with "Now who are you?" Or "Where are your people from?" Or "Who is your mom?" Or "Are you a Furey from St. Mary's or Conception Bay?"

The conversation can take so many twists and turns that it is as jagged and beautiful as the rugged coastline itself. What is almost certain is that it will not stop until each person finds some relative or friend in common. And you'd be surprised how little or long that takes. I'm not sure if this is unique to the province, but it is something I have not witnessed anywhere else.

I get it from patients at least twice a day. "Are you one of the Fureys from Holyrood or Avondale?" "Is your dad Chuck, George, or Leo?" "Who do you belong to?" This has always been a somewhat uncomfortable question for me to answer. Of course, Dad is from Avondale, but he grew up in Mount Cashel, so it is unlikely that I know Bill or Bob Furey from around the corner. In a strange twist, and making the conversation more odd, is that I spent every summer of my young life in Holyrood, a town almost immediately adjacent to Avondale. Not with the Fureys, though, but with my mom's family.

Holyrood is nestled in the head of Conception Bay. By virtue of its geography and the hills that wrap around it, it's one of the most protected areas on the Northeast Avalon Peninsula. It's only a short thirty-minute drive from St. John's and yet the weather is always a little warmer, the sun a little brighter, and the bustle a lot less.

So many childhood memories linger in the spruce trees here. This is where my grandparents had a summer home when I was growing up. Holyrood was then a community experiencing a growth spurt. It was home to two fish plants and an oil refinery and was one of the stops for the train. It was also cabin country for townies who wanted to get away for the weekend.

(A side note . . . there are two types of people on the island of Newfoundland: townies and baymen. A townie is anyone from St. John's. A bayman is pretty much everyone else, no matter if you live in, near, or nowhere near a bay. Of course if you are from outside of the province, you are a come from away, or CFA for short—hence the name of the hit musical.)

My grandfather built a place in the early 1960s and my mom's family would spend every weekend and all the summer months there. This tradition extended to me. I have incredibly fond memories of watching squid being jigged, cod flaked, and the train rumbling by my grandparents' place. (The train, affectionately known as the Newfie Bullet, has not existed on the island since the 1980s.)

I made some friends there every summer, but I was always the townie and would never quite break into the community.

This despite the fact that my great-uncle raised the iconic cross on the highest point on the mountain that is the namesake of the community. It is now electric and lit at night, glowing like a floating holy cross. You can see it for miles.

My parents loved the proximity of Holyrood to St. John's. Though it's not even a half-hour drive and you can often see the glow of the city at night, it can feel a world away. St. John's is funny that way. So many communities, like Torbay or Alan Doyle's hometown of Petty Harbour, or even Quidi Vidi, which feels like a town hiding within the city, are all in the vicinity of St. John's. Yet if you're standing on the Topsail Beach you may as well be a thousand miles from Water Street. It's a place of curious boroughs, a collective of villages on the collar of the old city. My parents loved that. I do too. And I'm sure the tranquility of the place helped as well. So much that my parents eventually built their own place there. It has become for all of us a place of comfort, family, and reflection.

I have made many of my life's biggest decisions in Holyrood. There is a beach just a two-minute walk from my grandparents' place. I used to walk there all the time with my Poppy O'Keefe, who would be on the way to the store for cigarettes and some penny candy for me. They say that in a child's memory everything is twice the size that it actually is. This beach is like that. It seemed huge then, but it is a small beach that is well protected and has a gentle calm about it.

There is a rock that juts out along the far side like a small peninsula, creating a division and protection from the rest of the bay. There's a healthy tradition of superstition throughout Newfoundland and Labrador. You couldn't go into the woods in case the fairies would take you away. And there was always some tale of a rogue wave that carried a bunch of children far out to sea.

This is probably why when we were small we were not allowed to play on "the big rock," but as I grew I was able to adventure over the sides and explore this protecting piece of granite.

It's a place I feel drawn to. There is a comfort in the gentle crashing waves, the safety on one side and the open ocean on the other. It's where I have sat alone and made a lot of my life decisions. It was where I sat when I decided to go to St. Francis Xavier University in Nova Scotia instead of Memorial. The same bump on the same rock is where I perched when I decided to turn down law school offers and go to medical school. It's the same place I decided I would propose to Allison, although the actual proposal was made on the top of the mountain bearing the cross overlooking Conception Bay. This lone piece of rock was also where I went to think about Dad's advice not to go to Haiti.

As the teams expanded, we developed a routine at the hospital and at home, packing red bags full of equipment weeks before leaving, and organizing more efficiently the fundraising efforts and communication between teams. We seemed to be in a groove. It was then that I thought it may be a good idea, in the serenity of a warm Holyrood summer day, to talk to Dad again about what we were doing in Haiti. I'm not sure what I was hoping to achieve. Maybe to get a little of that approval every boy seeks from his father. A nod. A wink. A slap on the back. Something that said *You were right to go, you did good there*. Or maybe I just wanted to hear that voice of reason on where this was all going because, to be frank, I didn't know myself.

So on a Sunday afternoon, with the kids gone for a walk with Allison and Mom, Dad and I sat on the deck, the sun shining over the trees with the crucifix mountaintop behind us. We have had many chats like this over the years, but this time was different. There was a subtle shift in the tone. He was no longer chatting like I was a child, an adolescent, or even a young man. He had suddenly become the senior statesman, the grandparent. I guess it was not all that sudden, but it suddenly became evident to me. His ambition more tempered and about legacy, mine more driven by change.

The conversation drifted from Haiti to public service in general. Perhaps because of his chaotic upbringing, my dad had been given incredible exposure to people who dedicated themselves to the betterment and advancement of those around them rather than to themselves. My grandmother herself, giving until she died to keep her unusual family unit strong and together. My aunt Rose, leaving the often heavy disciplinary hands of the Sisters to devote herself to the plight of the poor. She'd often venture outside the walls of the convent to provide for those in some of the poorest communities around the province.

It's no wonder Dad was drawn in his own way to the service of others. Of course it made sense that he chose a life of teaching, and we talked about his time in Stephenville, and Dunville, and the pure joy he got from seeing children reach new heights, set new goals and reach them again. In the past I have thought that these were positions forced on him. I'm not sure why, I guess oversimplifying his starting position, but it became clear from the passion he spoke with that it had been his calling.

I told him of the patients I had who were his former students or staff and how they all spoke with such admiration for him. But it was clear in the look on his face and the musing and laughing of different stories that it was not the accolades that had kept him motivated. It was the service to the communities and to the children themselves.

Education, he has often proclaimed, is the answer to all our society's woes. When I was younger I would often argue that point, that an education was not a given right, and that degrees and diplomas were not guarantees in life. My immaturity made me completely miss the point. So as we sat on the deck that day talking about the foundations of a society, I was the one arguing that education, in every sense of the word, needed to be a pillar of who we are. Reconciling differences, understanding, and tolerance are all made easier with education. And, more specifically, medical education can do more for the future of healthcare in impoverished countries than a thousand relief missions. I saw a twinkle in the corner of my old man's eye when I was done my spiel.

The conversation then drifted to my practice, as he was curious how it worked—how I dealt with the pressure of people's lives, making split-second decisions that profoundly changed people. I never thought it much different than his second job. That was the opening he needed to talk about his practice at a small mom-and-pop law office, struggling to pay bills yet never sending anyone away because they couldn't pay.

He spoke of the law—not the practice of it but the law itself— as though he missed it, as though it were a piece of him he almost longed to have back. In a different time and place, I wonder if instead of the political world, would he have chosen to become a law professor. I could see him at the lectern now challenging young lawyers to become passionate yet compassionate in their interpretation and practice of the law.

Finally, our attention turned to a subject that is the one we have the most fun with and the most in common. Some fathers and sons have hockey and have great long chats recalling past Stanley Cup games and shared heroes. Others play golf together.

For Dad and me, our common love has always been politics. Not so much the partisan red versus blue, although there was plenty of strategy talk, which generally involved me listening to old stories of how conventions were won and lost. The real love was in the power of the political system, and how policies were the true documents that would shape and advance our society, and that anyone who quickly dismissed the system or those working in it was doomed to reap their malcontent.

On this particular day we spent the lion's share of our time talking about Lincoln and the two books we had recently read, both portraying him in a different light. *Team of Rivals: The Political Genius of Abraham Lincoln* is one of Dad's favourite books, and *Leadership: In Turbulent Times* is one of mine. Both books are by the same author, Pulitzer Prize–winning American historian Doris Kearns Goodwin, but both have a slightly different take. The former is more confident and calculated; the latter more human and soft. Regardless of the slant on the president, the common theme of how the power of democracy can literally free a people came through in spades. What a marvellous space, politics, where the will of women and men could be articulated and organized and change how we operate, how we see each other, and how we act.

One thing Dad and I always agreed on is that good, righteous, noble people answering the call to public service is the only way the system could survive and thrive. Neither of us subscribed to the belief that the system was corrupt or that it attracted only self-serving players. We were not so naive to think they didn't exist, but realize they are only a small part of many millions of people serving in the public service across the country.

Since childhood I have been on the receiving end of snide remarks and barbs about my dad and the political profession he chose. One in particular was from someone supposed to be a mentor. There's a widely held opinion that the Senate should be elected, not appointed. This individual was asking how my dad slept at night being a senator. I would simply respond, "If not for people like Dad, who has dedicated his life to public service, then who? And I am pretty sure he sleeps just fine, thank you."

On this warm summer afternoon we agreed on almost every issue of the day. There have been many times where Dad and I did not agree. Some arguments were never again opened, each of us assuming the other would not budge, while others moved towards common ground. Regardless, almost all of them were argued through the lens of the public and where we thought society should be on issues, not personal but in a more global sense. There was never personal gain in any argument, be it about capital punishment or abortion or what have you, but we would always discuss it as if society was an individual and what we wanted that person to look like.

I think that is the essence of public service, the essence of why my grandmother left her husband, why my grandfather served overseas, why my father devoted his life to politics. To realize your time on earth is not about you, but rather is about making those around you better, and fighting to make the place better than you found it.

As the sun was setting and the kids were skipping into sight, I said to him, "Now do you understand why I went to Haiti? If not me, who?" The twinkle in his eye was a little brighter, but he shared no words. I wanted to tell him more about Broken Earth and our plans for expansion and our efforts to help the orphanages, like Maison des Enfants de Dieu. Haiti has been called "the land of a million orphans," so it seemed natural to see if we could help. We had seen many orphans in Haiti, in the ER and the pediatric wards, but had never seen first-hand the orphanages themselves.

My first visit to an orphanage changed me. I don't have the fortitude to handle the despair in children's eyes, so sometimes I feel I have deliberately avoided it. I do not routinely treat children as a part of my practice, in part because of these feelings. But this particular trip involved a stop at one of the places just outside Port-au-Prince from which we had received children. They asked us to come and visit.

In the middle of the chaos that is Port-au-Prince, on the best of days and in the depths of a poverty-stricken area with no real road, we drove through the back streets. Past the howling horns and screaming voices, we drove through the gates of the orphanage, and there seemed to be a sudden switch to calm and tranquility. A small oasis surrounded by walls, it was separated from the havoc beyond. It even felt cooler there. Fully grown trees offered shelter, and in the middle of the courtyard there was a playground with a rudimentary soccer pitch.

This orphanage hosted and cared for many special-needs children: those in wheelchairs, those with cognitive delay issues, and some with amputations. The tranquility of the place was interrupted only by the excitement of the children as we began passing out toys and books. They surrounded us, smiling and little hands reaching out. It was overwhelming. These kids wanted the toys, but they were also starved for attention, and we provided all we had.

After the toys were distributed and the kids had settled a little, it was time for lunch. That is, the organizers were about to start lunch when they realized there was too much excitement. So instead they passed out snacks of mangoes and water.

As we were chatting with the organizers of the orphanage, out of the corner of my eye I noticed a soccer game start, and they were using one of the balls we had brought. The children did not have shoes on, but were ecstatic to be playing soccer, a Haitian addiction. They were playing on a flattened gravel area where the hot sun was shining like a spotlight on the game.

At first glance it was a simple game of soccer being played by a group of kids ranging in age from eight to ten. On closer examination, there was something special going on. This was more than a game of soccer they were playing. This was a game of keep-away, where the person with the ball tries to keep the ball away from all the other players. In this case, the boy with the ball was dominating the other two kids his age. Try and try as they may, they could not get the ball from him.

The feat of holding on to the ball for as long as this boy did would be an accomplishment enough for anyone else. However, this boy was an above-knee amputee. He had lost his leg in the earthquake. He'd use a crutch for balance and his leg to control the ball. For added showmanship, he was eating one of the recently dispensed mangoes with his other hand. Crutch in one hand, mango in the other, and one leg, he could easily outplay the other two kids in keep-away.

There was ruin, poverty, and despair beyond the walls, yet here in this moment was the human spirit. Human determination on the stage of a gravel soccer pitch for all to see. Hope, courage, and determination all wrapped around a soccer ball. I stood in silence trying my best to take in every last second of the moment. Sometimes life stops you. Like a hand to your chest just stopping you right in place and it tells you, *Look at this, this is symbolic, this will now reside within you*. A medicine reserve. A soul bandage. This was a memory I could use when I fell down, felt down, or when things felt impossible. When the mountain seemed too high to climb or when I was ready to throw in the towel. It's there when I need it. I project it like a movie onto whatever surface is in front of me. Onto whatever impedes me.

Leaving the orphanage was harder than I thought it would be. When it was time to go, the kids hung on, hungry for attention, for the outside world to come and help. Or maybe it was just the toys. But prying away little hands trying to hold on to your legs as you walk out of an orphanage is not easy.

The ride back to the hospital was sobering. A strange imbalance of the joy of seeing the orphans and the uplifting visual of the soccer game against the pangs of having to leave them. Knowing that even when I was at home in Canada, this life, this orphanage, would be full. From an organizational perspective, I was unsure whether orphanage support was something we would do in the future. Those are the toughest decisions to live with, because it comes with remembering those little arms wrapped around your legs.

At home, looking from a window out to the ocean, my kids playing on the hardwood floor as Allison prepared a bite for everyone, I could not shake pictures of the orphans from my mind's eye. Their smiles, their want of even just the tiniest bit of attention. The little hands pulling at my leg. Sometimes those tough decisions come back to you at the strangest moments. I hear a whispering voice asking if the orphanage was worth the visit. Could we help? How? My youngest, Mark, took his seat comfortably on my lap. His thick blond curls hid his eyes, which were transfixed on the Legos in his hands. Not a care in the world. Not a worry either. Little hands.

Yeah. I knew that during the next trip, I'd have to revisit the idea.

———

Part of my role on these trips to Haiti has become building relationships. I often visit different stakeholders, government officials, and people who I think it is important to reach out to and let know what we are doing. Help can come from anywhere, and support is a job that's never finished.

One early morning I left the security of the hospital to go meet with some stakeholders, and I had taken the opportunity to add an orphanage to the schedule. By now I had grown accustomed to the confusion in the streets of Port-au-Prince. I know what to expect when I arrive. I know how bad the situation is, and it rarely becomes personal or emotional anymore. But this trip outside the gates was an exception, and it shook me. I felt my father's history in my journey. It caught me off guard. It overwhelmed me. And at times, I broke down. I see him now, sitting in the sun in Holyrood. That half-smile on Dad's face that says he's ten fathoms deep in thought.

We started the day in an orphanage, one very different from the others we had visited so far. It was being run by a former orphan. The children admitted to this facility all had one thing in common: they had lost both their parents. They were being cared for as best as possible given the circumstances. In the dorm rooms, there were bunk beds and bare mattresses. Some of the children were in cage-like cribs for their own protection. But protection from what? In each child's eyes, I could see my father's. I could see my own children's. The weight of it made it hard for me to breathe. It broke me.

And yet there was a shining light here. It was the people dedicating their lives to looking after these special children. Without them, these kids would be left to the streets and a darker fate. Here, there physically wasn't much. But there was love, in great store.

Our tour guide was a young dedicated teacher named Joey. He was born and raised in Haiti, and his smile lit up the room. He took us through the loose collection of buildings with the pride of a new homeowner. He was of modest stature but his enthusiasm made him seem larger. He saw this place differently than we did. Where we saw despair, he saw hope and the opportunity for a brighter future.

From there we drove through the poverty-ridden streets, up broken winding roads to a school. As we pulled into the guarded courtyard, we could hear the singing of children. It was beautiful. There were dedicated teachers working with children in an outdoor semi-enclosed classroom. They were learning to read and write. Doing math. And of course singing. These teachers were working hard, and the children listened and interacted. This could have been a school anywhere. Its impact and implication were universal. Education is always the answer.

It made me think/hope/believe that there was a child amongst them who would change Haiti. In every child's face there is that spark of hope. That same hope from the face of the little girl after her grandfather's hip surgery. That look, that feeling, recharges me every time.

From there, that day, I put on my political hat and met with the vice-president of the Haitian Senate, Andris Riché. I felt like I was continuing my family's history and journey through different eyes in a much different place.

Haitian government buildings are nothing like those Washington or Ottawa, although before the earthquake, the National Palace looked like the Capitol Building in D.C. It completely collapsed during the quake and was left in ruins. You could still drive by the old building and see the twisted dome leaning towards the ground. It was a full floor lower than where it should have sat, and the sun always managed to make it that much brighter. Illuminating it as a reminder that this was a gravesite. This dome is now a massive headstone for the countless number of people who died in the building that day.

The temporary Haitian government buildings used to be in the centre of the city but were later moved closer to the water. These are a series of heavily guarded buildings in the centre of Cité Soleil, one of the most dangerous areas in the city. The buildings were compartmentalized container-like structures, stacked one on top of the other and divided between the Senate, the Chamber of Deputies, the prime minister's offices, and the president's.

Compared to the outside, the security within these offices seemed light at best as we were led into the Senate offices. Dad of course is a senator, and I have spent some time in the Senate of Canada. Those Ottawa offices reflect the significance of the office the members represent, and a level of decorum is expected. I thought there would be some of the same here. Not the exact same, but a similar element of grandiosity. But there was none. The office was simple, with a Haitian flag in the corner and a picture of the president in an inexpensive frame, ironically hanging askew. It was minimalistic. The furniture did not match. There was no computer or phone. The degree of bureaucratic business that I have been accustomed to in Canadian government offices was completely absent.

Senator Riché was well dressed and polite, gracious and interested. I quickly forgot about my surroundings as we became immersed in conversation. He talked openly about the earthquake and the dire financial situation facing the country. He spoke proudly of his previous trips to Canada. This is not an unusual scenario. Haitians feel extremely close to Canada and Canadians. Canada and Haiti, after all, are two of the twenty-nine French-speaking countries in the world, and two of the four in North America. Canada has the fourth-highest number of Haitian-born residents outside Haiti, with Montreal boasting a vibrant community. Haitians often have stories of friends and families living in Canada, and at least four or five times each trip I am asked if I can get a visa for someone to travel to Canada. Although we cannot often fulfill these requests, it fills my heart with pride to hear my homeland being held in such regard.

The senator and I continued to chat for about an hour, using a combination of English and an interpreter for the French. In the chaos, the government has the same responsibilities as our own: funds, education, healthcare, roads, safety, and so on. The difference, of course, is the scale. They have so little. We are incredibly privileged in Canada to be able to engage in open debate about how our tax dollars are spent. Are we spending the right amount on healthcare? Are we getting good return on investment?

As I write this, Canada is spending approximately $7,000 per person per year on healthcare. In Haiti, they spend approximately $130. In Canada that wouldn't even provide food for a few people in a hospital for one day, yet this is what Haiti has to spend on all healthcare in a year, and even with that they are going further into debt. But much like Canada, their natural resources are vast and represent potential for the future.

After we shared a coffee, Senator Riché asked me about Dad. He clearly had done some research, as he knew Dad was a senator, and he asked about the Senate of Canada. What he did not know about was my journey earlier in the day. The orphanage, the school, now the Senate: the parallels of my family's story were real and deep.

Despite the temporary buildings, the poverty outside, and the armed guards, there was hope. That allowed me to collect myself. Riché spoke with passion and vision about a better Haiti. It's not what I've come to expect from government officials here, but admittedly, my opinion comes from reading the papers. You expect corruption. To encounter the opposite caught me off guard. In retrospect, perhaps I projected my own hope on him. If there wasn't hope in government officials, we would not find it anywhere else. These container offices had to deliver more than perhaps any government in Canada. Their job was larger. Establishing and delivering on a vision of hope has lives literally dependent on it.

It's funny how one conversation with one hopeful person can change your mood and perspective. As we were leaving the government buildings, I felt more settled, and it helped to know some people out there were working towards a brighter, sustainable Haiti. But this was still one of the hardest days I ever had in Haiti.

It was then that I decided two things. First, with the kids being cared for at the orphanage, in the schools, and with a government trying its best, there's a path forward for Haiti. Second, I would never return to a Haitian orphanage.

Okay, I know that sounds harsh. Selfish, even. I think it's good for teams to go and see the children we treat and take them toys, assess them for medical issues, and treat diseases, but I would not go again. To this day I have not returned to a Haitian orphanage. It is just too hard on me. It reaches deep inside, and the last thing these kids need to see is some tourist with tears in his eyes.

I can't help it. I look at those little faces and see Maggie's smile, Rachael's eyes, and Mark playing. I cannot reconcile it. I've seen a lot during my years in Haiti. But this is what brings me to my knees. It is something that I struggle with daily still.

On one of the first team visits to the orphanage, there was a child of only a few days or weeks old who had been abandoned in the streets, found by a dumpster. The orphanage took him in. One of our nurses, Heather Flight, recognized that this child was sick and needed the support of a hospital and pediatric team. As is always the case with Team Broken Earth, the team rallied.

The boy's name was Jonathan. He was thin, so thin that from across the room you could count his ribs and see his skeletal structure. His breathing was laboured, and he didn't make the usual sounds and movements of a baby. He was flat. Heather gathered Jonathan in a blanket and held him close as we loaded him into the front seat of our transport. No one said it, but everyone was thinking it: the clock was ticking on Jonathan's young life.

The truck pulled through the gates of the hospital, the mid-afternoon sun beating down relentlessly. Pediatricians Natalie Bridger and Leigh Anne Newhook stood waiting with the calm and caring faces that only pediatricians carry in medicine. Jonathan was rushed into the pediatric unit, placed on a crib bed, IVs were inserted, followed by a feeding tube, and immunizations were administered. Now it was a game of wait and see how he would respond. *If* he would respond.

Children truly are resilient. Or maybe it was just a case of the universe saying *No, not this kid*. Jonathan improved throughout our week. He became less lethargic and more responsive. He even began to gain weight. Eventually the tubes were removed and he was released back to the care of the orphanage.

We could not let the story stop there. What would happen to him? Would he return to his previous state, or would he continue to get the care he needed? We have sent teams back to the same orphanage every time we return to Haiti. Jonathan has grown. He has one of those little round bellies young kids have. He is interactive, growing, playing, and developing. Seeing the picture of him sent from a different team was a highlight for me in this adventure. He was sitting on the knee of a team member, bouncing and laughing. A large, healthy boy.

Today, Jonathan is three years old and has been assessed by multiple teams. Yes, he is just one child, but it's a win for us, a win for him, for everyone. Maybe he will be the one. The one who benefits from the security of the orphanage, from the value of an education, and maybe even from a free and democratic society. Maybe he will be the one to bring change, big or small, to his community, to Haiti, or to the world. Maybe Jonathan will be Dad. He will sit on a deck with his son someday and quietly reflect on how the universe is hard at work for us all. That fate can be made. That the hope you give comes from the hope you've been given.

13

TACTILE NATURE OF CHANGE

Port-au-Prince: October 2015

YOU'D BE SURPRISED what you can get used to sometimes. Even chaos can become routine. Our missions to Haiti had become like that. We always have to keep our guard up, especially when it comes to the safety and security of others. But the mayhem of the airport in Port-au-Prince, the way the traffic in the city moves like a school of fish, and the ever-present armed guards, this has all become white noise for those of us whose trips now number in the double digits.

Despite the frequency of the trips, there is something the same every time. A familiarity of the unknown. We are more comfortable with the locations, the people and staff, but as in life, in medicine there are always unknowns. The difference being that in medicine they often come with greater risks.

October 2015. The ritual begins at two in the morning Newfoundland time. Thirty people get up in the middle of the cool autumn night and get ready to go. They have given up their vacation for this. Some take cabs to the airport, letting loved ones stay in bed, while others come with families for early-morning smiles and last-minute hugs. This particular trip was a special one for me. It would be the first time Allison had returned since 2010.

Allison has been so supportive, so giving, so loving through all this. I was curious to see how she would see Haiti today. Would she see the results of her hard work and support? We're a team, and we each can do what we do only because of the other. She is a lens through which I see an honest perspective on things. I can read her as well as she reads me. So I'd know right away if the sacrifices had been worth it.

This would be the first time I was leading a team with Allison on it. We're both doctors but, apart from our first trip to Haiti, we've never worked together. Even during the four years of medical school, we were only ever partners on some skills sessions. I don't think we even studied together! But look at us now. Waiting to board a flight in the middle of the night.

So, leaving St. John's this time was much different. A lot had happened in six years. Rachael was only an infant when we'd first left, and now we were going to miss her soccer practices and homework. Maggie was now nine and had a fuller appreciation for what we were doing and how it was going to affect her. And Mark wasn't even born when we made our first trip. He was five now and just starting kindergarten. These trips seemed to affect him the most. It's not that the others don't miss me when I go, but Mark has been the only one to tug at my arm and ask me not to leave, or to snuggle in bed some morning and ask me, "Why?" I have this photo that Allison took at the airport one time when she brought the kids to greet me when I returned from a trip. It's the area at the foot of the escalator in arrivals where travellers are met by family and friends. In the picture, Mark sits by himself on the floor, legs folded, head in hands, waiting for me to come down. It broke my heart the first time I saw it. Now it's in my head every time the announcement is made on the flight that we'll soon be landing in St. John's.

Then there is what Allison refers to as our as "our hidden family member," Team Broken Earth. I've heard Allison use this description several times, telling people it eats most meals with us. When we all sit down to dinner, the conversation frequently turns to Team Broken Earth, as if it is sitting at the table. It's not a bad thing. Quite the opposite. We've put our hearts and souls into it. Nurtured it. We've watched as it has grown at this point to be in seven provinces with multiple teams going from around the country several times a year. We couldn't be prouder of our fourth child!

As we deplaned in Port-au-Prince, Allison immediately began noticing differences, the obvious improvements that I had just taken for granted. A quasi-functioning airport, no longer with tents surrounding it, and much less rubble. The drive was less chaotic by Haitian standards, meaning still chaotic but less life-threatening. At the hospital, her face lit up when she saw the much-improved pediatric and emergency units. Any previous concern had left her face, and her confidence and caring nature were now in full force.

This was a special trip for another reason. For the first time we would be using the new hospital and volunteer quarters, a legacy project that was now finally completed. I couldn't wait for Allison to see it. Couldn't wait myself.

The original volunteer quarters had consisted of four rooms separated from the operating room by a seventy-five-foot corridor, whose different-coloured plastic and metal roof shaded it from the sun and rain. At the end of the corridor stood a wall with barbed wire on the top; this separated us from the main street beyond. This last section was not covered, allowing for natural light to illuminate the covered section. The balance of light was such that the dust would sparkle and dance in the air, random beauty.

The corridor became a natural place for people to hang out and chat, to take a break when needed. There were remnants and mementoes of earlier teams and volunteers from around the world: half-used bottles of fly repellent and sunscreen and left-behind pens and paper. The walls were painted a combination of light green and an orange-pink that I have not seen anywhere else. It became so hot at times under the roof that you could feel the walls sweat.

In the dorm, the old bent wooden doors creaked when you opened them. Each door bore a room number on a piece of paper, 1 through 4. We would divide the staff based on their specialities and schedules, so people would not be disturbed when they were off shift.

Each room was divided by a wall with a door in it. There were one or two bunk beds on one side and three or four bunk beds on the slightly larger other side. The bunk beds were built of solid wood, with old, heavily used mattresses. Remnants of mosquito nets hung in a tangled mess of mesh and hooks. The beds were lined head to toe, on the right and left sides, leaving little room to even turn around. In each side of the room, a single light bulb hung from the ceiling; these didn't always work, electricity in Haiti being rather spontaneous. On the back wall was a small window with an air conditioner that frequently stopped working or, worse, leaked all over the tiled floor.

At the end of each room was a ten-by-ten-foot bathroom containing a sink (with water you could not drink), a toilet (which could not flush away even the flimsiest of tissue paper), and a shower that consisted of a pipe, a raised tile area, and a drain. The showers were full of leftover soaps and shampoos. A large garbage can next to the toilet was for materials that would normally be flushed.

We encouraged everyone to bring only one bag of personal items. This would not only reduce our baggage expense but allow us room to bring equipment as well. Still, we usually ended up with sixty bags for a team of thirty people. All these bags needed to be stored somewhere in these already cramped rooms. There was no other storage space. Even the bags with medical equipment were split between the rooms, with lists of their contents taped to the door of each room. Frequently, in the middle of the night, a nurse or doctor would come in and rummage through a bag in search of an essential piece of equipment or medication. We all got used to this pretty quickly.

On day one of a trip, people respected the limited amount of space, and bags were neatly stowed under the bunks. By the end of day two, the rooms looked like they belonged to university students on a road trip. But still, it worked.

After I returned from a trip in the winter of 2012, I was introduced over dinner to Brendan and Renee Paddick. I had never met Brendan, but I had heard of him. I knew that he was a successful businessman, the founder and CEO of Columbus Communications, a cable and communications company that did business in several Caribbean countries. It turns out we had several friends in common.

It was Alan Doyle's idea. Alan has known Brendan for a long time and thought it would be a good idea for the two of us to meet. Alan's always been a huge supporter of Team Broken Earth. He and Great Big Sea played our first fundraiser, and Alan did the second one solo. Of course Alan never really does any-thing solo. He's the first to get up-and-coming musicians like the Fortunate Ones up on stage with him. Always the generous soul. So when he said, "You gotta meet Brendan," I knew this would be good, as there was synergy in Newfoundlanders doing work in the Caribbean.

At that time, I had yet to really speak to anyone in the busi-ness community about Team Broken Earth. I was a doctor; what the hell did I know about fundraising? I managed to talk Allison into coming to dinner. I'm pretty sure my pressure was of the "don't make me do this by myself" variety. When we arrived, I sat next to Brendan, and Allison sat next to Renee, and we hit it off immediately. I remember someone saying that you don't make close friends after you turn thirty, but that dinner cer-tainly disproved it. Brendan and Renee remain some of our best friends, and we take vacations and spend Christmases together. It is even a ritual for them to come to our home and watch Harry Potter movies with the kids.

There was a warmth generating from them both. It was obvi-ous from the second we said hello that they were incredibly car-ing and kind people who, despite their business successes, were grounded and had a real desire to make a difference. We spoke of what Team Broken Earth was doing in Haiti. I could tell Brendan was genuinely curious and searching for an opportu-nity to help. He offered that his company might want to support the team and the project. He said Columbus received requests from Newfoundlanders all the time for support and donations, but given their operations were in the Caribbean, usually they couldn't make it happen. Team Broken Earth, though, was a natural fit. After all, we were both Newfoundlanders working in the Caribbean.

I've come to know that Brendan is not one to give from afar. He's hands-on. He likes to see things for himself and base decisions on that in-the-trenches experience. I knew at that moment this guy was going to Haiti with us.

"Of course," I said, "come along. It will be rewarding." I felt I needed a full-disclosure moment with him, to tell him about the conditions the teams worked in there. But I don't think anything could've dissuaded him. We decided to link him up with our next team and he could see for himself what we were doing. But in the car on the way home, I said to Allison that I didn't know what I'd just done. What if it didn't work out? Could a cable tycoon handle eating Pop-Tarts and putting used toilet paper in a garbage can?

Months passed and we were once again on the ground in Port-au-Prince. Brendan was scheduled to arrive in a few days. I was still questioning this decision. But I needn't have worried. Brendan integrated into the team immediately. He set up in a top bunk in my room, unpacked his bag, and tossed it onto the rest of the jumble on the floor. And then he got right to work, helping move things around the hospital and transporting patients. He fit in as if he had been part of the team from the very beginning. He never complained about the cramped conditions or the showers or anything else. He never faltered, and he did more than was asked. He's a guy who wants to be doing the heavy lifting, the kind of person who knows the names of all his employees and their families and has never forgotten where he came from. Brendan is a proud Newfoundlander through and through. He's humble, committed, funny, and hard-working. He has always flown the Newfoundland and Labrador flag with pride, regardless of the size of the boardroom or the players at the table. It is no wonder he is such a successful business leader.

Brendan is not one for publicity moments, something New-foundlanders refer to as "being grand." That's not Brendan at all. At the end of his trip, he pulled the team aside and, in the blistering sun of the courtyard, presented us with a cheque for $250,000. He told me he wanted us to use the funds for construction—to build better rooms for patients and volunteers alike. We were all a little stunned in a "what just happened?" way. Brendan's quiet generosity was speaking to the sustainability of Team Broken Earth for the first time.

The team had discussed the buildings and hospital infrastructure from time to time, but we never had the resources and never thought we would. We thought it was beyond our scope. But maybe we were just being naive; maybe our focus was too narrow. When our teams expanded across the country, it had broadened our idea of what Team Broken Earth can be. What we can do.

If we could build new hospital and volunteer quarters, it would raise patient care at Bernard Mevs Hospital to the next level.

The first hurdle to jump was finding the space to build. On the compound, there was an area that had previously been occupied by a tent morgue. Once a day or so a truck would come and take the bodies to the local morgue. It was not a great use of the space. It could accommodate a building, and anyway, it was the only square footage available on the compound. One problem: it was surrounded by other buildings and was therefore locked in.

I approached the Bernard Mevs board. They were incredibly excited and wanted us to proceed as fast as possible. At the time, the local hospital volunteer coordinator, Scott Gillenwater, was handling special projects. He's a nice guy from the United

States who had been in Haiti for a couple of years. I figured he had the expertise to coordinate the project.

Scott worked with a hospital architect, Michael Day, who travelled from Miami several times to ensure the site was right and the plans were correct. Designing a hospital requires more than just putting up walls. We had to consider things like the size of doors for wheelchairs, how to run oxygen in the walls, the arrangement and placement of nursing stations, and so on and so on, and all had to adhere to local building codes. We eventually landed on a two-storey design that would have patient rooms on the ground floor that would double the capacity of the hospital. The volunteer quarters, a dorm-style living space, would occupy the top floor.

With the plans, however, came the budget. It was more than I had expected, and more than Brendan had committed to. The hospital agreed to contribute some funds. And between Scott and me—well, really Scott—we managed to secure more funds from other sources, including Project Medishare and Food For The Poor.

So we had the land and the funds. Now we needed a contractor. This would prove to be the most challenging part. We needed to find a reliable, trustworthy contractor who was going to build what we wanted, not what they wanted. One who was not going to cut corners and who would build something all Haitians could be proud of. I wanted to meet them in person, so Scott arranged several meetings, but none left me feeling confident.

The construction business in Haiti is not closely regulated or monitored, and I had heard too many stories of projects being started and then spiralling out of control as budgets skyrocketed in less than honourable ways. I was petrified that would happen to us. I didn't want Brendan's donation or the other money we'd raised to be wasted in such a way, leaving us with a half-built building and no more funds. The streets of Port-au-Prince are full of half-built buildings that sit as a constant reminder.

Things changed when I met Jean-Marc de Matteis and his charming family. Jean-Marc is a middle-aged Haitian who was educated in the United States and returned to Port-au-Prince with his young family to run a construction and contracting company. We met at his house in the centre of Port-au-Prince, surrounded by lush trees. I met his wife, Verena, and their kids and we all hit it off.

We sat down to dinner, and as we discussed Jean-Marc's history in the country and the buildings he had completed, he could sense I was uneasy. When he asked me directly what the issue was, I explained to him that the budget was fixed and I was worried about cost overruns. I told him that when I start something, I want to finish it. He smiled and told me not to worry. He and his family wanted to give back as well. They would assume any cost overruns, and that would be his contribution to the building. It was settled with a handshake. I've got a pretty good read on people, and I just knew Jean-Marc was the real deal. Any worry I had evaporated in the afternoon air.

Within a year we had our two-storey earthquake-proof building.

This would be my first time walking through the doors. As soon as the team arrived from the airport, we gathered for a formal walk-through. It was as if we had just purchased a house. They actually handed me the keys. I am not going to lie, it was a proud day. This infrastructure will live beyond me, beyond our efforts here, a game-changing building for the people inside the walls of the hospital.

The top floor was for the volunteer quarters. Each room had four bunk beds and access to proper showers and toilets. The bedrooms surrounded a common eating area with tables and a TV. We had moved from the equivalent of tents to a college dorm.

My smile grew bigger as we went downstairs. There were private patient rooms and a large central nursing station close to multiple beds with curtains as partitions. It was a far cry from the single crammed room with a central fan pointing to the ceiling. This was progress. Overwhelmed by it, I threw my arms around Allison. More than a mission report or statistics, this was tactile. This was change that you could actually touch.

The team's excitement and energy lasted only a moment, as everyone got straight to work. The new operating rooms were busy right away. Pediatrics was overwhelmed. At one point the crew was so busy they had me doing chest compressions on a newborn while they were doing compressions on two others. From the earlier high, it was a sobering reminder of why we were there.

At the end of that day everyone seemed spent. I often get asked that question: Aren't you exhausted? That day I felt myself, for the first time in a long time, getting completely tired. As I was lying down on a stretcher in an empty operating room, I thought about how I was going to get the energy to do the next big case. But the usual battery rechargers kicked in. I thought about the team here and at home. I thought about this space we had built and how many people will come through these doors. It's moments like that when you realize that the universe is fluid. Always in motion. Its energy is movement in all forms. I can feel it fill the building. In turn, it fills me, and I'm ready for what's next.

There have been so many roller-coaster moments along the way but, if anything, they give us some great views. I witnessed some of those views on that trip. An ambulance sits with its lights flashing in the hospital parking lot. Of course, you say, it's a hospital after all. But this ambulance is brand new and shines with the logo of Team Broken Earth painted on its side. Thanks to a couple of businesses back in Newfoundland and New Brunswick, PF Collins and Malley Industries, we are able to better and more safely transfer patients to get the care they need. In the new OR, from seven in the morning to late into the evening, never complaining, and never slowing down, the nurses barely have time to sit down. The team has more work to do than we can ever get done, and the push is on. The eye clinic, run with the help of the Lions Club of Newfoundland, has proven to be a big success as well, with long lines of patients receiving eye care and free glasses. It is another win, and I make a mental note that it's something we need to do again.

As part of our outreach, we had visited other hospitals in Port-au-Prince, such as the State University of Haiti hospital. It had hundreds of patients, all in desperate need of care. People were lying on the floor because all the beds were full. And those beds were falling apart so, in some cases, the floor was the safer option. Patients outnumbered nurses about ten to one, and the doctors (the few we saw) were seriously overworked. We passed through the emergency department and there were people waiting with all kinds of ailments, all acute. They'd been waiting for days to be seen. As we passed by the pediatric ward, I felt a pang as I thought of my own kids. These visits are sobering. Suddenly our little wins seem so small you'd need a microscope to see them. But they are still wins. It is still progress. It just reminds me that we must keep going.

Doctors learn from doctors. It's an important part of professional growth. That's why on every trip we continue to work alongside surgical residents, and over the years have forged some strong bonds. Part of working with them involves teaching, and part of that teaching involves visiting their hospitals to see where they work and also to evaluate patients who we may be able to help throughout our week. One resident in particular made a lasting impression.

I first met Pierre Woolley when he was a junior resident and his passion for questions and his eagerness to learn stood out. He was our man on the ground for organizing local residents from La Paix University Hospital, and we have since solicited his help in organizing and recruiting for the courses we offer. He has since completed extra training in America and returned to Haiti to become a leader in orthopedics and general healthcare. I get this almost paternal pride when I think of his trajectory. We still email regularly.

It is election day at home. The country and the world seem to be captivated by Justin Trudeau, the leader of the Liberal Party. Stephen Harper has been prime minister for nearly a decade, but there is an undercurrent of youth and change in the air. It adds to the excitement. Given my family's involvement in politics, I am even more keen to watch it all unfold, especially as I know several people running. As the votes are being counted, we all watch the results on TV in the common room.

Coincidentally, it is election time here in Haiti, too. That explains the escalated violence that has caused us to be on lockdown, which means we cannot leave the compound. There have been gunshots in the streets and it would be unsafe. Everyone is tense. At home, a new government will replace a governing one, all without a single shot fired. Here, it's unpredictable. Things could get better or much, much worse.

One of the surgeons sitting in front of me is wearing a scrub cap with red maple leaves all over it. I am a lucky man, I think. My kids will grow up in Canada. They will never wonder who is going to pay a medical bill, they will not have to worry that they will be shot while trying to vote, and they will have the freedom to chase their dreams. A lucky man indeed.

Just like previous trips, the volume and intensity of the workload makes the week fly by. But more so this trip than others. There were so many highs and lows. As we are packing to leave, Allison takes my hand and leads me to the roof of the new building. We stand there in silence thinking about what the team has accomplished. What Brendan has helped us do here, and what the team, by working alongside Haitians, has unlocked.

A simple concept, really. Using your talents to help others, not for money or for fame, but just because you can. You cannot always enact the change you would like to see, but you always can make a difference. When it is all over, I think that that will be what I hope my kids learn, what Mark can answer for himself ten or twenty years from now when he wonders, "Why?"

Allison and I deplane in Newfoundland, and we step onto the escalator, hoping to see the kids waiting. She takes my hand and whispers to me, "You've done something good here, you know." It lifts me more than anything else could. The only reward, the only reassurance I thought I wanted was a patient's smile. I was wrong. That whisper in one quick moment provided every ounce of validation that I never knew I needed.

14

THE STILLNESS OF COMPLETE DESPAIR

Dhaka: February 2015

THIS WHOLE THING was changing. What had started as a small volunteer relief effort was taking on a life of its own. Bigger. More people. More logistics. A broader scope. As Team Broken Earth expanded and grew, I was faced with a blunt truth: I didn't have the skills needed to operate and sustain the business at such an expanding scale. I kept telling myself, I'm just a doctor. I had two choices. I could walk away from this (believe me, it was tempting at times) and hire a staff to take over. Or I could develop the skills myself. And that's exactly what I did.

Oxford, England, is as beautiful as it is intimidating. Centuries of history and tradition surround you in those smoky grey buildings. Scholars, scientists, authors, and politicians have roamed the halls of its colleges and enjoyed the pubs. People who have changed the world left their footprints here. I don't frighten easily, but you feel the weight of expectation here, and even the most confident can be left asking if they're good enough to cross the lawns, grace the echoing stone halls. I chose Oxford to take a business diploma in organizational leadership. Most doctors are not known for their business savvy. The only thing heavier than the expectation was the self-doubt.

I brought all those emotions to class with me but kept them just below the surface. I was one of only two Canadians there. I don't know why—maybe in moments of doubt we retreat to clichés for comfort—but I expected the room to be full of stuffy white people in long black robes. The grown children of privilege. Instead, I was struck by how multicultural my classmates were. People from all walks of life, from every corner of the world were there to share the experience. It put me at ease.

The first classes were built strongly on decision-making and small group work. For one of the first exercises, I was paired in a group with Zahida Fizza Kabir, a woman from Bangladesh. Dressed in Bangladeshi dress, she had a quiet and confident demeanour. She spoke deliberately, as though every word was carefully thought out before it was spoken.

After the exercise, we spoke about our individual projects. Zahida, it turned out, was a social worker running a large not-for-profit hospital network in Dhaka. It seemed we were on the same knowledge pilgrimage. She had read my class biography and asked if Team Broken Earth had ever thought of travelling to Bangladesh. I quickly dismissed the idea. Between commitments at home and my work in Haiti, I had a full plate. I told her our teams were fully committed to Haiti at this time.

Over the next two years, I returned to Oxford as the classes continued. My relationship with Zahida grew, and she continued to suggest that her charity, the SAJIDA Foundation, could use a Canadian partner. Her compassion for the people she helped, her belief that changes could be made, that things in Bangladesh would be better, these stayed with me. I could blame post-exam euphoria, or maybe being at the pub helped, but I found myself agreeing with Zahida more and more. Yes, it would be a good idea for Team Broken Earth to check out what they were doing in Dhaka and complete a needs assessment to see how we might help.

The flight home was long, made longer as I thought about the million and one logistics involved in adding another point on the map for our team. I was embarrassed that I did not know much about Bangladesh. I wasn't even exactly sure where it was, and I knew little of its history or current situation. Whenever I speak about Haiti to people, I remind them that the country is right in our backyard, just an hour's flight from Miami. Dhaka, on the other hand, was on the opposite side of the planet. I had to do a lot more research to learn what the team would be getting into.

Bangladesh is a young country, born out of a short war with Pakistan but now anchored in peace. Bangladeshis pride themselves on being socially progressive. But the first thing that really struck me was the population: 160 million. I read the number over and over. That many people in a small landmass meant a density reaching fifty thousand people per square kilometre at times. In some places, a population the size of Newfoundland and Labrador's was packed into ten square kilometres. What could our team from spacious Canada possibly have to offer?

As with Haiti, it felt like a leap of faith was in order. In those moments you often wonder when your luck will run out. I committed to a visit, but given the distance, I did not want to commit a full team until we knew what we were getting into. Art Rideout was in. He had some experience in South Asian countries and had been to India before. And with the support of my sister Meghan, who helped with the parameters for a needs assessment, we booked our flight.

The commute would be brutal. St. John's to Toronto: four hours. Toronto to Istanbul: twelve hours. And Istanbul to Dhaka: another ten hours with stops along the way. Even for the seasoned flyer, this would be utterly draining. With our visas and a fresh batch of self-doubt fully in hand, Art and I boarded the plane on a cold February afternoon.

It is something I do not like to admit, but I was nervous. I rarely get nervous. Put me on a flight to Haiti, the security and safety of thirty people on my shoulders and going to a place that's often lawless and can experience violence daily, and my hands do not shake. But here I was, somewhere over the Atlantic, and I could feel the tension in me. I could feel the nerves twitch in my gut. What the hell was I doing? I hate to admit it, but I just didn't want to go there. Bangladesh was too different. Different airlines, different customs, different people, different food, different safety concerns. Different all round. My hands tightened.

I realized I was being selfish and not confident. I justified my not wanting to go by telling myself I was trying to protect the resources we had for Haiti. But as quick as I said it to myself, it struck me why I had gone to Haiti in the first place. If someone needs help and you are able to, you should help.

But how? Haiti had and still has a specific set of needs that required a specific response. What would Bangladesh need? There was an opportunity here, I told myself, not something to avoid. I thought long about what Team Broken Earth could do in a different country without changing our focus from Haiti. The answer was born out of our progress in Haiti. It was in the education element that had become part of every mission. We could offer to support teaching and education in Bangladesh while not diluting our efforts in Haiti.

If I had stopped to think about the work, the risks, and the sacrifices before going to Haiti, I don't know that I would ever have gone in the first place. But I did. I have often wondered what mountains lie beyond Haiti, what tasks and opportunities would present themselves next. I had never dreamed it would be Bangladesh, but then again, I had never dreamed I'd work in Haiti either. As the plane descended, I couldn't help but think that this was the next mountain.

You can tell a lot about a place by its airport. We arrive in Hazrat Shahjalal International Airport after thirty-odd hours of travel, and the first thing I notice is how small the airport is. It's one of around five or so airports in Bangladesh but considered the largest. It's of medium to small size by any standards, but incredibly small to service 160 million people. There are few gates and fewer amenities. The infrastructure is in better shape than the airport in Haiti, though. I catch myself constantly making comparisons with Haiti. I remind myself that the week cannot unfold that way. These are very different worlds, histories, and cultures. To compare everything would just be wrong.

There's a long lineup at the visa checkpoint. It's four thirty in the morning. I don't know what time it is at home. Don't know if I am tired or sick, but I find it hard to stand. We slowly move along and it feels like this will take forever. My mood is grey till I spot a familiar face. It's Zahida. I have not seen her for some time, since Oxford, and there is that immediate connection again. I introduce her to Art and in turn we are introduced to Dr. Shamsher Ali Khan, her right-hand man. He's about sixty and has a magnetic warmth; he reminds me of a storybook grandfather. He is immediately welcoming us, looking after us, anxious to tell us stories and introduce us to his country.

Even though it's close to five in the morning, the streets are packed with people, animals, all manner of vehicles, people pulling things, driving things, or travelling in or on some form of bus. The energy of it is overwhelming. Shamsher reassures us that our journey to the hotel will be short, as traffic is not that bad yet. Not that bad? If it's this crazy at five, what constitutes bad?

Ahead of us, we have a full day of meetings and site visits. We're informed in the hotel lobby that there are some security issues and as a result they will be transporting us to different sites in the back of an ambulance. Art and I climb in the back of the ambulance, we pull out of the hotel, and immediately come to a stop. The serious traffic has started. There are millions of people on the move. It's wall to wall to wall, three to four lanes deep in the middle of the city, with vehicles moving inches at a time. Rickshaws appear to move quicker than any gas vehicle. It's claustrophobic and nerve-racking. And the noise. I've never experienced anything like it.

The slow drive continues inch by inch. I can barely keep my eyes open. It must be two or three in the morning back home. I have never felt true jet lag until now. God knows how long this drive will take. I am punch-drunk. I have to excuse myself to our hosts and lie down on the stretcher, take a nap before our first meeting.

I am not sure if it's from seeing it all through tired eyes, but the day is a whirlwind adventure through various hospitals and charity offices. It becomes obvious that our being white is a novelty to most. As we tour hospitals, patients, nurses, and doctors all stare. People stop and take pictures of us with their phones. Some even want selfies. It's strange being regarded as a novelty.

That night I can't sleep. Eyes on the ceiling, mind racing. I think it is just the time change, but I cannot stop thinking about the sights of the day. The density. The millions of faces. The energy of countless people trying to squeeze through the same small space.

First stop of the day had been a tour of SAJIDA's Amrao Manush, a facility for those given the unfortunate designation of "pavement dwellers." These are people who literally lie on the street at night. No cover overhead, no blanket, no place to call home. In fact, they do not even exist in the eyes of the government (no name, no address, no citizenship). At first I wondered why they were not referred to as the homeless, until I saw the pictures. People just putting their heads down directly on the pavement at the end of the day. Half a million of them. A hundred thousand in Dhaka alone. One-third of them children. Even typing this I can't believe those numbers.

If there's a glimmer of hope, it comes from Zahida. She has created an amazing institute to help some of these people, especially some of the kids. We arrived to one hundred singing children wishing us well. They sang and danced and did a presentation. Through this you almost forget the imbalance. These kids, sleeping in the streets, yet dancing and singing for the two gents from Canada. They were lively, engaged, as if they had new life because of the help that was being provided for them. In front of us they were just kids being kids, yet the reality for them outside these walls was as harsh as it gets.

Amrao Manush looks after around eleven thousand people. The building was poorly lit and was a bit like a warehouse divided into an eating area and classrooms. We heard the stories of children who were found wandering aimlessly, not knowing who they were, no name, no parents. *No name.* That in partic-ular struck me hard. How does a child not even have a name? How does that happen?

Out on the streets these children organize into groups if they're lucky. The less fortunate ones are taken and abused. The ones that make it into a group organize into street gangs and survive on raw instinct. Here in front of our eyes was a real-life *Lord of the Flies.* Instead of an island, they were lost in a city. The results were the same. Lawlessness and violence.

When you see something like that, it often gives you cause to reflect. I know I'm a lucky guy. But I often wonder, if I was born in a different time and place, how I would react. Would I have had the courage to charge forward to certain death at Beaumont-Hamel? How would I have behaved in a concentration camp or, for that matter, as a German in that situation? How would I have survived in Mount Cashel Orphanage? As a four-year-old with no name and living on the streets, how would I have grown and developed? Would I have survived here in Bangladesh?

Suddenly there are five-year-old girls standing in front of me, dressed in plaid uniforms. Orphaned, abandoned, and living on the street. Words cannot do justice to the feeling it creates deep inside of you. A combination of guilt, nervousness, anger, and grief. It's just not right. We live in the shadow of such gigantic divides. We have to do better. I believe that we are all part of something bigger; we are all in this together. When a five-year-old lays her head on the pavement in Bangladesh at night, we should all feel it. When an adolescent boy cries for help in the streets of Dhaka and no one responds, we should all hear it. Isn't that what it means to be part of a global community?

The five-year-olds snap me out of it with a song. Five-year-olds are five-year-olds no matter where they are. Big smiles. Dancing carefree. It brings smiles to all our faces. Despite the poverty, despite the fact that some of these kids will have to leave the building tonight and come back tomorrow, they smile. There is something more to their smiles, their eyes. It's more than child-hood innocence. It's hope. And in hope, they are richer than any of us.

The children in gangs are allowed in only during the day, for food, water, and shelter. The others can stay overnight. They are given clothing, shelter, and, most important, love. You can see the appreciation in the children's faces as they dance and sing, not for us but for their teachers and their instructors.

I find it so hard to call these kids "pavement dwellers." I guess I'm just a little in denial of their reality. Why? Because the real-ity just wraps tightly around your heart and squeezes with tiny hands. It was harder than I thought it would be. But truth be told, what I saw in the afternoon was what has been keeping me up. Haunting me.

We visited a combination clinic and school. The school was amazing, and there were more pavement children there to get protection and education. But at the clinic, we saw patient after patient who were young women in the sex trade. They had a common request. They all asked to have the scars on their faces removed. All had been cut in the same fashion on both cheeks. These were the badges of the sex trade. A blatant, horrible marker of who these women were. I felt gut-wrenched. I bit down on my own outrage. Fists so tight that my fingernails dug into my palms.

Then it got worse. One girl was twelve. She had scars on both cheeks and one across her neck. She was four years older than my Maggie. She should be in Grade 7. Instead, she was begging for us to help take the brand of prostitution off her face. Prostitution is the wrong word here. This is sex-trafficking. This is the monetized rape of a minor. She sat in silence as we explained there was nothing we could do for her. She sat with blank eyes for what felt like an eternity.

Then it got much worse. As she stood up, I could see she was at least six months pregnant. My heart just emptied. I've seen a lot in my medical career, but I have never been so shaken as I was then. What do you do in that moment? Shake your fist at a world that let this happen? Scream out what the hell is wrong with us? What would happen to this poor girl, to her child? Would this cycle continue? My feeling of utter helplessness in that moment is something that I will carry with me for a long time.

I couldn't sleep that night, not because of jet lag, not because of the busy city, not because of some other excuse, but because I kept seeing that little girl's blank stare. This was the opposite of hope. This was the stillness of complete despair.

The next day we travelled to the older part of Dhaka to visit a SAJIDA hospital. It was without a doubt one of the more interesting drives I have taken. It took us close to three hours to travel a short distance through what I can only describe as an ocean of people, not waves or even groups, but constant people, side by side, rickshaw by rickshaw for kilometres.

At the hospital we discussed how Team Broken Earth and SAJIDA could collaborate. They had the equipment and skills but needed more education and support. I thought that was where we could help. They averaged three or four C-sections a day, but needed more training in infant resuscitation, a course we could teach them. Then, more importantly, they could pass that knowledge on to others.

Then it was time for some hands-on work. We ran a busy clinic with the help of local doctors and nurses. It was incredibly rewarding to work alongside such remarkable people, to work with and learn from them. I liked this. Everything came from muscle memory. Results were immediate and tangible. Patients in and out. Healing began. It helped my heavy heart, just a little.

From the clinic, it was into the operating room, where Art Rideout helped alter the fate of a child who might otherwise have gone through life with just three fingers. She had a condition called syndactyly, and her fingers were fused together, creating two thicker fingers and a thumb. It was a relatively uncomplicated surgery that would make a world of difference for this child in a society that ostracizes those who are different.

We met one patient who was born with no legs and only two fingers on one hand. He lived in rural Bangladesh, and despite his perceived disability, he was a successful farmer (farming the land himself), husband, and father. He was so thankful to see us, he sang us a song of appreciation.

When the trip wound down, we were invited to a party in our honour. Shamsher and Zahida presented us with traditional Bangladeshi dress to wear for the evening. When we arrived, many of the people we had met throughout the week were on the roof with food and a band. Everyone had come out to meet us again. They had done this on their time off and battled the traffic to show their gratitude.

For the first time I started to really think about how this could be the start of a longer, more sustainable relationship. On the plane home, I began to sketch out a plan for the next trip. The place had gripped me, and despite my initial reservations, I thought we could contribute in education, quality assurance, and joint relationships on strategy, as well as collaborate on

Canadian and international governmental grants. I felt the hard part would be convincing Allison and Broken Earth's board that it was a good idea.

It occurred to me fairly quickly that we could repeat in Dhaka the trauma course that we had been doing in Haiti easily enough. The equipment was the same, the instructors could be the same, and the content was universal. And it was an area they had specifically requested educational support in.

Art was on-board with this. Armed with the idea, we mapped out a team and secured a date. That turned out to be the easy part. Allison and I do not usually disagree, but when I told her about the plan to return to Bangladesh, it was not met with the glowing endorsement I had hoped. We sat one long evening discussing the pros and cons of it, how much it would take away from my being at home, how much it would cost, and where we were going from there. She was no different than I had been at first: nervous, afraid, and concerned. But like me, she eventually agreed that this was the right thing to do when someone asks for help.

One year after our first trip to Dhaka we are on the ground again, this time to teach. And this time I take Allison. I'm convinced that she will fall in love with the people just as I had.

It all comes back to me at once. The traffic. The endless waves of people. I wonder how the rest of the team will respond. Will they see the same poverty and sadness but also the hope that I saw? I had my heart torn out here last year. I don't wish that on anyone. I want them to see the reality but feel the hope.

As we pull away from the airport, this time travelling in a bus and not an ambulance, there is still the mass of humanity that breathes and moves like one gigantic organism; there is still the abject poverty everywhere you look. The city's population grows at an alarming 4 per cent a year; it is estimated it will be 25 million by 2025. The per capita income is about $3,100 a year, the lowest among the world's mega-cities.

Yet among the poverty and the density is a candle of hope. Here, a modern-day Mother Teresa exists. It's our hostess, Zahida. I'd heard a story that Dhaka is named for the hidden goddess Dhakeshwari. Well, we may have found that hidden goddess in Zahida. She again welcomes us with open arms at the airport and takes us for the tour of their operations.

I want the team to have the full experience, not just teach the course. So we start with a visit with some low-income families for whom SAJIDA provided business loans. Ten families live in an area no bigger than two Tim Hortons coffee shops. A dozen women gathered in a small hut to show us pottery and textiles they have made with funding from the business loan. These are empowered women in a developing country.

We move then to the hospital and are greeted by familiar faces. On the wall outside the ER is a big poster of Team Broken Earth and the SAJIDA Foundation working together during our last visit. I look over to see Allison smiling.

The final trip of the day is to revisit the pavement dwellers. There is a lump in my throat as we walk into the building. On the first floor, twenty or so boys from ten to thirteen are being taught basic life skills such as reading, writing, basic math, music, and personal hygiene. They'll leave this building in an hour or so and go to the streets in the same way any of our kids would head home after school. There's still a cold chill that comes with that realization.

We go upstairs, where dozens of five- and six-year-olds are waiting for us. They have smiles as big as my five-year-old son's.

Some have single mothers who will come to collect them later. Some of the young ones will stay here overnight. Others will have to leave and, with the boys, find a dry corner of pavement to lay their heads—if they're lucky.

Lucky. There's nothing lucky about this.

It has been six years since I first travelled to Haiti, in 2010. Six years since a little girl's smile compelled me to act, changed my life. That day in Dhaka I saw that smile and that hope again. Despite the adversity, the poverty, the abuse, the chaos, a smile and eyes filled with hope. It's a testament to people like Zahida, determined to make a difference, to keep that candle of hope burning.

The education portion of the trip is executed perfectly. The course is opened by the Canadian high commissioner to Bangladesh, Benoît-Pierre Laramée, and the president of the Bangladesh Orthopaedic Society, Dr. M. Amjad Hossain. We run the trauma training over two days for one hundred trainees from multiple hospitals throughout Dhaka, with the mannequins and simulation that we had used in Haiti. The feedback is fantastic, and it confirms my belief that we have a model that is more sustainable than providing clinical care in Bangladesh. Education answers their needs and matches our skills.

The flight home is easier and more comfortable with Allison by my side. She has forged the same connection with the people, the children, and the country that I have. As is often the case, I do a lot of my thinking on the plane. On this particular flight, I am focused on women's health. From the beginning of Team Broken Earth, I have recognized the importance of maternal fetal health, the importance of women's health, and how poverty around the world weighs most heavily and unjustly on women.

Of the 1.6 billion people that live in poverty, the majority are women. Every single day around the world, thousands of women are subject to violence, forced marriage, and sexual abuse. This is a global problem. It belongs to all of us, and we all need to be part of the solution.

It was on my first trip to Bangladesh—when I witnessed this problem literally and figuratively on the faces of women in the sex trade and in the thousands of homeless young girls in a shelter—that the facts and figures bluntly became reality for me. I knew we needed to be more proactive in the area of women's health.

Bangladesh still has a long way to go in a lot of areas, but they are moving in a positive direction. They have made incredible strides in healthcare and in maternal medicine in particular. In the 1980s, the maternal death rate was 600 out of every 100,000 mothers, an incredibly high number. (Canada's was 6 per 100,000.) Yet with the help of countries like Canada, that rate has plunged to approximately 100 per 100,000.

This is a challenge for me. I'm a bit of a fish out of water here. I'm not an obstetrician or gynecologist. I'm a bone surgeon. I see broken bones and I fix them. But how do you fix this gigantic problem of gender? I have daughters, a wife, a mother, and strong grandmothers and aunts who have risen to challenges, shaken stigmas, and succeeded. Every woman everywhere deserves the same chances. I can't shake the emotions of it. I won't.

Some may say that the problem is just too big, that a difference can't be made. But that's nonsense. To do nothing is a coward's way out. We need to ensure that women in these vulnerable countries are afforded greater opportunities. And if there's one thing I've learned through Team Broken Earth, it's that the answers lie in safe health and education. That's why we are here. Bangladesh is a developing country with high maternal and neonatal mortality rates. But dedicated medical professionals are working hard to change those statistics and outcomes for women in their country.

When we return home, I approach our obstetrics and gynecology department about putting together a course similar to our trauma course but this time in maternal fetal medicine, covering topics like domestic violence. Over a coffee with the department chair, Dr. Atamjit Gill, the idea takes shape. He assures me that we can accomplish this.

A third trip to Bangladesh starts to take shape in August 2017. The team includes nurses, residents, and doctors from Newfoundland and Labrador. Everyone is engaged and committed, and with the right equipment, the course should be a successful one.

Leaving never gets easier. The kids clinging tight the way only kids can, asking you in little voices not to go. The look in Allison's eyes and that extra-long squeeze. It's just so damn hard sometimes. But these trips make me appreciate them so much more. Still, it weighs on me. As does this trip, taking another new and uncharted step with Team Broken Earth.

In Dhaka, seeing the obstetricians and nurses from Newfoundland and Labrador teaching seventy obstetrics doctors and nurses is rewarding enough. Watching the group of mostly women discuss and teach about delivery, social stigmas, preterm labour, abortion, violence, and how to improve women's place not just in healthcare but in society in general is reassurance that this is a life-changing course for many. But it is when I hear the CEO of a Bangladesh pharmaceutical company express the ramifications this training will have that it really hits home. He says that the thing about Bangladesh is that teaching and education are immediately scalable. In a country of 160 million, he says, these seventy providers trained by Team Broken Earth will influence thousands of lives, and the impact will be felt not in six months or a year but tomorrow. That is overwhelming, and it will forever silence those "the problem is too big" voices in my head.

On our way to the airport the traffic is again dense. On this day, one of the rickshaws gets stuck in mud. However, instead of responding with anger, competing rickshaw drivers lay down their own bikes and cargo to help push him out of trouble. They push and pull and struggle in the sweltering heat to help a stranger. In a mass of humanity beyond most of our comprehension, these daily acts of kindness are precious to this place.

I always love the approach into St. John's airport. The cliffs towering above the white-capped ocean. I can't wait to get off the plane, squeeze my kids so tight for so long. The faces and the laughter of the children in Bangladesh are still in my thoughts. There are not fifty thousand homeless children on the streets of St. John's. The contrasts are more than theoretical; they are real and they weigh so heavily on us.

But we know where taking little steps can lead us. Team Broken Earth started as a group of three people and has now expanded around the world. And teaching courses in Bangladesh will, literally, save and help thousands of lives in the near future. The ripple effect of the idea of hope is what balances the internal conflict of contrast. We need to all keep pushing the rickshaw, keep that ripple expanding far and wide.

15

FORCES AT WORK IN THE UNIVERSE

Haiti and Nicaragua: October 2016

WHEN YOUR DAY job is a hands-on endeavour of mediating the opposites, you get wise to a thing or two. Like how the universe is a scale and there's a secret balance at work. How every action has a reaction. Every day has a night. How under one roof, life is brought into the world and as often escorted out. Balance. There may also be a healthy dose of that Newfoundland skepticism I've seen so many times over the years. That something good can only mean something bad will happen.

Our Halifax and Ottawa teams were both scheduled to return to Haiti in the winter of 2016. We had been in Haiti during an election before, but this time things were different. The president, Michel Martelly, was not allowed to run for a consecutive term, and so a full set of candidates had put their names forward. In the first vote, in October 2015, no candidate received a majority and a runoff was scheduled for right after Christmas. There were, however, massive protests after the first vote over the legitimacy of the result and the balloting. Subsequently, the runoff was postponed until January 17 and then to January 24.

This was the day when our Ottawa team would be arriving.

The situation had its own difficult balance. On one side were the cost and logistics of rescheduling. On the other was team safety. There is no debate, I thought: safety is always paramount. We had to call the team in Ottawa and postpone their trip. We've had to reschedule trips before, but never with such short notice and never with such a degree of threat.

This is never an easy call to make, and I did not know what to expect. People make sacrifices to do these missions. They give up their vacation time to do it. Often family arrangements are made, and money is spent on shots and medications needed to travel. It's always easy to say "safety first," but I suspected there would be disappointment and frustration. This would mean lost income, lost vacation, and potentially a lost team. But I could not have been more wrong. Everyone was so incredibly under-standing, and I felt a measure of guilt for having thought they wouldn't be.

As the date for the runoff vote approached, there were riots in the streets, with demonstrators burning tires and hurling rocks at police. For me it just reinforced that we had made the right decision. But tensions were escalating in Haiti, and I knew that would have a ripple effect for our teams. The runoff was post-poned yet again, with a rumoured date of April 26, this time when our Halifax team was scheduled to be there.

Like trying to predict the Newfoundland weather, this was becoming futile. Elections are supposed to happen on a set date, not float around in the air for months. You can't blame the people of Haiti for being upset about it. In a place with a long history of political corruption, things had boiled over like this before and probably will again. As angered as I was about our teams having to reschedule, my thoughts also kept returning to Haiti's government. The president was no longer legitimate. Who was running the treasury? Who was running the police, and with what authority?

Fresh off the experience with Ottawa, we wanted to make sure that we gave the Halifax team ample notice to readjust their work schedules, reschedule vacations, and allow us to rebook them without excessive airline fees. Part of the beauty of the model we'd created is that we can be agile, we can be dynamic and try new things without endless committees, approvals, and bureaucratic time wasted. We are able to take chances, and if they do not work out, then so be it. The situation in Haiti was testing this agility.

The Halifax team completely understood and, although disappointed, they recognized that conditions in Haiti were constantly shifting beyond our control. But it was not long after the decision was made that we heard rumours that the April deadline was now postponed, this time indefinitely. At what point, I wondered, is this no longer a democracy? Were we witnessing the gradual return to a dictatorship?

Whatever we were feeling, our Haitian colleagues were more distressed. They were frustrated and disheartened, and worried that the political turmoil would cause us to re-evaluate our commitment to their country. I couldn't blame them. They'd seen aid groups come and go for years.

This last postponement was the tipping point for the UN. They registered their disappointment and concern. In the spring of 2016, the Haitian elections committee hit reset and started the whole election process over again. This time the first vote would happen in October of 2016, right around the time I was supposed to be there with a Newfoundland and Labrador team.

This now felt like playing darts on a boat in rough seas. All you could do was hope for the best. But too many of these delays and cancellations could stall the organization's momentum. People are eager to be a part of a team and go on our missions. They want to make the necessary sacrifices. But if that's met with a "not now, maybe in the spring—maybe," we could start losing volunteers. And rightfully so.

I had many sleepless nights worrying about this. I was torn apart inside. I felt so attached to Haiti. It's where all this started, and we'd come so far there. But I think my devotion to it may have impaired my vision of where our organization was going, where it could expand to. Team Broken Earth will always be about Haiti. But it can also be about more than Haiti. Other countries in need. We had a large Newfoundland and Labrador team gearing up for action, and I wondered if there was some way to salvage the mission, even if it did not involve Haiti.

We could not quickly pivot to or from Bangladesh the way we could Haiti. The geography made it too complex. More cost would be involved. But if we had other countries we could send missions to, Team Broken Earth could maintain its momentum despite political uncertainty or civil unrest in Haiti, or anywhere else for that matter. Flexibility would allow us to be more robust and to extend our reach to others in need.

It was a big risk. We knew Haiti and knew what to expect. I didn't feel comfortable sending anyone to a place where I had not personally done the recon and assessed the need. But if we were going to make this work, we would have to move quickly.

Carlos Enriquez is a fixture at the children's emergency room in St. John's. He was the one who hired Allison, and she has always considered him a mentor. He is loved by all. He fled Nicaragua in the 1980s, during the civil war. A thoracic surgeon there, he took his family and fled to Canada, eventually landing in Newfoundland. He is a short, bald man who speaks with a thick Spanish accent and always wears a white lab coat. His sense of humour is gigantic, and the only thing as big as his laugh is his heart and his love for his family.

Carlos came with us on one of our Haiti missions. After the trip, he kept insisting that we could do this kind of mission in his hometown of Chinandega, a rural city in Nicaragua. We had been open to the idea, and he had given us a presentation on the facilities and what the city could offer. But we had never been ready; resources were running thin as it was.

Until now.

Chinandega is a city of around 135,000 people just a short distance from the Pacific coast and close to the border with Honduras to the north. It's far more developed than the cities of Haiti, but still far less than those of Canada. It's a beautiful spot, with a lush canopy of trees and the Pacific Ocean air flowing through. There are gas stations and open-air restaurants that remind me of those near the all-inclusive resorts I have been to in the Dominican Republic or Cuba. Despite the commerce, poverty is ever-present. Families are reduced to living in the local dump, rummaging for any items of substance. It's a peaceful place today, but you don't have to look further than the names of the missing painted on a wall to see how the history of the Contras lurks in the shadows.

I ran into Carlos one day in St. John's. It was the summer of 2016. The turmoil in Haiti was still on my mind, but his presentation flashed in my head again, and I asked him what he thought of our team going to Nicaragua in the fall instead of to Haiti.

His face lit up, and in a musical Spanish accent he gave his best Newfoundland "Yes, b'y!"

The team quickly pivoted. We downsized it by half, and instead of booking tickets to Port-au-Prince, we booked flights to Managua. Instead of doing surgery, we would provide clinics in family medicine, pediatrics, plastic surgery for cleft lips and burns, and orthopedics, as well as run an eyeglass clinic. We would also do a complete site visit for future trips.

The first thing that struck me was the beauty of the landscape. Lush, rolling hills just like Haiti, but real roads. And order. It just felt safer. We didn't need an armed guard. We drove out of Managua on a highway with Carlos entertaining us all with stories of the history of the country and his family.

When we arrived at Chinandega, we quickly set up three clinic spaces, along with the eyeglass clinic. I think glasses are something we all take for granted, and they're not something that immediately comes to mind when you think about donating items from home. But it's a huge need in countries that don't have the same access as we do.

The eyeglass clinic was a good example of how we were able to experiment with different programs as additions to the healthcare and education we usually provide. A few years earlier, a St. John's Lions Club champion, Brad Moss, had emailed me and said he had some eyeglasses to donate. We chatted on the phone, and it turned out there wasn't just a few pairs of eyeglasses. He had crates of them. They had been donated to the Lions by thousands of Newfoundlanders and Labradorians. I admit I had never thought about what happens to pairs of eyeglasses after people are done with them. Well, they are collected at a correctional facility, and after they are sorted, fixed, cleaned, and bagged, they are given back to the Lions Club.

Brad wanted to know if we would take all the glasses. I immediately said yes, but suggested we conduct an eyeglass clinic as well. Brad could come with us, and we could set up a clinic where patients would be assessed by the team's optometrists and then fitted with the right glasses. I threw in a catch, though: I wanted Brad to organize it, to take this idea and run with it. And he did.

Our first eyeglass clinic was in Haiti, and it was such a success that we'd needed to call in extra security. The queue was just that big. We all realized that the clinic was portable; we could do it anywhere. We even conducted the clinic in St. John's for newly arrived refugees.

Brad had sent a good team to Nicaragua that included one of my best friends, Chris Jackman, an ophthalmologist, which made this an extra-special trip for me. As we were setting up the clinic, there was just such a good vibe about it. I knew this would be an excellent team. The next day they got right to work, asking people to read the big E on the exam poster, followed by eye drops, then an eye exam and a fitting for glasses if needed.

The stories from this clinic are always touching. There was one from a Haiti clinic where a child was examined and required eyeglasses. After he was fitted with his new spectacles, he began to walk with his knees high up in the air, as if he was trying to step over something high or clear a puddle. Turned out he was trying to step over the lines in the tiled floor. He had never seen them before. It filled every heart in the room. A woman came with her elderly mother to another clinic. They waited patiently and were the last patients of the day. There was some suggestion they may not be assessed, but they had sat in the bright sun so long waiting for their number to be called, we had to see them. They progressed through the exam, daughter by her mother's side, holding her arm as a guide. At the end, when fitted with her glasses, the mom cried with joy. It was the first time she had seen her daughter in years. Many of the clinic staff had to look away. Not a dry eye in the place. To date, I am proud to say we have continued these clinics in several countries and have distributed over five thousand pairs of eyeglasses.

Balance. Yin and yang. Or again that old Newfoundland skepticism that when something's so right, there must be something wrong. Either way, around the time we were all still riding high on the spirit of the Nicaraguan eye clinic, news reached us of another impending natural disaster in Haiti just as it was preparing for its overdue elections.

Hurricane Matthew was brewing in the Caribbean and was headed straight for Port-au-Prince and our colleagues, our friends, and our hospital. In distant Nicaragua, we were all glued to our phones for updates, watching CNN as the swirling terror advanced. My impulse was to jump on a plane and go there, as if I could do anything to stop it. But at least I'd be doing *something*. This was personal. This wasn't a distant "them," it was us. I felt incredibly helpless standing on the sidelines watching, waiting, hoping for a miracle. Surely the universe could not be this cruel. Haiti had barely recovered from the devastation of 2010's earthquake. Now, just six years later, an epic Category 4 hurricane was bearing down on them.

People living in tents and makeshift huts should not have to face 1000 millimetres of rain and 220-kilometre-an-hour winds. It is not a fair fight. Team Broken Earth immediately committed to participating in the relief effort, though we did not know yet what that effort would look like or what would be involved. The news was getting harder and harder to watch.

We did our best to keep in contact with the folks in Port-au-Prince, but it provided little solace. Jenny Bitar was the CEO of Bernard Mevs and one of our most crucial supporters. I could tell by her voice that she just wanted reassurance of our commitment, not just to the hospital but to Haiti itself. That sentiment was echoed by Dr. Hans Larsen, the president of the Haitian Orthopaedic and Traumatology Association, and Dr. Joanna Cherry, a dear friend and the medical director at Bernard Mevs.

Everyone braced for the worst. For us, it was like hearing on the phone about a sick loved one in another country—your heart aches as your mind knows you are helpless. I wanted to be with our Team Broken Earth family during this time, but the only thing to do was to carry on in Nicaragua, making a difference to those who would not otherwise have access to care. Strength returned in watching the pediatric team treat a very sick child with antibiotics. Solace came with knowing that we would be there to help with the rebuild in Haiti as soon as the storm had passed. We had to be there. We'd been asked before the storm even landed to begin to assemble a team. But we couldn't do a lot before we knew what to expect or who we would need.

Jo Cherry helped assess what the needs might be. We now had a list of the skill sets needed, but we still weren't sure that, even logistically, we could meet the last-minute emergency demands. This caused a lot of stress. But if there's one thing I've learned from everyone who has ever volunteered with Team Broken Earth, all you have to do is ask and they will answer. So, from rural Nicaragua, we started organizing. And with one email to our national family, we had what we needed. Flying into the centre of a natural disaster was not going to be easy. But not only did our volunteers rise to the occasion, they stood out as a force that was able to partner with Project Medishare, Carris (another non-profit in Haiti), the Sow A Seed Foundation, and others, prepared to collectively see over four thousand patients.

The massive storm veered to the west of Port-au-Prince and instead struck with full force on the southwest coast of the country, taking out the only road to the city of Jérémie. In its wake, the hurricane left people without homes, without water or food, and with no road to get those to them. The national death toll hit nine hundred and would rise in the wake of the storm. It surely would have been five times that amount had its largest city taken a direct hit.

It quickly became clear they would not need surgeons. I would watch from the sidelines, hard for me, but it was the right thing to do. It's one of our strengths to be able to provide what is needed, not what we want to deliver. Our volunteers rallied from coast to coast, a truly Canadian effort. Flying in on a small Cessna, they were warmly welcomed in Jérémie and celebrated for being front and centre in the relief effort.

These are the heroes that walk among us every day. This is where I get my inspiration. From people like team leader Dr. Dick Barter, as well as Jim Maher, a nurse from the Southern Shore of Newfoundland, who step up and leave work and family on a moment's notice, risking health and safety to help the people of Haiti. Not because it is a part of their job, not because they are getting paid overtime, not for fame or accolades, but because they want to.

There was so much going on, with the stress of the Haitian election, the hurricane, and teams expanding across the country. But in the middle of it all, I received a message from a parent at my children's school. She told me how her daughter, for her ninth birthday party, asked her friends, in lieu of gifts, could they please bring articles of clothing for Haiti. This random child, turning nine, offering not just to help but to sacrifice her own birthday gifts to help those in need. Think to when you were nine. I know I would not have been so altruistic.

It occurred to me then: this is how we strike the balance.

When you feel all is lost, or when the forecast calls for the darkest moments for the ones you love, you have to see it as being one hand. One heavy hand. Now look for the other hand. Seek out that counterbalance. That nine-year-old girl did more for me in that moment than any accolade could ever do. She's there with people like Brad, Jim, and Carlos. Bringing balance. Being an inspiration.

The forces at work in the universe are indifferent. Sometimes they devastate us, and sometimes they lift us up, if only for a moment. But emotions work in an entirely different dimension, one where physics mean nothing. Every action does not necessarily generate an equal reaction. Sometimes the positive reaction is far greater, so much richer. Maybe there is no balance in it, and it all comes down to the smallest voice and some nine-year-old wisdom. It says: inspiration is everywhere.

16

THE CURRENCY OF HOPE

St. John's: Summer 2018

THERE'S AN OLD story about St. John's. Someone arriving at the airport asks, "How do I get downtown?" The answer: "You keep going downhill till you hit water."

First-time visitors are often surprised by the rolling hills in the city. They probably have seen the craggy cliffs that drop hundreds of feet to the ocean. But the hills? Prescott Street alone feels like a sixty-degree angle.

One of the most popular hikes within the city is around Signal Hill. This is an iconic St. John's location. It's visible all over the city because it sits high above the entrance to the harbour known as "the Narrows." The stone building at the top is where Guglielmo Marconi received the first transatlantic wireless message in 1901.

The trail at Signal Hill starts or ends with a steep climb, depending where you park. Then there's the wind. Sunny days in St. John's often go hand in hand with gale-force winds. Okay, maybe that's a bit of an exaggeration. But not by much. Besides all that, there's absolutely nothing better than a warm, sunny day in St. John's. Just one is worth ten sunny days anywhere else. People in the city know it. Bannerman Park fills up with families near the playground, and friends picnic in the shadow of those massive old trees. The shops and sidewalks on Duckworth and Water Streets bustle with people soaking up every minute of sun. All the decks on George are jammed solid. There's an energy at work that makes you instantly forget the three weeks of rain, drizzle, and fog that may have preceded this day. Or maybe it's because everyone knows that at any moment a fog bank could roll in and drop the temperature by ten degrees in two minutes. Either way, we enjoy it while it lasts, or at least till the Royal St. John's Regatta comes and marks the unofficial beginning of the end of the summer season. Everyone lives like this could be the last time the sun turns our way for some time.

It's hot today. A little breeze rustles the trees. Not enough though to keep you cool. I love walking in this city. It's such a wonderfully odd place. The different neighbourhoods, like Rabbittown or the Brow. The old merchant buildings leading new lives as trendy restaurants and boutiques. And inevitably there's music. Either a busker or an open door to a pub where an afternoon jam session is well under way. It's not all jams and jigs, though. The city has changed a lot. The boom and bust of the last decade has taken a toll. There are more drugs here now and, as I've heard from the ER staff, all the horror that comes with that.

As I hit the corner of Prescott and Duckworth, my thoughts go back to when I was a kid and seeing the traffic cop who directed this four-way stop for years before they put in the lights. His choreography was thrilling, and it was all I wanted to be when I grew up. The moment is interrupted by a woman asking for change. I hand over the few coins I was going to use for the meter. She smiles and nods. I continue my trek up Prescott. A bead of sweat rolls down and I can feel my breaths get deeper with each step.

Then it's Haiti and I'm the hottest I've ever been in my life and on my way to meet the greatest example of hope I've ever known.

The years after the earthquake in Haiti revealed the long-term damage it had done to the country's healthcare system. For example, there was the great need for, and the subsequent burden of, amputations. Not just from the earthquake but from all sorts of diseases and trauma. Without advanced technology and knowledge of current surgical procedures, local medical staff often chose the simplest option: an amputation. It can be life-saving. It is still often the right surgical decision. Functioning with a prosthesis can be hard enough in Canada, where infrastructure is more easily navigated. But in Haiti? On the winding, uneven, unforgiving streets and hills of Port-au-Prince? And that assumes you could even get a prosthesis to begin with.

Team Broken Earth had been thinking about expanding our reach to provide for patients who needed prostheses and post-amputation care. I'll be honest, until this point, I had never followed patients in their homes. I saw them in follow-up at the hospital, but orthopedics is not the kind of practice that usually warrants a house call. In Haiti, I can reach more people at the hospital. But today we would make an exception. Today, a few of us would go visit Rose Ann.

I met our guide for the day's adventure, Wilfred, in the courtyard of the hospital. The sun felt closer than normal, and it had to be pushing forty degrees with no wind. Wilfred himself is an amputee. He is in his late twenties or early thirties and has the happy smile of a child. He lost his leg in the earth-quake and has made it his life mission to help amputees in Haiti become fitted with a prosthesis. Always clad in cargo shorts, he wears his prosthesis as a badge of honour. It says, "I'm here. I'm a survivor." We have worked with Wilfred over the years as a consultant to patients considering amputation. In fact, he used to run his own prosthetic-fitting lab in the hospital. But, like many such programs, the earthquake ended that. If we could potentially reinvigorate it, he could return to fitting patients and giving them a chance at a normal life.

I climbed into the back of an old SUV hoping for a little reprieve from the heat. No such luck. The air conditioner was only partly working, but at least there was shade. We travelled a convoluted route through Port-au-Prince in a direction that was not familiar to me until we reached the bottom of one of the many hills that frame the city. We stopped briefly so I could see the small market where Rose Anne sells food. It occupied the corner of a dirt road, a space large enough for one vehicle, and was draped on the sides by brightly coloured umbrellas in different states of use and age, most plastered with the logos of cell phone companies.

The small SUV lunged and sputtered as Wilfred switched it into four-wheel drive. I realized I had no seat belt. The vehicle struggled up the narrow paths as we ascended the mountainside, switchback after switchback, kilometre after kilometre, over rough, weather-torn terrain that was barely a path, let alone a road. All along the way we passed women and children walking up and down this bizarre maze.

We were nearing the top as the steepest part came into view. It was so steep that we needed to get out and walk the rest of the way so the SUV could make the last stretch without our weight holding it back. From the summit, we could see for miles. The valley below was now in full view, and I had a better appreciation for the huts built directly into the hillsides. They were everywhere. Far below was a weathered-bright drying riverbed. The sun hit the river rocks like a highlighter.

We continued our journey on foot until we reached Rose Anne's house. As we walked down a slight grade to her home, a little girl came walking uphill with two jugs of water. I could still see the river from where we were standing; it must have been at least a two-hour walk. As I wiped my brow, she smiled and said, *"Bonjour."* I was struggling with the heat and terrain while Wilfred, with his prosthesis, navigated with ease.

Rose Anne's house consisted of four rough walls made of a combination of discarded wood and sheet metal in different stages of rusting. They were latched together with rope held to a pole that seemed to have only a foot of purchase in the soil. The roof was also a combination of sheet metal, with large openings where light and rain could enter. An open-air kitchen comprised a well-trodden sitting area around a firepit no larger than a medium-sized pot and full of burnt coal and debris. There were no seats even to sit and share a meal. I have seen more established eating areas in the middle of the Newfoundland wilderness. The sun was relentless.

The kitchen area was immediately adjacent to the home, and Wilfred gently tapped on the sheet metal next to an opening in the hut that I assume was the front door. There was no answer, but Wilfred entered. I poked my head in. It was dark and blessedly a little cooler. The space was roughly fifteen by fifteen feet. There was a dirt floor, and in one corner the sun poked through a hole in the roof, illuminating mattresses and clothing piled in the corner. A table that seemed to be an old computer desk listed to one side. There was no electricity and no running water.

Wilfred told me that Rose Anne is a single mother with five children. I tried to picture the daily routine. How would they all fit in this tiny space? How would they have enough to eat? No toilet. No washing machine. No toys or books. The weight of it was tough to digest.

With the agility of an athlete, Wilfred quickly negotiated the steep, narrow path down to her neighbour's hut. The next hut was so close you could almost touch it, but strangely difficult to get to despite its proximity. Her neighbour told Wilfred that Rose Ann was down at the river washing clothes and gathering water. We jumped back into the SUV and headed down the switchbacks until we reached the river. After brushing several donkeys aside, the SUV turned into the riverbed along a path that I was not convinced was wide enough for our little vehicle. My back was soaked. A lump was in my throat.

Hundreds of families were washing their clothes and collecting water in the beautiful, pale-stoned river. You could see how large the river either gets or was in the past.

We pulled up to the water's edge and got out of the vehicle. The sun was now more intense than I had ever felt. Instantly I could feel my white skin burning and sweating as it had never before, and I was completely soaked.

Following Wilfred, I walked down to the riverbed to meet Rose Anne. Along the way we passed some kids playing soccer. There was a flatter area of the riverbed that was more sand than stone, and the kids were using two stones as goalposts and a soccer ball they'd made of bags taped together. They had no shoes. I thought of my own little soccer star, Rachael.

———

Rose Ann had been in a car accident sixteen years earlier and was a bilateral (meaning right and left) lower limb amputee. Her incredible story had reached us at the hospital. Dr. Frank O'Dea had assessed her, recommended prostheses, and the rest of the team jumped into action. She received two prosthetics, and walked this year for the first time in sixteen years. It was a huge moment for her. As a single mother, though, she still struggles to make money for food and education for her children. The same journey we had made in an SUV, she makes every single day. On stumps. Carrying water, food, and hope. The sweat in my eyes stings. It's mixed with tears.

From across the river, Rose Anne spots us. She immediately smiles and waves and rapidly, on her knees, makes her way through the river towards us. Her children follow in a row behind her like ducklings. She navigates seamlessly across the rugged riverbed where I am struggling not to slip and fall in. Water splashes on either side of her like a car pulling through a large puddle, but all you can see is her bright yellow shirt and even brighter smile.

I kneel to give her a handshake, but she waves that off and embraces me in a hug, kissing both cheeks. Her children stand behind her, committed to following their mom no matter where she goes. The love between the kids and Rose Ann is obvious, but equally obvious is the malnutrition of the children. They are not hungry or skinny, but malnourished through a medical lens. They have discoloured hair and teeth and slightly bent bones, signs of a lack of essential nutrients. The medical term is kwashiorkor, and it refers to extreme protein deficiency resulting in lethargy, skin changes, and an orange-red hair discoloration. It is most common in places of extreme poverty after children are weaned from breast milk.

Wilfred had fitted Rose Anne with prostheses some time ago, yet here she is on her knee stumps. Rose Anne tells us that she cannot wear the prosthetics in the riverbed. It's not hard to see why. I had to jump over river rocks and running water to meet her halfway, and I'm sure I could not have done it with bad shoes, let alone prostheses. But when I ask how she felt about the prostheses, she smiles and says those steps were the first steps in the rest of her life.

Suddenly my awareness of the heat disappears. My heart is full. Little mercies are sometimes as big as a mountain, as simple as a first step. On the way back to the hospital I forget about how cramped I am and how sweat-soaked my clothing is. A million things run through my head. So many questions. Economics, politics, faith, humanity, and hope. How can Rose Anne move forward? How can she have a smile? How can her kids smile? By all appearances, the odds are against her. She is poor. Disabled. The single mother of five. But her smile is still there. And each day she goes about making a difference for her family. I don't know where she finds the strength. I can't help but think of Nan. The answer has to be hope.

This much I know: hope is everywhere, hope is real. Hope is what drives Rose Anne to try to make a better life for her children, to make the world a better place—even if that world is the hillside where she lives and works. We need to help keep the river of hope running, to keep Wilfred and Rose Anne moving forward.

The first real step for us is to believe it possible. One thing I've discovered about this journey with Team Broken Earth is that the answers present themselves to you, often rendering the question rhetorical. That when you see Rose Anne and Wilfred and what they accomplish, you don't ask how can we not do a prosthetic program. You just know we need to do it. And we do.

My phone rings, startling me from this memory. I let it go to voicemail. Allison notices and asks what I am thinking about, as I seem to be somewhere else as we walk through the streets with the kids. It's still sunny and the rays are hitting the harbour, its dark emerald surface rippling in the breeze. It's like a scene from a tourism commercial.

I tell Allison it's nothing, but she knows better than that. "Haiti?" she asks. She knows Rose Anne's story well. I've told it many times since, to everyone from a primary school class to a conference hall filled with CEOs and politicians. I often wonder what Rose Anne would think of her fame. If she'd be proud that her story has inspired so many to give or join or just strive to do better.

Rose Anne is richer than all of us combined. Her currency is hope.

17

ONE POINT TWO MILLION CASES OF COMPLICITY

Cox's Bazar: September 2018

NOTHING JARS YOU from sleep like a clap of thunder. I gasp and I'm awake. The kind of awake where you feel your heart pounding in your chest and you know there's no getting back to sleep tonight. Lightning fills every corner of the room. It takes only a second for me to remember where I am and what I've seen today. I'm in Cox's Bazar. It sounds like an exotic spice market, but it's a district in Bangladesh that hosts the largest of the Rohingya refugee camps in the country. I try to digest what I have witnessed here. The picture of a sick little girl in the arms of her mother is in my head. My thoughts immediately go to home.

Home. It has to mean more than bricks and a roof. More than 2.3 kids and a picket fence. For me, home is my own profound sense of place and belonging in the world. A place where I know I am safe and loved. What happens when that is taken away? Violently, cruelly taken away? Yesterday I witnessed exactly that.

Early in the morning, the team and I had departed Dhaka by plane for Cox's Bazar. The flight was long and everyone carried a measure of quiet anxiousness, not knowing exactly what we were getting into here. We were met by the friendliest of crew from the SAJIDA Foundation doing work in the refugee camps. We then took a two-hour van ride along winding mud streets and partially paved highways along the longest beach in the world.

The long ride gave us a chance to discuss with our hosts what was happening on the ground and to get more of a history of what we were about to witness. But no lesson could prepare us. A friend of mine had explained the situation to me over a coffee in St. John's two years earlier, before the massive migration. But at the time, we had just begun doing work in Bangladesh, and I did not feel that we had the capacity to address his concerns. I know hindsight is twenty-twenty, but I feel now that I should have done something.

Although the Rohingya people resided in Myanmar, they were not recognized by the government or its Nobel Peace Prize–winning leader, Aung San Suu Kyi. Not recognized as people, any people. No nationality, no citizenship, and thereby persecuted first bureaucratically and then physically, primarily because of their religious beliefs. In 2013 the UN recognized the Rohingyas as "one of the most persecuted minorities in the world." Our host explains that the Rohingya people have been trying to seek refuge in Bangladesh since the 1970s. There have been discussions between the two governments about how to handle them, with Myanmar maintaining that they were not entitled to be in their country and are not their problem. They even banned the word *Rohingya*.

Since 2017, there has been a mass exodus of Rohingyas by foot and boat. More than 1.2 million people fled Myanmar, fearing for their safety. Our host tells stories of the early days, seeing the refugees arrive while smoke rose from the border, evidence that the Myanmar military was burning their homes. There were horror stories every day of men and young boys being brutally beaten and murdered. The UN eventually called it a "textbook example of ethnic cleansing."

In my head, 1.2 million people became a single family. I had envisioned a series of tents, and a mother and child, perhaps, on the side of the road. But 1.2 million people is of course more than that. It cannot be easily comprehended. That's the population of Calgary. Picture it like this: take the population of Nova Scotia and Newfoundland and Labrador combined and force them to live in an area no bigger than Lethbridge, with no sewers and no running water.

The area itself is rolling hills of pure green. The rain and foothills soil make it fertile, almost like a jungle. That is, until we reach the camp. The hills suddenly and dramatically turn to tents. A mile back it was dense green; now it is clear-cut, with tents and shanties clinging to the sides of cliffs as far as the eye can see.

We pass the security checkpoint and proceed through the gates. The camp itself is organized into blocks, and the blocks are organized into a grid of makeshift roads that have a feel of permanence to them. As we drive along, we notice that along these roads, full commerce is taking place. There is a man selling shrimp from a gigantic pot. At a makeshift tent, men barter over a bag of mangoes. Immediately across the road, two blacksmiths heat iron over an open fire, forging what look like knives with a hammer. Thousands of people buying and selling everything and anything. I'm struck by how normal it all looks.

We visit the SAJIDA health clinic, which is on a side street where cars cannot pass. As the van doors open, we are immediately hit by the wall of thirty-five-degree heat and the harsh smell of the open sewers. It pierces my nostrils sharply and brings back memories of Haiti after the earthquake. But this is worse; this is everywhere. We walk down the brick and dirt road, being swarmed by kids screaming "Hello!" and parroting English from other foreign visitors, laughing and playing, holding our hands, and skipping in front of us. They are all in various states of dress and some are completely naked. There are at least fifty of them walking with us, just being kids.

The bustle of the main street ends as we move along. As the road turns I see more vividly that the tents are built into the soil of the hills and they are a combination of tarps of different colours and bamboo. Sandbags have been fashioned into rough steps between the makeshift homes, allowing access to them. Unlike the streets of Haiti, it feels safe here, and there are no convoys of white armoured UN vehicles on every corner. In fact, I see little evidence of the UN at all.

We are shown the medical tent, yet another temporary structure that looks like it will probably be there permanently. It serves as the primary care facility for that block of the camp and is divided into three rooms. We change our footwear in the waiting room that is lined with twenty or so young women and children. It strikes me that there is a massive gender discrepancy in the streets. The majority of residents we have seen so far are women and children. I initially think that this reflects the global health burden that affects more women than men, but our host explains that it's because during the migration families would often send women and children first. Many of the young boys and men were then murdered by the Myanmar army.

We step into the clinic and I still cannot shake the smell from earlier. In the first room there is a young physician with a surgical mask and a white lab coat. She is young and seems intimidated by the presence of a surgeon. The room is small, with two windows crammed with the faces of the kids that accompanied us. There's no electricity and only a single table. At the other end of the table is a young mother dressed in a traditional niqab, holding one child in her arms; another child huddles at her side, peeking shyly around her to watch us. The niqab is black and gold and remarkably clean.

The child in her arms is not well. Allison often says that in pediatric ER, you know when a child is sick just by looking at them; it's intuition. The two-year-old girl is lethargic. Even when the young doctor pokes at the child to take vitals there is little response. The girl has a rash on her neck and back, and she is motionless and feverish. The mother says nothing and sits still during the entire encounter, yet you can see the concern and panic in her eyes. I try to look a little closer and the child opens her eyes and cries. A good sign, I think, but she is definitely sick. The mother is given a script for antibiotics and a return appointment and then they are gone.

In my gut, my medical intuition tells me that the child will need more than a few pills. It's hard to watch. Harder still to forget. The mother's becomes one of those many faces in my memory. From here, from Haiti and Dhaka. Faces that haunt me. The distant yet concerned look of a mother's eyes.

The clinic sees two hundred patients each day. A sign on the wall lifts my spirit a bit. I see that the clinic was sponsored by SAJIDA and in turn Team Broken Earth. This is where our donations went, to front-line services. This is *all* of our efforts in action.

The clinic is in a valley, and looking up, I can see families in their tents, their homes, with curious children poking their heads from behind the tarp. We decide to make our way up the makeshift stairs to see the view from the top. In the forty-degree heat, we step from sandbag to sandbag along the twisting, turning path. Along the way we catch glimpses into the tents, see families lying on the dirt of the mountainside, ten to twelve people per tent. Peering past the open flaps, you can see they have nothing, no possessions, not a bag in the corner or chair or pile of clothing. They are shockingly empty.

I again notice the smell, and see a river of fluid running alongside the stairs. It comes from the communal outhouse on the side of the hill. Just before the peak, next to the outhouse, is a well, and kids are pumping the handle up and down, showing it off like a new toy.

From the top the view is frightening. The camp is so dense. As far as the eye can see, hills beyond hills are covered in tents. Literally hundreds of thousands of people living on top of each other as far as you can see. Is this temporary? Is this generational? Is this their new home?

It feels like a city. A rudimentary one but still a city. The high-rises are replaced by the rolling hills covered with tents, the cars replaced by foot traffic. But the human spirit is here, you can feel it.

We go back down the stairs to visit a school and what they refer to as a "child safe" place. Walking along the paths, you can see the waste leaking from the orange- and blue-tarped shallow latrines all down the hillsides. Twisting and turning, this path seems like an ancient riverbed that was etched out over time. A naked three-year-old boy, alone, plays in a puddle of what I assume—or hope—is just muddy water. He's smiling from ear to ear. Two men argue over a live chicken that one of them holds firmly. A woman passes me carrying a bag of rice. This is the day-to-day camp life. It just seems so normal, so far from temporary.

The school is a one-room tent with a wooden roof and divider screens. It's filled with children, playing and being taught by three teachers. They all smile and stand to greet us when we arrive. Again, there is no electricity. There are barely even mats on the floor for them to sit on. I think of the classrooms of my kids. I think of France banning cell phones in the classroom. I think of school hockey team photos and kids in jerseys offering to pack your groceries to raise money for their trips. These kids in front of me have none of that. Still they smile and laugh and play and learn. Innocence knows nothing of what surrounds it.

Before we leave, we pass the market area again, and despite the distraction of bartering, I cannot help but think of the little girl I saw at the clinic. I keep running the diagnosis in my head. Was that rash meningitis? How long had she been that lethargic? What was the last thing she ate? Will she be okay? Will she ever make it to a new home, or even live long enough to hope so? Behind my sunglasses, my eyes fill up. I'm sure the last thing these people need is more tears. But I can't help it. Tears of guilt. Tears of rage. Tears.

No one speaks during the two-hour drive back to Cox's Bazar. Home crosses my mind again. It's more than a sense of place; it is a basic human right. In the pursuit of a better life for our children, we all need a place we can call home. The world has seen genocide and witnessed ethnic cleansing before. But to paraphrase Einstein, if we remain silent we are guilty of complicity. In that camp is a full generation of people displaced, unwanted, unrecognized, raped, and forced to leave their homes. We have seen this movie before, and we know it does not end well.

Failing to act is being complicit in the atrocity itself. Countries that can act should act. Those that are acting should do more. We cannot sit idly by. Can we?

I'm suddenly gripped by, even relieved by, the knowledge that I'm headed home. This feeling of safety, maybe even escape, trickles through my mind. I think of my grandmother leaving Avondale with just whatever she had in her purse and eight kids in tow. Fleeing a hard situation into the unknown. The scenery rushes by outside and I pretend I'm on the train with her. Her hand in mine. I feel safe. I don't know where we are going. I don't know what we will do. I just know that I'm safe.

I remember hearing this story once about when General Patton liberated the Nazi death camps in Germany at the end of the Second World War. How he had his troops march the people living in the towns nearby to the sites and made them witness what had happened there. Made them help with the burials and recovery. The reality of complicity doesn't hit harder than that.

I think more governments need to witness what is happening here in Bangladesh and in other parts of the world. To not just say the word *refugees* but to understand, first-hand, what that even means. Someone needs to speak up for the Rohingya. To speak for the voiceless little girl. To give them all some sense that the dream of a home beyond those rolling hills of tarps and sewers can be real. I have to believe it can be within reach.

18

EVERY WALL HAS ITS DOOR

St. John's: January 2019

NOTHING? I THOUGHT. I suddenly stopped at the realization that I didn't have anything to do. It was such an odd feeling, like everything that was in motion had suddenly stopped. And I could see my surroundings. Ever have that experience where even your most familiar surroundings all of a sudden seem new to you? Like you're revisiting a place for the first time in a long time, and it surprises you? I was at home. I sat down on the couch and looked around. The kids were out. Allison was at the store. The dog was asleep. My usually jammed inbox was empty. I had scrolled through my social channels and read the news.

Perhaps it was the calm after the storm or just the clarity of the moment, but I sat there and reflected, and it was nice. I felt I was still recovering from last fall, meeting the Rohingya refugees one week and Haitian amputees the next. It was a lot to digest, and a massive dissonance to reconcile at home.

Between patients at my clinic, I would often close my eyes and see the faces of the kids running in the refugee camps. Or I'd be watching TV at night and catch myself staring straight through it, wondering how the boy with no leg would get to school in Port-au-Prince. Strange feelings to reconcile. These images don't haunt me. They're just there. They appear at random times and in the strangest of places. I wondered why. In the serenity of this moment and the post-Christmas season, I think the answer is clear: they are there to remind me.

There's a lot of negativity around us. It's hard to watch the news these days without being drawn into the issues, locally, nationally, internationally. It can jade you if you let it. And often it does. We grow immune to it or, even worse, apathetic. We experience our own hurdles, barriers, and heartache in Team Broken Earth as well. We've had failed trips, broken equipment, upset team members, and failed pitches for donations. It sometimes feels like we are taking two steps forward and three back. But I don't think that is really the case. That is why the faces of those children appear. We are not taking three steps back. We may stumble and even at times fall, but we are moving forward. The faces appear to show me that walls are actually doors. They open. We move forward, always forward.

As a team, we've lately been reflecting on who we are. I have heard from people that we should be focusing on changing the country, changing the people, that is what will change Haiti and make it better. That wall can seem daunting until you realize the only way to change a people is through individuals. Helping change the lives of individuals is what we are good at. It is why we do what we do. Changing the life of one individual can change others' lives. It can have everlasting downstream consequences. And that will change the people. It starts with the one, as one will influence many.

I'm reminded of a little boy in Haiti, the one who received his new glasses and could see properly for the first time and was high-stepping, knees up to his chest so he didn't trip over the lines on the tiled floor. For him, we made a wall a door.

Then there was Rudy, a boy we had treated in Haiti who needed a prosthesis for an amputation. We visited him in his home and then went to his school, walking along unstable walkways knitted between the sheet-metal-roofed huts all down the mountainside in unbearable heat. Yet Rudy handled the twisting, turning steep maze with ease, never breaking a sweat. It took us thirty minutes to get from Rudy's home to his school, a single classroom, no toilet and infrequent electricity. Yet when we asked his teacher how Rudy was doing in school, she raved about his dedication and how the only thing bigger than his spirit was his smile. For Rudy, a wall became a door.

Just the week before, I'd been part of seeing how another charity I work with was having a direct impact in people's lives. I've been working with Brendan Paddick and Alan Doyle on A Dollar A Day, collecting funds for mental health and addictions services. We visited Thrive, an organization that provides help for youth and young adults who suffer from mental health or addiction issues. These guys are on the front lines. The office was full of donated essentials like socks, deodorant, food, and shoes, all organized into packages for people. I overheard someone say, "People's future should not be defined by their past." How far does a dollar go? A long way. These donations together will help organizations like Thrive continue to help youth, some of whom are homeless but not forgotten. It'll help these youth realize their future is still a blank page, unwritten and ready. It felt good to know that we are helping people open new doors in their lives.

Finally, there was a family from Dhaka. Determined to make a better life for their two boys, and after hearing Team Broken

Earth speak about Memorial University, they immigrated to Canada so the parents could further their university studies. They may be pursuing education, but they are fuelled by the hope to create a better future for their children. They see Canada as a land of hope, positivity, and opportunity. They don't focus on the negativity. They see Canada and Newfoundland and Labrador as we are unable to at times. They see it as an amazing place to live and raise a family.

So, the population of Newfoundland and Labrador has grown by four. The community gets bigger, brighter, and more diverse. Same for the future. Shake off the negativity and place a hand on any wall in front of you. You can't see it—you have to feel your way through—but there is always a door. You just have to reach for it.

There's never a shortage of things to be done after the holidays. And maybe it's the warmth of the Christmas tree (in Newfoundland, your Christmas tree stays up till Old Christmas Day on January 6) or the nostalgia it welcomes this time of year, but it all makes me smile. I believe that contentment is found in the simplest of things. A card from a friend. A smile to a stranger. And the love we give and get through charitable acts, great and small. We're all the better for it when we see the goodness and the opportunities it brings. We must always strive to choose that. To not see walls but find the doors. Easier said than done sometimes, I know. February is just around the corner. It's always a tough month in Newfoundland and Labrador.

During the middle of February 2019, around Valentine's Day, we received word that there were violent protests in Haiti. We had two teams on the ground. There was a team of twenty from Saskatoon in Port-au-Prince and a team of ten from Ontario in the north. What started as planned protests got out of control. Frustrations among citizens and police alike exploded one day, and the fiery protests were right outside the gates of our hospital.

We needed to move quickly. All volunteers went to immediate lockdown on the secured second floor of the hospital. Rapid assessment with our partners on the ground in Haiti and at home in Canada led us to the decision to evacuate.

We had talked about this, planned for it, but this was the first time we needed to actually do it. Within two hours of the decision being made, we had booked flights and organized secured vehicles to get the teams to the airport.

What I had not expected was what happens in the aftermath of asking people to stop working. It was clear to our team members that it was not safe for them to be in an open area of the hospital. But when everyone is locked down like that, what happens if someone comes in who desperately needs help? That's exactly what happened next.

I was on the phone with the team from their locked-down position. They told me a man had been brought in with a gunshot wound and needed urgent attention. The violence was still growing outside the gates. I could hear the tension in each voice on the phone. Then one of the surgeons asked, "Can I go down to help him?"

That question hung in the air, still air, for what felt like an eternity. I could hear the depth of each of my breaths, the click of each thought. There was a life in my hands. And I was thousands of miles away.

Surgeons do not often struggle with decisions. And the good ones make them efficiently, not necessarily quickly but efficiently and effectively. However, I struggled with this one. I was there but I wasn't there. God forbid something happened to one of our volunteers. But this man's fate was in my hands. And my heart sank hard and fast. I knew what needed to be done. I just hated having to do it.

"Evacuate. As soon as possible." The phone felt like a fifty-pound weight in my hand.

The team got out. I was relieved, but I knew it came with a heavy price for the patients they left behind. I'll carry that for the team. They were the ones on the front line. They were the ones with so much to lose. The violence continued to escalate. The Canadian embassy was shut down. Evacuations were occurring. Leaving was the right thing to do. It was also far from the easiest thing to do.

February. Why does the second week of February in particular always feel like it's cursed in this province? Those of us just old enough might still remember when the *Daily News* published in the province (it stopped running in 1984, after ninety years) and their bold headline: SHE'S GONE. During the early morning hours of February 15, 1982, an oil rig, the *Ocean Ranger*, listed heavily off the Grand Banks. It began to take on water and a mayday call was sent out. Eventually they had to make a decision, and there was an eerie message that turned out to be the last words from the rig: "There will be no further radio communications from *Ocean Ranger*. We are going to lifeboat stations."

The rig was lost, and all eighty-four men on-board died in the chilly dark waters of the North Atlantic. Most Newfoundlanders knew someone on-board or knew someone who lost someone. It is one of those moments that defined who we are. Many things changed in the offshore oil and gas industry after that.

It's been close to four decades since that happened, but it's still hard to savour roses and chocolates here in mid-February.

Newfoundlanders and Labradorians never forget. That can be a blessing and a curse. A grudge and an homage. From the slaughter of the Newfoundland Regiment at Beaumont-Hamel in 1916 to the cod moratorium of 1992, we either honour who was there or reminisce the event ourselves. I'm sure there are a lot of places that do that. But here, there are people still genuinely passionate about the outcome of Confederation as if it occurred last week, and that happened in 1949.

Closer to home, it was February 15, 2017, again in the middle of a vicious snowstorm, that I got a panicked call from Allison's mom. Between the sobs and gasps, she was saying she could not reach Allison and that Rick, Allison's father, had died suddenly. Rick had a superhuman heart, just not the arteries to hold it. He was a larger-than-life man who loved his family, loved to golf, and, above all, loved life. As much as I will miss Rick, the thing that brings the biggest tear to my eye to this day is seeing his sense of humour and his smile in my son, Mark. Yeah, Newfoundlanders never forget.

A patient not long ago ranted at me because his knee surgery wasn't healing quickly enough for his liking. He did not want to hear me say, "There is nothing wrong. This is part of the process. Healing takes time." As he listed the things he couldn't do yet, I admit I let my mind wander. Up dusty hillside paths overlooking Port-au-Prince. Through dense and overcrowded streets in Bangladesh. To Nan singing under her breath as she makes tea and toast, the Newfoundland cure-all.

I put my hand on the patient's shoulder and in the kindest tone I could muster, I told him that everything he just told me will be a list of what he can no longer do if he doesn't exercise patience and let his knee heal. He seemed a little deflated as he leaned back in his chair and said, "Okay, Doc, okay."

I've built a warehouse of memories in my head. How I organize it is how I cope. Everything in its place but strategically located. February's aisle is there, but I've learned to surround it with months of joy and reasons to look forward. Things are only as big as what stands next to them. That's balance at heart as well.

I find myself here at the helm of what's now a national and international volunteer organization. Our next step will be onto the continent of Africa. A much-anticipated trip to Ethiopia. More walls to touch. More doors to find.

19

UNDER AFRICAN SKIES

Ethiopia: February 2019

I ALWAYS THOUGHT the term "African skies" was kind of non-sensical. I mean really, how different can the sky in Africa be from the sky in Newfoundland and Labrador? How can the clouds in Ethiopia be different from those in Calgary? The earth may be large, but we all share the same sky, and the geophysics of clouds is the same no matter where you live. Or so I thought.

A team of ten leaves Canada in the middle of winter in 2019, arrives after a thirteen-hour flight from Toronto in Addis Ababa in Ethiopia, and then takes a one-and-a-half-hour flight to Goba, a rural town of about thirty thousand people. The thing that is most striking as soon as I step out of the plane is the sky. It seems larger, bluer, the clouds closer, with their borders more exact as if they were carefully placed by an obsessive artist.

The town is like many found in the developing world: make-shift markets surrounded by donkeys, chickens running along-side the car, refuse and old cans embedded into the uneven surfaces of the roads. Tin huts and partially constructed small buildings line the streets. This is set against the backdrop of the mountains jutting up to touch the bluest sky you've ever seen. This country is as beautiful as it is poor.

In the hotel at last, it felt good to lie back on a bed for a few moments after such a long trek. I took a deep breath but found my chest feeling a little tighter and my lungs a little stiffer. Which is exactly when I heard one of the team members say, "Did you know we're at almost ten thousand feet above sea level?" Well, that explained it. Perhaps it explained the sky as well, but I don't think so. That was something more than altitude.

There is no water in the hotel for showers (I know, I know, first-world problem), so the team decides to investigate the town. It's safe here and easy to explore. Goba is full of incredibly friendly people, waving and stopping to speak. The familiar smell hits me immediately. It's a mixture of a burning open-fire kitchen, coal and dust, balanced with sweet aromas of flowers, evergreen trees, and fresh air. It's an odd blend of the smells of Haiti and those of British Columbia wilderness.

It's incredibly dry here, with seemingly no humidity. Even though the sun is bright, none of us sweat as we walk. It's the type of dryness that sucks the moisture from your breath before it leaves your lungs. As the sun sets, we return to the hotel as the temperature drops quickly.

The next day we depart with our host, Dr. David Allison, for a tour of the Madda Walabu University Goba Referral Hospital and to meet some of the participants of the trauma course we are here to teach. The hospital consists of a series of buildings connected by a maze of loose, partially covered walkways. It's a sight all too familiar from my past tours of medical facilities in low-income countries. Patients huddle in the walkways to get shade from the direct sun. Inside the buildings, the halls are exceptionally crowded, and poorly lit, often with a single light bulb hanging from a wire.

The patient rooms are full of patients and their families trying to help with care. The beds are all too familiar as well. All are of different makes and models and in various states of disrepair. In one room there are a couple of a bunk beds. That sight is a first for me. The rooms carry the smell of spilled sterilizing alcohol and human despair. The patients all smile as we are toured through the rooms, and I wonder what they must be thinking of the parade of Canadians with North Face backpacks.

There are patients everywhere. Our host tells us that the hospital provides services for up to five hundred thousand people. It is the regional referral centre for a population the size of Newfoundland. And there are only two operating rooms, each with one light and antiquated but functioning equipment. At times, David tells us, the hospital goes without water for weeks at a time. Weeks? Did I hear that right?

As we move from one room to another, I check out. I actually stop paying attention. My mind wanders to this documentary I saw on Netflix as well as tonight's NHL game. I catch myself and immediately give myself a lecture that would rival any Catholic-guilt sermon. But I also realize that it isn't the not-paying-attention that's bothering me. It's the fact that I have become numb to it all. I've often wondered whether and how long-term exposure to what I've seen on these missions would manifest itself. I've always guarded against it. Don't get used to it, I tell myself. Don't ever get used to it. The shock of what I see is often the fuel I use to drive change.

But apathy can creep in. You don't see it coming. I remember being in a staff lounge one time and overhearing a group nearby reminisce about where they were on 9/11. How some of them saw the second plane go in. There was a jovial feeling to it. How many times have we all seen that footage? At what point did we stop realizing we're watching the murder of thousands of people?

In Haiti I was so moved by the tents and the collapsed hospital. I knew then that we must help change this. If we turned our heads, shame on us. It's a small country in the grand scheme of the globe, but surely we could make a difference. I was so naive. I thought that this was as bad as things can get. An earthquake did this, but goodness will prevail. Change is within reach. Blah, blah, blah. How foolishly naive.

In Bangladesh, touring hospitals that had thousands and thousands of patients in various states of illness and injury, I thought: This is just like Haiti—how could there be two countries struggling like this? Again in Nicaragua and Guatemala—hospital room after hospital room with no air conditioning or consistent electricity or sanitation. Patients lying waiting for care they didn't know would ever come.

I slow my pace and pull to the back of the group. Low moments like this make me wonder if the critics are right. Maybe there is too much to do here. How can our team possibly help? The problem is beyond the reach of any woman or man. It is beyond politics or forms of government. It is unfixable. Maybe I should quit. I was born in Canada and have and will continue to live a privileged life. Sacrifice and altruism will not change the endless rooms of patients. People. Those whom the developed world has forgotten. I've often said that the most aggressive and damaging disease I know is apathy.

I have fallen behind now, and I don't even think I am on the tour anymore. I can no longer see the group through the maze of poorly lit corridors. No matter, there will be nothing new or encouraging around the corner. What the hell am I doing here?

It feels like every mountain climbed only reveals a bigger, higher mountain behind it.

I don't like thinking this way. I can usually change the direction in my head. Move on. But it's hard to do at this moment, when I realize that as far as we've come, there's still so far to go. It tires me. I want to go back to the hotel. I want to talk to my kids. Dad. Anyone. As I move deeper into the hospital, I come across a class of nurses. They all wear crisp uniforms, freshly pressed. They can go without water and electricity here for weeks at a time and yet these nurses' uniforms are spotless. They're learning how to do their clinical work and being mentored by senior nurses.

I go through a roll call of the many Team Broken Earth nurses I've worked with over the years. People like Kristi, Michelle, and Shirley. It's their passion, energy, and undying commitment that lift the team up. I have seen them give until I thought they would break yet then give more. I have witnessed them sweating through endless hours in the operating room, running around frantically looking for life-saving equipment, and have seen them tenderly hold and wrap and cuddle an infant who had recently died, waiting for the parents to arrive. They are the beating heart of the team. Our heart and soul. They carry us.

Common feedback from the nurses on the teams is that these missions away make them better at their jobs at home. Sometimes the practice of medicine can become overwhelming, and not in the way you would expect. It's not the blood, or the highs and lows of dealing with patients, or even having to deliver bad news. Sometimes it's the bureaucracy of medicine that cripples you. No one I know practising medicine has not felt this to some degree. Doctors, nurses, and other health professionals have all mentioned it.

Most of us go into medicine for the personal contact, to be part of patients' lives, helping them through vulnerable moments and getting them back on their feet. But there is little, if any, training for how to manage the practice of medicine. How to properly or effectively manage the bookings and billings and insurance forms and letters and on and on.

Most of us just want to fix things. But this volume of work can be all-consuming. It can be frustrating and lead to stressful situations. Not the artery or nerve in your hand, but the system itself. I remember one nurse saying she was on the verge of quitting her career, moving on from the medical realm to the private sector. But it was her experience on a team, caring for one child in particular, that made her realize that it is not about the system. It's about the patient. One patient at a time.

Seeing the nurses working closely together in that crammed hospital in Ethiopia lifted me back up. It was another reminder not to accept the status quo. A lot of the hospitals we tour look the same, and the issues of global health discrepancies are real and vast. But fixing that was never our goal. Our goal has always been about the patient, and regardless of the colour of the walls, the state of the gurneys, or the lack of sinks and latrines, patients are in need, and if we can help one, then that is motivation enough. Again, the words of Dr. Jeremy Pridham run through my mind: we're not trying to change the world, just someone's world.

I quickly snap back and run to catch up with the rest of the tour.

The next day is the first day of the trauma course. We will be providing training for fifty front-line providers. We teach a team approach to trauma, nurses, doctors, and surgeons all working together to treat the most critical patients. One thing that was evident at yesterday's tour was the high number of traffic accident patients at this hospital. This course is welcomed and needed.

The course is divided between lectures and skills stations. The participants will have a chance to learn and then practise. We have completed this course in four countries now and I've noticed this each time: the participants are shy and don't answer questions at the beginning and then they are laughing, sharing, and asking for more at the end. People are people no matter where you go. When I see teachers demonstrating life-saving emergency procedures on mannequins, or teaching basic airway management, I can't help but be aware that these opportunities would not exist without the sacrifice of our volunteers or the support of our donors.

At the last exercise of the day, the Ethiopian students and surgeons gather to perform a simulated trauma scenario being directed and evaluated by our staff. Dr. Chris Patey is the director and the fake patient is Karl Smith. Karl, our newest board member and a former CFO, is getting into the action and letting the students examine him while he responds to their interventions. I love it. These same students who were too shy to say hello this morning are now yelling for IVs and X-rays.

That night, the president of the university, which has twenty-three thousand students, welcomes us with a traditional Ethiopian dinner. We are seated outside, and the air is cool and dry. In the middle of an open space, logs are stacked in a pyramid six feet high. A traditional bonfire. It feels like home. Like I'm on Topsail Beach with the lights of Bell Island twinkling across the tickle. Here we are in the middle of Africa with people gathered around a fire telling stories and laughing. The only thing missing is the gentle wash of waves on a rocky beach and we could be at home.

Ethiopia is known as the birthplace of coffee, where its origins can be traced back to ninth-century goat herders. Coffee is to Ethiopia what cod is to Newfoundland and Labrador: it is more than a commodity, it is something almost spiritual. Our host invites us to experience an Ethiopian coffee ceremony in the Bale Mountains just outside Goba, home to a national park and one of the highest mountains in Ethiopia.

I almost decide against going but don't want to disappoint our hosts. And so I go, but I harbour a secret: I'm not a coffee drinker! I know, I know, it almost feels traitorous to my profession. It's a part of the gig. Truth is, I used to drink it by the truckload. I would have five or six extra-larges a day. Then on one of the trips back home from Haiti, I became violently ill. I don't think it was from the coffee I'd just had, but in a Pavlovian manner I associated it with the coffee and I haven't taken a sip since. That was two years ago.

The drive was long and tiresome over rough terrain. My mind drifts again, wondering if the course is worth it, will it make a difference, will it change the long corridors of beds and gurneys of patients waiting for care. We finally stop ascending and the convoy of vehicles comes to a stop outside of a small series of handmade huts. We then drive through an opening of a hand-woven fence of bamboo that extends for as far as the eye can see.

We are seated in a semicircle around a firepit and presented with a series of traditional foods. I am not feeling particularly adventurous, so I pass on the food, though the aromas are exquisite. Then the coffee is presented. We listen to a brief description of how it is processed and then, from a piping hot metal kettle, they pour the correct number of cups. It is so hot I fear the porcelain will melt.

I am about to pass on it, but it seems to be one of those moments in life that is special, even mystical. I know I'll regret it later if I don't try it. So, for the first time in two years, I take a sip of this hot black syrup. I'm glad I do. It is the best coffee I have ever smelled or tasted. It instantly brings back a flood of memories. Like baking bread, the scent of freshly brewed coffee takes me back to my grandparents' house, and from there to so many different times and places over the years. It proves again that smell is the biggest trigger of memory.

Everyone's enjoying it and conversations spark up as evening grows sharper around us. Bluer blues. Brighter yellows. But me? I'm thousands of miles away in a coffee shop in Newfoundland. I was there to meet a friend. I was a bit down on medicine at the time. I was frustrated and deflated, a bit like I was during the recent tour of the hospital. As I was in line waiting to order, the woman in front of me turned around and asked, "Are you Dr. Furey?"

Now, Furey is a fairly common name in Newfoundland and there are several Dr. Fureys at the hospital in St. John's. So I replied, "I am *a* Dr. Furey." You never really know how these conversations will go. I could be about to get an earful about how her knee is not perfect or how she had to wait too long to see me. You just never know.

"You don't remember me, do you?" she continued. "Well, ten years ago you saved my life." It caught me off guard and I didn't quite know what to say. She reached out and touched my arm, looking me warmly in the eyes. "I was so down and out at the time and jumped from a bridge. I should have died there. But you put my legs and pelvis back together." All the images of her X-rays and trauma code came rushing back. She tugged up her jeans to reveal the scars on her shins. She took my hand and said simply, "Thank you. You gave me another shot."

My fingers close around the hot cup in my hand. The coffee burns my lips a little. But there I am, in Ethiopia, and a little more changed. Or just reminded. I look at the faces around me. Team members laughing, enjoying this special experience. I hear that lyric from the Talking Heads. *Well, how did I get here?* The doubts leave me and drift off into the African night like embers from a bonfire. I think of the nurses at the hospital in Goba. The optimism on their faces as they're being taught. Change is a singularity that influences the plural. One life, I think. Change one life at a time.

We are treated to other traditional activities, like harvesting honey from a beehive that sits forty feet up in a tree. We see waterfalls and stroll around the Ethiopian hills, each step feeling better than the last.

One of my New Year's resolutions this year is to run more. It's not my favourite activity, but I am determined to run several times a week. I have my gear with me, and Art Rideout and I decide that we will head out at five thirty in the morning. As we are running, what is immediately evident, other than the physiologic effects of the altitude, is the sky. The stars are still up, and they are the brightest, clearest stars I have ever seen. It is as if I could reach out and touch them. It makes me aware of our tiny place in the universe. It's humbling.

As we run, the sun begins to rise, and some locals join us, running alongside for short stretches. Others we pass wave and give the thumbs-up in encouragement. In the distance, across the plains of browned sunburnt grass, are mountains that provide an amazing backdrop to this incredible sunrise. Cattle herders are now bringing their cows to the pastures, and we have to stop several times to let them cross the road. They move slowly, with the bulls in the front. Their guide says good morning with almost a Newfoundland nod.

You can see hope on the faces here, whether it's a patient hoping for a positive outcome or the cattle herder about his daily business while always offering a prayer for rain, or the medical staff we are teaching who are eager for better health for their community. I remember as a kid hearing someone say the sky is blue because it is a reflection of the earth. I now know that's not true, but I like the poetry of it. Maybe that is what's special, even magical, about this African sky. It's a reflection of this place. A mirror held to the face of hope. The bright colour of a better tomorrow.

Hope is like a compass. It works the same way no matter where you go. As we are driving to the airport to begin our long trek home, we pass some kids playing in the streets. This could be any street anywhere in the world. Kids playing street hockey in Brampton. Kids riding bikes by Quidi Vidi Lake in St. John's. The truck has to swerve to the right to avoid them. One of the kids looks up as we are passing and gives us that innocent smile of a kid just being a kid. A tiny seed of hope, I think. After the long, exhausting trip home, I pull into the driveway and see Mark and Rachael out playing. The similarity and the contrast are palpable, poetic. Little seeds of hope. Change one life. Change life. Change, always focus on change.

You should've seen the look on Allison's face when I asked if we had any coffee.

20

A LEGACY OF QUESTIONS

Port-au-Prince: May 2017

DEEP, DEEP GASP and I'm suddenly awake. It's midnight and I am in a hotel room in Haiti. I'm usually an early-to-bed, early-to-rise guy, and you could usually dance the St. John's Waltz on my chest and I won't stir. But not tonight. Tonight, I woke in a cold sweat. Dreams of faces causing me to stir. Undefined panic, like losing lights in the middle of a surgery.

People often ask me how this Broken Earth journey has affected me. Do I suffer from any sort of post-traumatic stress after some of the things I have witnessed? I don't think I do. I know the signs and I've seen them in others, front-line workers like ER staff and paramedics, soldiers and veterans. I never thought I was immune to it, but I guess I just didn't see it coming. Does anyone? I know I shouldn't self-diagnose, but in moments like tonight, in that quiet void of sleep when the patients come to visit, I'm left to wonder. Still they come. And like everything in medicine, they are never the ones you helped.

Again I see the face of the young girl in Haiti as she shook my hand and cared for her grandfather. She's been a regular for years, and I often wonder how things turned out for them both. God, she must be in her early twenties by now. In the dream she is wearing a yellow dress and she smiles and turns away in the bright blinding sun so that all I see is her silhouette. Behind her are the faces of the ones who I couldn't help. They appear briefly, fleeting. The boy with cancer. The young girl who succumbed to her internal injuries in the operating room. The patient who bled out in the ER after being shot in the streets of Port-au-Prince. They say nothing. They just look me straight in the eyes. I call to the girl in the yellow dress to turn around, and she does. She casts another smile and then all goes black. It wakes me every time.

I can't fall back asleep. Wide eyes staring at the ceiling with my mind now racing through a litany of to-do lists, conversations, and images, all moving fast like I'm skimming through a book. I think of the course we are teaching this week in Haiti. I hear the echoing comment by a Canadian bureaucrat about how Team Broken Earth are not making, and will not make, a difference.

Really?

Tomorrow will be a big day. I'll be in a room containing over 90 per cent of the orthopedic surgery residents of Haiti. Education. Collaboration. This will be our legacy here and will live long after many Team Broken Earth members have moved on.

Yesterday, we toured the hospital we've been working in for years now. We walked through the OR we helped build. We saw the new hospital ward full of patients and the volunteer quarters we built (and which the locals call "the Canada tower" or "Broken Earth tower"). The millions of dollars worth of equipment we have secured is being used every day, and the staff greeted us with the kind of warm embraces reserved for family. The team even had time to see a few patients yesterday. We looked at the

X-rays of the first bilateral total hip replacements the team had done in Haiti with surgeons from Canada and Haiti working side by side. It was a proud moment.

This week, we're giving lectures and skills-simulation labs, in which the residents practise on artificial bones using real surgical equipment, for residents who have come from across Haiti. This is the third time we have hosted this course. To watch the senior residents (who were juniors when we first did this) teach the new junior residents, well, it just fills me with pride. It's these young surgeons, full of energy and enthusiasm, who will change orthopedic care in Haiti. And Team Broken Earth is now a critical part of their education, year after year.

Still, though, the criticisms are always there. Always politely present in the back of the room. Always somewhere on the periphery, keeping me awake like low noise outside the bedroom. As odd as it sounds, I actually owe the critics a debt of gratitude. Why? Because progress is made by doubt. It makes you ask important questions. It shows you the gaps. Doubt makes you seek answers. It reassures you. It makes you better at what you do. Doubt everything, I say, because the end result will be that much more solid.

So, a thank-you is in order for the criticisms. Thank you for inspiring the necessary reflection and the confidence to know we are moving in the right direction. When people ask if we're making a difference, I think about the cleft palate of a patient that Art Rideout corrected. He literally gave that person back her smile. I think of the patient with two new hip replacements who would otherwise be in a wheelchair. We, all of us on and supporting Team Broken Earth, made a difference for those patients. Capacity and sustainability? We got that. We're establishing infrastructure, building relationships, and advancing education. We are creating a legacy. A Canadian legacy here and abroad. I feel better about that. And to the critics I say this: It's okay to have doubts, but you must always believe in the existence of solutions.

My mind is an issue-seeking missile sometimes. Critics aside, I still cannot sleep. I think about my parents. They're scheduled to come to Haiti this week, their first visit, which opens a whole other box of anxieties. I replay every conversation I have ever had with them about the place. About Team Broken Earth. About its evolution. And about the toll it can take. Dad knows more about the sacrifice of public service than anyone I know. I keep telling myself this is different, but is it? Will he see that? Funny how so many of us never stop seeking our father's approval, no matter how old we are or what we've accomplished.

My parents. For me, theirs are giant shoulders to stand on. Theirs are the largest shoes to fill. They've heard my stories, read my blog, and seen the pictures. But will the real thing live up to their expectations of me? All of a sudden, I'm ten years old and bringing home a report card.

Flashback to 2010. When I first said I was going to help the medical relief effort after the earthquake, my father tried to talk me out of it. It wasn't because of what was happening in Haiti; it was about concern for me. He said I should really think about my young family. Maybe the time was not right for me, I should probably wait and do this kind of work when my career was more established and my family was grown. To not take the risk, not just for my safety but for my future. I'm not sure I would have given different advice to my kids if I were in my father's shoes. He is always right. I always listen. But something in my heart told me this time was different. I took this step untethered, and it was terrifying.

Seven years later I try to see all this through his eyes. Will he see what the critics see—the unsolvable problem, the unclimbable mountain? Will he see the unceasing despair and the faces of need? Most important, will he see the hope that I see? Countless people come here and do not see the progress. But if you didn't see it when it was hopeless, what are you gauging it against?

Of course my parents will see the tangible accomplishments: the new hospital building and the new ambulance. They will not witness the rubble in the streets or the tent ORs we once worked in. But will they see how far we have come? Will they see what our team has accomplished, and also how far we still have to go? I am nervous that what they see will not match what I see, will not meet their expectations. Will Dad now agree that the decision I made to come here in the first place was the right one?

Around the time I was finishing this book, I took a trip to Ottawa to visit Dad. There's no more iconic image of Canada than Parliament Hill, and it is bright in my early-morning memory today. I'm sure I've seen it a hundred times but it never fails to give me goosebumps. It's something about the history, or just that kinship you feel in the heart of the nation. Standing in front of the Eternal Flame with the Peace Tower in the background, it is hard not to feel your heart grow with pride. It's a beacon of hope to the rest of the world. I know that sounds grand, but I really feel that it's true.

For me, that trip also doubled as a twist on "take your kid to work day." This time, I was the kid and loving it. We rarely get to see people we love and care for working at their jobs. We hear about them, hear from others how they perform, but rarely do we get to experience it first-hand. I was so proud to be here with Dad.

I was asked to give a talk that trip, up on "the Hill," as they say in Ottawa. This was more nerve-racking than usual, but the strength of the collaboration with our partners in Haiti made it easier. Meeting with the Haitian ambassador and seeing the passion and commitment he has for this partnership with Canada was inspiring. The relationship between Haiti and Team Broken Earth has grown from a few individuals providing emergency relief to the people of Port-au-Prince, to a Canada-wide team of over a thousand volunteers providing medical care and education to the people of Haiti. Rural teams, eye care teams, teams expanding beyond our borders and across the ocean.

On behalf of our entire team, from Vancouver to St. John's, I assured the ambassador and our audience that Team Broken Earth would continue to be a sustained medical and educational presence in their country. Together, Canada and Haiti can be an example of how collaboration can not only change the life of one desperate patient, but in fact change a people and indeed the world.

I remember walking along Sparks Street in the dark with Dad after that event and him telling me how proud he was of Team Broken Earth and what we have accomplished. Maybe today would not be that bad. It was time to see. It was time for me to take Mom and Dad to work.

This would be the first time I had travelled with Dad in his official capacity as Speaker of the Senate. I've always assumed I understood the significance of the office he holds. I was wrong. He arrived at the hotel escorted by an entourage of ten people and surrounded by armed guards, with dignitaries and everyone tripping over themselves to ensure he was safe and doted on. Staff scurried about with baggage and BlackBerries like a scene from a political action movie. Hand in hand, Mom and Dad got out of an armoured vehicle and were escorted by the Canadian ambassador herself and other embassy staff into the hotel lobby. Dad always seems uncomfortable with attention, and he probably just wanted to check into his room like anyone else. It was tough to make eye contact with either of them through the swarm of bodies.

Here was a kid from Mount Cashel being treated as if he was the prime minister of Canada. I knew when Dad was appointed Speaker of the Senate that he was, constitutionally speaking, fourth in the order of precedence. I had seen him many times in the uniform of his position amid the pomp and regal parade that exists when the upper chamber sits. But this was different. From the Mount to the Senate to an international representative for Canada. Could he have possibly dreamed this outcome that first night in his bunk bed–filled dorm away from his brothers, sisters, and his mom? Could Nan have imagined such an outcome when she fled Avondale in the dead of night? I'm not sure if it is pride or guilt that is running through me. Has it really taken a scene of foreigners doting on him for me to realize how special he is? It is a strange dissonance that I fear will take years for me to reconcile. Like the culture of Newfoundlanders and Labradorians, sometimes when you are surrounded by something your whole life it takes an outsider to make you truly realize it.

Mom sees me first and is able to break free from the circus of it all and give me the biggest, longest hug. She is overwhelmed with simply the drive from the airport. It's something that I've gotten so used to, but it is a story I've heard from almost every first-time volunteer. Some are on the verge of tears just from that drive from the airport. Everyone, regardless of position, profession, or experience, gets a huge reality check just from that simple drive.

Dad gives me a nod as he continues the conversation he's in and I barely have time to speak with Mom before they are both whisked upstairs to private meetings with the ambassador. It's a quick reminder for me that they are here on official business, and family time will have to wait.

For the next couple of hours I'm like a kid waiting for the green light to go downstairs on Christmas morning. The sun is setting by the time there's finally some one-on-one time. Dad and I sit on the hotel's deck, and it's as though we've been transported back to the deck in Holyrood. Maybe it's the time of day, but there is a sense of calmness and serenity. It's just Dad and me again, father and son.

We can see the smoke from burning tires in the distance. The streets are humming with activity. The conversation begins about the drive in from the airport, and Dad asks how I do it. How can I hold on to those scenes and how can I keep coming back? He says he is stressed just from one drive, and he has not even seen the hospital or the patients or the true Port-au-Prince yet.

I confess to him that I'm worried. Canadian officials and Newfoundland and Labrador officials are here to see one thing: progress. I feel I am about to be judged. They haven't seen the girl in the yellow dress. They haven't held somebody's somebody, or seen Rose Anne cross a river. There is no way for them to truly appreciate the progress. But would they see hope?

Dad reassures me in a fatherly way, saying not to worry, things will be fine. His words feel empty. He gets up to head to bed as the last rays of sunset fade. He smiles at me and says, "I'm still not sure I understand why you do this."

There's a siren in the distance. There always is.

———

The next morning we meet in the lobby, the full group of senators and diplomats with a convoy of armed vehicles readying to make the short trip to the hospital. Following that, there's to be a tour of a school and then more meetings. It's a typical political agenda, except it has Team Broken Earth on full display.

The journey to the hospital is the typical rugged, emotional experience, except this time with police escort and blaring sirens. For security reasons I am not allowed to travel in the same vehicle as Mom and Dad, which suits me just fine. Like Dad, I've never been a fan of attention. Staring out the window at the all too familiar scene of street vendors, motorcycles, and debris, I am able to lose myself in the action of the city. There is a woman with three kids on the sidewalk, she's holding their hands while balancing a basket of market goods on her head. I think of Nan.

I can still remember my hand in hers. Nan's fingers were always moving. Knitting some imaginary mitts or solving some puzzle, was how I thought of it. I think about the courage she mustered and her hope and determination for a brighter future. I would not be making this journey without it. I think about my grandfather and how, if he hadn't told others to mind their own business when they said Mom shouldn't marry a guy from the Mount, none of us would be here. I have been surrounded by loving, caring people my whole life. Surrounded by people willing to give when they had nothing, and to serve others when they could have been served. It was the twisting broken roads of Port-au-Prince, like strands of DNA, that made me realize why we did this, why Team Broken Earth exists. My family, me personally, owe our very existence to people who have given and sacrificed. This rugged island itself is a garden of neighbours helping, sacrificing, giving. I have been doubly blessed.

The gates of the hospital open and the convoy pulls in, occupying the entire parking lot. The Team Broken Earth ambulance is in full display. All the hospital staff are front and centre in bright white freshly pressed lab coats to meet the dignitaries. As soon as the formal introductions are done, the doctors, nurses, and administrators give me the more familiar kiss on the cheek.

Jo Cherry starts off the official tour. Mom looks prouder than on my wedding day, and I see Dad's smile get bigger as we move through the hospital. We go from the pediatric ward to the neonatal ward to the OR. Everywhere, pictures of Team Broken Earth hang on the walls. Everywhere, our logo is on equipment we've acquired.

We stop in the ER. A police officer has been shot in the hand, and I quickly examine the X-ray and give an opinion. The city doesn't know there are dignitaries here. Haiti goes on being Haiti.

When we tour the building with the new volunteer quarters, my heart fills as the guide explains that the structure is due in large part to Team Broken Earth funds and leadership. It was a huge step forward for the hospital, and our tour guide does it justice.

As the tour is winding down and we get to walk through the new bunkrooms and the kitchen area for volunteers, I am able to pull Dad away from the group and take him up to the roof. From above the second floor you are able to see the entire hospital. Dad asks about the patients we just saw and what will happen to the police officer. With the sun beating down, he places his hand on my shoulder. It feels like a fifty-pound weight tied to all my thoughts.

"I get it," he says. "I get it now. I'm proud of you. I understand why you do this. But I still do not know how." It catches me off guard and I wish I'd had the wherewithal then to say that it was you, Dad. It was Nan. It was Allison and the kids. It was growing up in Newfoundland and Labrador. It was all those things.

Dad continues asking about the patients he saw on tour, where they came from and would they be okay. I tell him about the hospital's procedures and what we do for post-discharge healthcare, but my mind is still on the last thing he said. *He knows why I do this.*

It feels like a current passed from his hand to my shoulder, and I realize the question that people always ask, perhaps it was a question I had been asking myself the whole time. Why? And I finally had an answer: my dad, my mom, my wife, my children, my province, my country, my world. Because there is no us and them, really. There is only us. We are all one. We're all fluid. All different harbours along the same ocean. And what touches one will eventually touch us all, connecting all of us together, from Haiti to Bangladesh to Avondale. The current pulls, pulses, and is always moving. The Atlantic bleeds into the Caribbean and vice versa. The waves that wash up on the shores of Newfoundland and Labrador are the same waves that crest on the beaches of Haiti and on the coast of Bangladesh. I have to believe our efforts will give people hope. That a ripple will occur, and it will eventually reach us all. Everything in me hopes that is true.

I'm looking at my hands, thinking of the wounded officer downstairs. One of the Haitian nurses finds us on the roof to ask if I could see another patient. Dad's looking out over the compound to the streets beyond the wall where Port-au-Prince never stops buzzing. Someone's shouting in French. Horns blare. He smiles at the scene. "Back to work," he says.

AS ANYONE WITH kids can attest, dinnertime can be a frenzied blend of negotiation, rebellion, and the odd bit of martial law in between. There's the countless activities the kids are involved in and the coming and going generated by each. Allison has her own workload at the hospital, and I'm usually tired after a long day in the OR or seeing all the patients in clinic. We tag-team as best we can with what the kids have on the go. So by the time dinner rolls around, patience can be in short order.

But the kids are just being kids. They've got that youthful energy working for them and are rarely fatigued (unless asked to do a chore!). Rachael practises the violin while Maggie works her way through the keys of the piano. Mark has Legos spread all over the floor as he assembles some fortress from his imagination. Allison tries to supervise it all while thinking about what to cook. She'd be the first to tell you that my culinary skills are not exactly top-notch. She says I have the Newfoundland palate . . . boiled or buttered. As Nan would say, there's nothing wrong with my appetite. I love to eat. I truly appreciate the artistry and skill behind magical culinary creations, but left to my own devices I would survive on cereal, bananas, and tea. My kids are often concerned about what I am going to eat when I'm away from them. Allison, on the other hand, likes to cook, and one thing we aim to do is eat together as a family. All of us sitting at the table, talking about how everyone's day was, what activities we had and what friends did and what the teachers had to say today. It reminds me of the dinners with Mom and Dad and everyone else. I want my kids to have those memories too. It's important.

Team Broken Earth has naturally become integrated into our dinner conversations. Allison has often said that Broken Earth is our fourth child, and that's nowhere more evident than at the dinner table. Early on, before cell phones were banned at the table, I have to admit sometimes I kept mine in my lap, out of Allison's line of sight.

One evening, while Mark was still eating baby food in a high-chair, and Rachael and Maggie were trying not to spill three glasses of milk per meal, my phone buzzed in my pocket with a text message. I took a sneak peek. It was from Dr. Workens Alexandre, a young orthopedic surgeon who had recently grad-uated and was working at Bernard Mevs. He would frequently send me messages seeking my advice. There, on the dinner table, were pictures of someone who was dying of a wound across her pelvis and a severe fracture underneath. It was a mess. No wonder he reached out. It was a complex case but one that was easy enough to provide advice about. Sometimes in medicine you get too deep into the weeds and can't see the solution, only the problem in front of you. This was one of those times. Dr. Alexandre just needed to take a deep breath, see beyond the extreme-looking fracture, and prioritize life-saving measures. In two minutes, with Mark throwing food from his highchair in the background, we had it sorted out. From the streets of Port-au-Prince to our dinner table in St. John's, the long-distance consult worked.

This scene has played out many, many times since, whether it's in the middle of family dinners or when out with friends or during my own working day. Friends are often shocked when my phone buzzes and it is someone from Haiti with X-rays or photos seeking advice. What initially excited me about these encounters was how technology had changed the practice of medicine by allowing access to expert opinion in seconds from anywhere in the world. But when I think about this a little deeper, look a little closer, the true marvel is the trust and relationships we have built in Haiti over the years.

From the very beginning of Team Broken Earth, we did not want to be a group of medical tourists on a one-time tour. After the earthquake, I got a sense that many well-intentioned doctors flew in, did much-needed and appreciated work, and then left with an all too often unmet promise to return. I knew building a relationship of trust was the only way we could get the locals to be a part of what we were trying to accomplish. They needed to know that they are as much Team Broken Earth as the rest of us. I wanted them to believe in our promise of sustained medical help.

Haitians are stoic, quiet people. They have an incredible ability to communicate through body language and facial gestures. They often have little use for words of any kind. I have been in meetings that seemed to go well until someone translated what occurred and I saw I was way off. What did I miss?

After many missions and many more hours spent in surgeries as well as at the hospital, I feel Team Broken Earth has a solid relationship with the local staff, nurses, residents, and fellow surgeons. When you walk into the OR in the hospital in Port-au-Prince, there is a framed picture of Newfoundland, and many pictures of nurses, residents, and staff are taped to the anesthesia cabinet. It is a real family.

On one of my first trips to Haiti, I reached out to the local orthopedic community, and one of the people who responded was Dr. Hans Larsen. He wanted to meet for dinner and see how we could work together. Hans was in his late fifties or early sixties, with a smaller stature and glasses. He carried himself with the quiet confidence of a university professor without the elbow patches on a tweed jacket. When we met it was clear that he was an influencer, a connector, someone who knew how to get things done and how to interact with people. He had to stop to talk to every table in the restaurant, asking about people's parents and children. I'd always thought that was just a Newfoundland thing.

It turned out that Hans was the president of the Haitian Orthopaedic and Traumatology Association. We hit it off immediately. He had many residents and connections to teaching programs. The timing was perfect. Team Broken Earth was looking for ways to advance our focus on education. His residents needed exposure to techniques, cases, and equipment that were not always available. Before we knew it, we were working out the details.

Hans and I have remained very good friends. I have invited him to Canada several times, and he was a guest lecturer at the Newfoundland Surgical Society Meeting in the late winter of 2013. The Newfoundland and Labrador winter wind was no doubt a shock to our Haitian friend, but all bundled up, Hans had the honour of dropping the puck for our annual hockey game, the Maroun Cup. In June of 2016, Hans had a national audience as he lectured at the Canadian Orthopaedic Association's annual meeting. Most important, however, Hans was instrumental in helping us start our first orthopedic trauma course in Haiti back in 2012, and we have repeated that four times now. We realized right away this was how best to extend Team Broken Earth's medical reach. One of the residents who took the course really stood out. He was a familiar face: he always seemed to be in the OR when we were at Bernard Mevs. Rain or shine, early or late, he was there. Dedicated, skilled, and smart, he was a shining star committed to staying in Haiti and making a difference. His name was Jean Hippolyte.

Jean is incredibly quiet beyond what any language barrier should allow. He has a big smile and carries himself like someone who has worked hard for everything he has. And he has. He's a young man, but you can see the years of hard work in his hands. He completed the public residency program but he didn't have access to many of the tools of the other programs. He had to find them and work at it, often without any guidance. We all felt that he earned his stripes.

Dr. John Durham, one of my colleagues from Arizona, and I recognized Jean's talent and suggested that he come to Canada to do some advanced training before returning to Haiti. A few phone calls, and with the support of Dr. Paul Duffy in Calgary, Jean became our first Dr. Spencer McLean Fellow, named in recognition of the Team Broken Earth member who had lost his battle with cancer in 2013. Jean spent three months in Calgary working alongside Alberta's finest surgeons. He then returned to Haiti, where he continues to work at the hospital, with us when we are there and solo when we are not. He is dedicated to improving the delivery of orthopedic trauma care in his country. I firmly believe that people like Jean will change Haiti for the better.

After Dr. Bernard Mevs passed away, two general surgeons began running the hospital. They are twin brothers, Marlon and Gerry Bitar. They are Haitian doctors who trained in France and returned home. Their dedication is as inspirational as it is compelling. They are committed to improvement, inside and outside the gates of the hospital. They are identical twins, and to this day I find it hard to tell them apart. They are the closest brothers too. I am not sure I have ever seen one without the other. They drive to the hospital together, they operate together, and they eat together. I have heard stories of this deep connection between identical twins, but thought it was a myth. They busted the myth for me. They move and talk similarly, and you have a strange sense that you are talking to one person while seeing two people and feeling the weight of influence and power of ten people. They remain some of my closest friends in Haiti and take great care of us while we are there.

As strong as the force of the Bitar brothers is, the real powerhouse is Jenny Bitar. In the many hospitals I've worked in across many different countries and continents, she's hands-down the strongest administrator I've ever worked with. The brothers may make the medical decisions, but she runs the hospital, she is in charge. Jenny manages all the staff and equipment as well as finances, payroll, patient beds, hospital flow, daily supply chain, gas for the generators, and oxygen for the OR. She does the job of what would be several departments at home. Her energy is contagious, and her no-nonsense approach to decision-making is exactly what is needed. I have approached her many times with various problems, and regardless of the question, the answer is never "No." It is always "Let me see." Jenny is a fixer. She doesn't see barriers; she sees hurdles to be jumped.

And it's the little things too. I have called her in Port-au-Prince and said, "Jenny, one of our team members has a birthday today. I know it's last-minute, but do you know how we could get a cake?" Two hours later, there is a cake on the table with the name of the volunteer and candles. In a land where it can be tough to find water, this is no small feat. Of all the people I have met throughout this adventure, Jenny is probably the one I remain in closest contact with at home, and she is truly one of my heroes.

One evening during a Haiti mission, I was invited to the Bitars' home for dinner. When you are on these trips, the sense of individual days of the week disappear. Being away from your regular routines and being so 24/7 busy, there is no way to tell if it is a Monday or a Thursday. We pulled through the secure gates with their armed guards to see, surprisingly, an average two-storey home. There were toys scattered about and a swing set out back. The aroma of dinner wafting from the kitchen, the laughter of children, the day-to-day life of any family anywhere. It made me miss home that much more.

Jenny was helping the kids with homework and readying lunches for tomorrow. The brothers were trying to fill out some form for the hospital. It was familiar. It was a Tuesday night, I thought. Maggie has piano on Tuesdays.

As we sat around the large dining room table, they were thanking us for all our help and patience in working in their home country. The children would come in and out, Jenny trying to get them to go to bed, while the brothers were answering calls about patients and trying to direct their care. Again, the familiarity transported me home. I could see Mark furrow his brow as he studied his Cheerios. I see Allison's face as she pretends not to see me check my phone. Rachael is singing a song she just learned. And Maggie calls out from the piano asking where her sheet music is.

In my professional medical opinion, it's hard for a heart to be in two places at once. But I wouldn't change any of it.

ACKNOWLEDGMENTS

THIS BOOK WOULD not have been possible without the help, dedication and friendship of many people, the most important of whom are patients here in Canada and around the world who have taught, humbled and inspired me. Thank you.

Thank you to my ever-patient wife, Allison. Your understanding, guidance and commitment make me love you more every day.

To my children Maggie, Rachael and Mark—you fill me with energy and pick me up when I am down. I only hope you are able to experience the same love, devotion and adventure in your own families some day.

There are no words to thank my dear friend Jim Mackey. You believed in Broken Earth before I did. You have given me the confidence and courage to find and develop my voice in telling this story. I could not have done it without you!

Art and Mary Rideout and Jeremy and Gillian Pridham—there have been many ups, downs and sideway paths, but through it all, and most importantly, I was always able to lean on you and laugh with you.

Heather Dalton, who I initially met to talk about a landing page for Team Broken Earth—it is your vision that has really helped direct what we have become and I can't thank you enough.

Joanne Pardy and Renee Paddick—thank you for being such good friends and offering guidance as to the evolution of the Team.

Thank you to Allan Hawco, Alan Doyle, Brendan Paddick and my sister Meghan Gardner for reading this book as I wrote it and offering suggestions and edits.

Thank you to my parents, George and Karen, my brother, David, and my sisters, Meghan and Rebecca. I stand on your shoulders every day. To Allison's parents, Rick and Deb—we could not have made any of the trips without your support at home.

There are so many others to thank, including my colleagues in many disciplines who believed in this crazy notion and supported me as it developed. Thank you in particular to my own orthopedic division for supporting me: Will Moores, Frank O'Dea, Frank Noftall, Rod Martin, Keegan Au, Carl Moores, Heather Jackman, Peter Rockwood, Nick Smith, Steve Croft, Danny Squire, Guy Hogan and Vic Sahajpal.

There are so many doctors and nurses to thank, but some have been extraordinary. Thank you to Chad and Jodi Coles, Kristi Lange and Jim Kim, Darryl and Heather Young, Carlos and Maria Eniquez, Paul and Suzanne Duffy, Tina Whitty and Ray Ryan, Sheldon Peddle and Dave Thomas, Huw and Henrike Rees, Eric Lenzer and Peter Jarzem, Demetrius Litwin, Nora

Fullington and John (Bull) Durham, Nat and Neil Segaren, Supriya Singh and Marjorie Johnson, and Steve Hunt and Monica Kidd, Atam Gill and Jennifer Mercer, Erin Marshall, and Ellie, Maria, Andrew, James and Jane Rideout.

A special thank you to Dick Barter. You have always stepped up when asked, and believed when others didn't. You are a true friend.

Thank you to Brad and Suzzette Moss and all the Lions for recognizing and executing on the value of partnerships.

The Bitar family and all the staff at Bernard Mevs Hospital have become our home away from home and are truly family. To Jenny in particular, thank you for never saying no and always finding solutions.

Jo Cherry, I miss our chats on the roof about how to change the world, or at least the campus. I hope you will return to Haiti after you are done in the UK. Equally, Travis Horn, who has captured so many of the experiences we have had—you are a true magician and friend.

The nurses are the heart and soul of Team Broken Earth. People like Jackie Williams Connolly, Brenda Earles, Rochelle McCarthy, Michelle Murphy, Geralyn Lamb, Pauline Malcomson, Jim Maher and many more. None of this would be possible without you.

To everyone at m5, thank you for believing in all of us. Special thank you to Krsyta Rudofsky who saw the potential before I did.

My friends, who I attended grade school, high school, undergraduate and medical school with, you have always been so supportive and I have been lucky enough to have two of them join us on missions. Thank you to Chris and Stephanie Jackman and Lisa and Shannon Goodyear. In particular to Lisa who took the first step and first flight to Haiti with us.

To all the Team Broken Earth board of directors, past and present, and to our staff, including Chris Bonnell, Gabe Cavallaro, Karl Smith, Mark Cook, James Goodridge, Jim Rourke, Derrick Langdon, Krista Bussy and Susan Keough—thank you for your skills and your belief.

Heartfelt thanks to my agent Michael Levine for championing this project from the very start.

To Lucina Mason, simply thank you for all you do.

To my editors at Penguin Random House, Scott Sellers and Tim Rostron—thank you for answering my silly questions, sorting out my jumbled work and for being my personal psychologists when needed.

Thank you to my uncle Leo, who is the real writer in the family. Your encouragement, advice and endless recommendations of books to read, helped in creating this piece of work. I will forever cherish our coffees.

Thank you to the first team who decided to leap with no net: Lisa Goodyear, Dave Pace, Art Rideout, Jeremy Pridham, Steve Hunt, Carolyn Churchill, Geralyn Lamb, Catherine Seviour, Jane Seviour, Peter Collins, Jane Martin, Brenda Earles, Mary O'Brien, Scott Wilson, Jackie Williams-Connoly, Theresa Peacock, Lynn Anderson, Rochelle McCarthy, Laila Brown, Shirely MacNeil, Robyn Noseworthy, Frank O'Dea, Daniel Martyn, Lorrine Pelley, Pam Griffiths and Malhoudi Tau.

Finally, thank you to some of my dear friends around the world. In Haiti: Jenny, Jerry and Marlon Bitar, Hans Larsen, Ben Nau, Jean Hippolyte, Pierre Wooley, Jean Marc deMatteis, Paula Caldwell, Nat Segaren, and Michelle Barjon. From Nicaragua, Alberto Balladares and all the staff at the 2001 Chinandega Foundation. In Bangladesh, Zahida Fizza Kabir and her entire family, and all staff at the SAJIDA foundation including our dear friend Kahdija Rhena. In Gautemala: Areil Marroquin and the staff at Partner for Surgery. In Ethiopia: David Allison, Dr. Abubeker and all the staff from Madda Walabu University.

Thank you to the Faculty of Medicine at Memorial, including Jill Allison and Eastern Health, especially all the behind the scenes people who helped especially at the beginning like George Butt.

To the many thousands I have not mentioned who have given of your time, talents or funds to Team Broken Earth—thank you!